HOLLYWOOD KRYPTONITE

SAM KASHNER AND NANCY SCHOENBERGER

HOLLYWOOD KRYPTONITE

The Bulldog, the Lady, and the Death of Superman

ST. MARTIN'S PRESS ❧ NEW YORK

This book is a work of nonfiction, not a "Superman" story. It has not been authorized or endorsed in any way by DC Comics or any other owner of rights in the "Superman" character.

HOLLYWOOD KRYPTONITE: THE BULLDOG, THE LADY, AND THE DEATH OF SUPERMAN. Copyright © 1996 by Sam Kashner and Nancy Schoenberger. Printed in the United States of America. No part of this book may be used or reproduced in any manner whatsoever without written permission except in the case of brief quotations embodied in critical articles or reviews. For information, address St. Martin's Press, 175 Fifth Avenue, New York, N.Y. 10010.

Design by Pei Loi Koay

Library of Congress Cataloging-in-Publication Data

Kashner, Sam.
   Hollywood Kryptonite : the bulldog, the lady, and the death of Superman / Sam Kashner and Nancy Schoenberger.
      p.   cm.
  ISBN 0-312-14616-7
  1. Reeves, George, 1914–1959.   2. Actors—United States—Biography.
I. Schoenberger, Nancy. II. Title.
PN2287.R293K37   1996
791.45'028'092—dc20
[B]   96-21658
                                           CIP

First edition: October 1996

10   9   8   7   6   5   4   3   2   1

For Fred and Deenah Mollin,

"Who killed Superman?"

and for Jan Alan Henderson,

Jim Beaver, and Jim Nolt,

keepers of the flame.

CONTENTS

Who by brave ascent? Who by accident? Who in solitude? Who in this mirror? Who by his lady's command? Who by his own hand? Who in mortal chains? Who in power? And who shall I say is calling?

—Leonard Cohen, "Who by Fire"

ACKNOWLEDGMENTS

Certain nonfiction books, like this one, are collaborative efforts. We could not have proceeded without the insights and information offered by many who have pursued the George Reeves case on their own. Chief among them are Jan Alan Henderson, author of "Speeding Bullet: George Reeves, The Man, the Myth, The Mystery" (*Cult Movies*, No. 14), and the actor and writer Jim Beaver, who has been researching the authorized biography of George Reeves for over a decade. Both Henderson and Beaver offered their expertise, opinions, and information with no strings attached; indeed, their enthusiasm and encouragement made this book possible.

Jim Hambrick completes this triad of Reeves experts. Hambrick, founder of The Super Museum in Metropolis, Illinois, provided us with Sergeant V. A. Peterson's files on the case, including copies of the police and autopsy reports pertaining to the death of George Reeves. Despite a bad cold in the depths of a midwestern winter, Hambrick graciously shared his information and theories with us.

Jim Nolt, editor of *The Adventures Continue*—the only publication in America devoted to the life and career of George Reeves—also provided essential keys to the puzzle. He and his wife, Gail, helped give Reeves's story a human face; through Nolt's encyclopedic knowledge of Reeves's life, we were able to corroborate much of our earlier information. More important, the Nolts gave us an understanding of the genuine impact Reeves-as-Superman had on that first TV generation of Superman aficionados.

We thank Bette Shayne for her revealing and detailed account of George Reeves's life as a suburbanite and behind the scenes at *The Ad-*

ventures of Superman; she helped us enormously in deepening our portrait of Reeves.

It was Jack Larson who offered a full, intimate picture of who George Reeves was during the making of *The Adventures of Superman.* Larson's grasp of the ironic moment and his poet's eye for detail helped us flesh out a ghost. His actor's insight into Reeves's dilemma helped us better understand our subject. Although we came to different conclusions as to Reeves's fate, we remain grateful to Larson—Superman's true pal—for his honesty and his superb memory.

Lee Saylor's remarkable conversations, which he recorded with Leonore Lemmon in the summer of 1989, proved an invaluable boon to our research. We are grateful for his generosity in sharing them with us; his own insights and theories were also enlightening and helped us to describe the last days of George Reeves. Without the discovery of his material, our book could never have been completed. Indeed, our recreation of the events that took place in the early morning hours of June 16, 1959, and all allegations regarding William "Bill" Bliss, Gwen Dailey, and Carol Van Ronkel, are based on Leonore Lemmon's own words, as recorded by Lee Saylor during his interview with her.

Our gratitude, also, to the following people who shared their thoughts and reminiscences with us, and who were far more helpful than they could have imagined: Henny Backus, Jan Bliss, Leo Boroskin (who wishes to remain pseudonymous), Eddie Bracken, Fred Crane, John Fields, Sydney Guilaroff, Joe Hyams, Gene La Belle, Peter Levinson, Michael Selsman, Constance Shirley (who, we're sad to report, died before this book was completed), Dr. John E. Smialek, Milo Spiriglio, Dr. Barry Taff, Dr. Philip Terman, Harry Thomas, Elaine Young, and Henny Youngman.

We also thank Arlene Hellerman, a fount of information on the ways of Hollywood and show business lore.

For Charles Spicer, our editor at St. Martin's Press, who brought this book into being, our deepest gratitude for his faith in us. He is part Pinkerton, part Max Perkins. We also thank his assistant, Katerina Christopoulos, for her many kindnesses. They were both a joy to work with, and, speaking of great joys, we thank our agent Joy Harris, who never lost faith in this project and who put her own considerable gifts at our disposal. There are others who helped us at the Robert Lantz-Joy Harris Literary Agency whom we would like to acknowledge: the luminous Leslie Daniels and the unflappable Paul Chung.

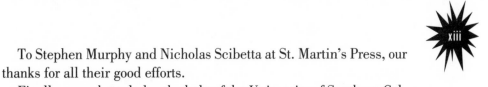

To Stephen Murphy and Nicholas Scibetta at St. Martin's Press, our thanks for all their good efforts.

Finally, we acknowledge the help of the University of Southern California Cinema-Television Library and Archive, the New York Public Library at Lincoln Center, as well as The Academy of Motion Picture Archives, which provided us with all the major news coverage of George Reeves's death and subsequent controversy over the verdict of suicide. Our gratitude, again, to Dan Einstein at the UCLA Film and Television Archive for making Reeves's early television work available to us.

Major published sources of information include Otto Friedrich's *City of Nets* (New York: Harper & Row, 1986); Jerry Giesler's *The Jerry Giesler Story* as told to Pete Martin (New York: Simon and Schuster, 1960); Stewart Granger's *Sparks Fly Upward* (New York: G.P. Putnam & Sons, 1981); Gary Grossman's *Superman, Serial to Cereal,* published as part of the Big Apple Film Series, edited by Leonard Maltin (New York: Popular Library, 1976); Jan Alan Henderson's "Speeding Bullet: George Reeves, the Man, the Myth, the Mystery" (*Cult Movies,* No. 14, 1995); and Samuel Marx and Joyce Vanderveen's *Deadly Illusions* (New York: Random House, 1990).

We have reconstructed conversations between George Reeves and other persons in this book based on firsthand accounts of his behavior and activities, as revealed to us over many hours of interviewing his friends and acquaintances. In other cases, dialogue attributed to Reeves, Helen Bessolo, the Mannixes, and Leonore Lemmon were taken from newspaper accounts of the day. Conversations between Toni Mannix, Samuel Marx, and Howard Strickling were taken from Samuel Marx and Joyce Vanderveen's *Deadly Illusions,* which we hereby acknowledge. Testimony from Phyllis Coates and Dr. Paul Hanson are from Jan Alan Henderson's article cited above. And conversations between Toni Mannix and Stewart Granger are from Granger's autobiography, acknowledged above, *Sparks Fly Upward.*

Otherwise, we don't claim that all dialogue represents verbatim quotations; rather it is a re-creation based on our best understanding of Reeves's personality, character, and mental state. For information from Helen Bessolo's relatives, we thank Jim Beaver, who has worked closely with the Bessolo family for several years and who shared much of his findings with us. Our solution to this mystery is entirely our own, differing from conclusions drawn by other researchers into the Reeves case.

Hollywood has a long rap sheet—from Fatty Arbuckle's final party to Johnny Stompanato's death at the hands of Lana Turner's teenage daughter—but some Hollywood crimes have never been solved. This is a story of sex and murder and the suppression of evidence. It is also about the death of Superman.

In the early morning hours of June 16, 1959, a shot rang out through the narrow street that winds tortuously through Benedict Canyon: a haunted street that runs through jagged hills and rocky terrain, rising gradually from the expensive real estate of Beverly Hills. While his fiancée drank with a handful of strangers gathered in the living room below, actor George Reeves—tucked away in his tiny upstairs bedroom—suffered a fatal gunshot wound to the head.

No one knew exactly how long it took the party of witnesses downstairs to call the police—it could have been anywhere from three quarters of an hour to four hours after finding the man who played Superman lying prone on his blood-soaked bed. Except for Leonore Lemmon, Reeves's flamboyant girlfriend of a few months, the other guests were virtual strangers: two Benedict Canyon residents named William Bliss and Carol Van Ronkel, and a visiting journalist named Robert Condon. There were rumors of heavy drinking, but the assembled guests managed to agree on two things, after the fact: that George Reeves, typecast by his role as Superman on the popular television series, had been out of work and severely depressed. And that moments before the shot broke the stillness of the canyon, Leonore predicted that George was going to shoot himself.

But many didn't believe their story. The rumors as to what really happened to George Reeves the night his life ended persist to this day: that he was depressed about the accounts of children maiming themselves trying to fly in their Superman costumes; that he thought he *could* fly and jumped out of a third-story window; that he liked to play Russian roulette because he was, after all, invincible; that he was suicidal over his inability to find acting work when *The Adventures of Superman* was canceled; that he was forever typecast; that he was murdered over gambling debts; that his girlfriend at the time, "international party girl" Leonore Lemmon, killed him when he called off their engagement; that he was murdered by a jealous husband, none other than powerful MGM executive Eddie Mannix, whose wife Toni had been George's lover for ten years.

One thing is clear. The Los Angeles Police Department did little to investigate his death, although the .30-caliber Luger found at George's feet had been so heavily oiled that no fingerprints showed up on the gun. None of those present the night George died attended his funeral, and his erstwhile fiancée skipped town, never to return.

For those old enough to understand, and for those who would one day come to know what had happened to Superman, the world would never again be the same, nor feel as safe. They knew that behind all that talk about "truth, justice, and the American way" some terrible secret lurked. Because he stood on top of the world in that thrilling opening of *The Adventures of Superman,* he had seemed invincible. But with George Reeves's death, how can you trust anything any adult told you about the world—a world in which not even Superman was safe?

Though the LAPD would finally insist upon an official verdict of suicide, Reeves's mother, his closest friends, a high-profile defense attorney, operatives of the Nick Harris Detective Agency, and at least one officer involved in the case were all convinced that the witnesses assembled at Reeves's Benedict Canyon house that night were not telling the truth.

1

MAD ABOUT THE BOY

There it was, that unmistakable voice. Even her friends described it as "imperious." Toni Mannix was in high dudgeon, which is Noel Coward for "pissed off." This was in 1972, some thirteen years after George Reeves's death and nine years after the death of Eddie Mannix, Toni's husband. She was cursing a blue streak and, for a minute, sounded like she was channeling some of her husband's best bits of dialogue.

"Get the fuck over here right now," Toni yelled into the phone. "Some asshole from the *Times* wants to do a piece on George. I told him to get lost. That I have nothing to say, but he won't leave me alone. I need some help. Now!"

Why Toni Mannix? Why was she calling after all this time? Howard Strickling hadn't heard that voice in over ten years. Strickling was the retired head of publicity at MGM—retired "publicity genius" was more like it. Toni used to call Strickling when she needed something—some big favor that she always referred to as some little favor. It used to drive Strickling crazy, and that voice! She used to lay it on, thick and heavy, for Strickling, like the kind of maple syrup he liked to pour over his flannel cakes at Musso & Frank's, that big, dark, workhorse of a restaurant over on Hollywood Boulevard. Howard used to sit with Gable in the great old days of MGM, in one of the booths toward the back of the cavernous room, inhaling martinis.

Strickling had some idea of what Toni Mannix wanted. Toni had been involved in one of Hollywood's enduring mysteries. She had been George Reeves's lover for ten years, though all that time she was married to Eddie Mannix, one of the most feared and powerful executives

3

in the movie business. Eddie Mannix had been Strickling's boss at MGM.

• • •

In 1959, Toni was too genteel for rough language. She was "high-society Hollywood." Reeves, who was born in Woolstock, Iowa, and grew up in Kentucky and California, was never her equal socially or financially. Sure, he moved in her circle, drank with her friends, attended her parties, because he and Toni Mannix, for about ten years, were inseparable.

Toni Mannix and George Reeves began their love affair around 1949. At fifty-two, Toni was seven years older than George and crazy about him. She called him "the boy" in that faux aristocratic accent employed by a lot of ex–New York showgirls of the era who suddenly found themselves with money and a social position in Hollywood. It's the dropped "r" accent of Mrs. Thurston Howell III in *Gilligan's Island,* of a slew of B-movie actresses playing society dames in romantic comedies. They made Chasen's sound like Buckingham Palace when it was actually filled with *shtarkers*—that's a Yiddish word for "tough guys." Lenny Bruce's definition of a *shtarker* is a guy who wears woolen suits without any underwear, which describes Toni's husband Eddie Mannix.

Of course, there were those who thought Toni's air of gentility was laid on with a shovel. She was capable of making a scene in a restaurant, but she would never have been thrown out of the Stork Club. George loved Toni's parties. He loved to have a lot of people around him, he loved to drink, and he loved people to drink around him.

Maybe because she was so much older than George—and though still a striking, handsome woman, past the age when a woman wants to compete for the hearts and souls of men—Toni was particularly possessive. "She was jealous in the sense that she was jealous of his time," a member of the cast of *The Adventures of Superman* said about their relationship. "She didn't like him to be alone with anybody without her being a part of it. Not just in a male-female sense. She didn't like for him to get into a conversation with his director!"

She could be a hellion if she thought another woman was moondogging her quail—then the glacé, three-quarter-length gloves would come off. Phyllis Coates, who played Lois Lane in the first year of the TV show, felt Toni's heat. "She wanted to be sure I had no designs on

George," she said. At their first meeting in a Mexican restaurant, Phyllis Coates felt Toni sizing her up, making sure that Lois Lane really didn't have the hots for Superman. She was satisfied by what she saw. Toni offered her the peace pipe by taking Phyllis to a health spa on La Cienega for steam baths and massages.

• • •

Eddie was a tough guy with a heart of tungsten. He was a vice president at MGM. That was his title, "president of vice," and that was his job. His work was to clean up the mess, to put the stars back into alignment whenever they started careening out of control and threatened to blow up the whole works. It was Eddie's job to be the eyes and ears for Louis B. Mayer. If the MGM lion had any cubs out of wedlock, Eddie Mannix would be the first to know about it and would find the little whelps a good home. Or drown them in the executive washroom.

Eddie Mannix was a *shlub* who got lucky, who provided a service to MGM, and who was paid handsomely for his street smarts. He seemed like someone who would hurt you, and that was his ace. The moguls at MGM kept him around because he made them look good. One of Eddie's cronies said, "In reality, he was like the toughest guy on your block who hung around the candy store. MGM was the candy store, and compared to Samuel Goldwyn, Eddie was tough."

An ex-bouncer from New Jersey, Eddie was invaluable to the studio in their battle with the unions. Even the more dignified studio chiefs like Irving Thalberg brought Eddie Mannix with him to meetings. Having Eddie around was like playing "good cop, bad cop": He made the studio chiefs look benevolent, as harmless as retired shoe salesmen at a Collins Avenue bingo tournament. Eddie had honed his union-busting skills back in Jersey, and by the mid-1930s, Hollywood was having its own troubles with the fledgling Screen Writers Guild, which the studios refused even to acknowledge. When the Screen Writers Guild considered joining forces with the Dramatists Guild, Eddie read the riot act to all of MGM's employees, reminding them not to pry open the fist that fed them.

Eddie was continually earning his stripes for the MGM paterfamilias. When Carole Lombard's plane strayed off course and smashed into a cliff near the top of Potosi Mountain in Las Vegas, it was Eddie Mannix who led the mules up into the snow-covered mountains to retrieve the actress's charred and decapitated body.

In the 1930s, MGM was wired for sound. Not only the pictures themselves, but the actors. Whenever an actor walked into the MGM Telegraph Office to send a telegram or pick up a message, a copy always went to Eddie Mannix. The dingy room was constantly busy, filled with studio personnel, sending and receiving the most intimate kinds of messages, but only Mayer's inner circle knew that copies of every telegram coming in or going out wound up in Eddie Mannix's powerful mitts. It was the equivalent of having your phone tapped. Mannix derived his power from knowing things about people, things that were none of his business. It gave him enormous clout as a kind of glorified blackmailer, one who wanted to be paid off only in silence. He would read those telegrams in his office, then take them home and read them in bed. Better than those novels Toni read with her gardenia bookmark, which just made the house smell like a funeral at a ladies' luncheon.

When Paul Bern was found dead soon after marrying Jean Harlow, it was Eddie who thought up the angle that made Paul Bern the most maligned husband in America. To prevent any suspicion of murder falling across MGM's hottest property, Eddie launched the story that Paul Bern had killed himself out of despair over being impotent. A big lie, but Bern could be sacrificed, Harlow could not. Irving Thalberg—he of the weak heart—once tried to talk Louis B. Mayer out of the practice of collecting information through Eddie's "subterranean pipeline," but Mayer insisted that the practice was invaluable, especially now, when East Coast–based unions were threatening to infiltrate MGM's "one big happy family."

Howard Strickling was Eddie's best customer for what he was peddling. "With the information that was available to him," according to MGM screenwriter-turned-executive Sam Marx, "Mannix was always able to pass on ultra-exclusive material to Howard Strickling about the private activities of studio personnel that nobody was ever supposed to know."

But Eddie's real power came from the niche in Hollywood that was filled by organized crime. Eddie thought such connections useful in keeping his stars in line. He had made friends with a number of gangsters when he was just a kid working construction at New Jersey's Palisades Park. He liked the company of bookmakers, bootleggers, prize fight promoters, and talent agents, in that order. They enjoyed dropping in on Eddie to reminisce. Plus, the Vegas hoods he hung with were good company. Eddie drank their bathwater to give him courage, and the palm trees of Hollywood made those gangsters feel like pharaohs being cooled down in the temple of beauty. Toni derived her power from Eddie's connections. And from the perception of Eddie's power, which would outlive even Eddie himself.

• • •

When Camille "Toni" Lanier, fresh from Broadway, walked onto a Culver City soundstage for the first time to appear in the film *Ziegfeld Follies*, Eddie picked her out of a production number and said to an assistant, "Give that girl $4,500 for the day's work and have her come see me." After that, Toni never had to work again.

Toni Mannix had been a big-time beauty, a real Ziegfeld Follies showgirl, billed as "the girl with the million-dollar legs." She was still a beauty—a classy, dark-haired woman who liked her bridge games, her charities, and her "boy." She would meet him on the set of *The Adventures of Superman* in the old RKO-Pathé Studio in Culver City and bring him his lunch in a brown paper bag. And help him drink it. She was a two-fisted drinker, like George. She enjoyed being teased by him in front of their friends. "You were real hot last night, baby, what set you off?" George would tease his lady love, or so Jack Larson, aka Jimmy Olsen, remembered. He also remembered Toni as a charming and generous woman, and that George seemed to be as mad about her as Toni was about him.

Gene Tierney could have played her in the movies. Everyone in Hollywood seemed to like her. She was high-spirited and looked good in hats. She remembered your birthday. She had great style in everything she did. Eddie was known as "the Bulldog," Toni was known as "Lady." She had an enviable position: She had the power and prestige of the movie business through her husband, but without the fishbowl existence movie stardom bestows. Toni and George both got involved with the Myasthenia Gravis Foundation and the leukemia research work at the City of Hope and other charities involving children. She tried to improve her mind by reading the books George gave her; she filled up her gated Beverly Hills mansion at 1120 El Retiro Way with all sorts of books. George liked to talk about Shakespeare, so Toni made every effort to read that weird stuff. George got her to read the scandalous new novel by that Russian emigré writer, what was his name—Nabokov—about the dirty old man with the double name and the hot young bombshell. (What did that queer writer on TV say about *Lolita*? That it was a great guide to motels.) She tried to educate herself. She worked on her accent. She wore white gloves. She advised George not to be photographed smoking a cigarette in public—it didn't jibe with his Superman image.

• • •

Eddie and Toni had been together a long time, so long in fact that Eddie was relieved when Toni fell for one of the Tarleton twins from *Gone With the Wind,* the one played by George Reeves. It took a lot of pressure off Eddie. And by the late 1950s his heart resembled a big fist of heavily marbled beef. His angina attacks were coming fast and furious. It was like José Greco dancing on his chest every time he went to brush his teeth. But every so often he would have a good day. He would get up out of bed, even go into work. Fire a few people and go home to take a nap. So he was grateful to have George Reeves do the heavy lifting for him. "Like they do in Europe," Eddie would say in his own defense whenever he had to think about it for too long.

Part of Eddie's appeal for Toni Mannix—besides his money and his power—was that he represented old Hollywood in all its glory. But by the mid-1950s, the studios were losing power, and television was the reason. People weren't going to the movies anymore. Everyone was staying home to watch those goddamn shows that were making stars out of character actors like Raymond Burr, Walter Brennan, Robert Young— even baseball players like Chuck Connors. George had become that new phenomenon in American life: a television star. The changes were affecting Eddie Mannix as well. Toni could hear him stumbling around in his bedroom at night like a caged bear. Her bedroom was just down the red-carpeted hall from Eddie's. "The red sea," she called it. It separated them the way her love for George kept her from having the marriage she and Eddie used to have.

• • •

Officers Don Johnson and Daniel E. Korby found a gruesome sight when they answered the call from George Reeves's home at 1579 Benedict Canyon. There was a lot of blood. Maybe because it was a small room and he was such a big guy. After all, he was Superman, and bullets were supposed to bounce off his chest. He wasn't supposed to die, not ever,

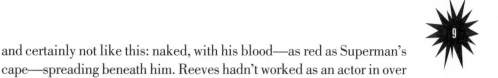
and certainly not like this: naked, with his blood—as red as Superman's cape—spreading beneath him. Reeves hadn't worked as an actor in over two years, but he was still Superman to 10 million American baby boomers—and the news hit them the next morning like a meteor crashing into a schoolyard. Superman, the man who couldn't die, was dead as a city pigeon.

Within hours of George's death, Sergeant V. A. Peterson was assigned to the case: #45426. His report is a one-page novel typed out on the chief medical examiner's stationery by P. Cain in prose that's pure *Dragnet:*

At approximately 12:00 A.M., June 16, 1959, decedent retired, leaving two house guests, Leonore Lemmon and Robert Condon, to retire to their respective rooms. At approximately 12:05 A.M., William Bliss and Carol Van Ronkel arrived and were admitted by Leonore Lemmon. The decedent came down from his upstairs bedroom wearing a bathrobe, upset and irritated by the arrival of the two guests at such a late hour. An argument ensued between the decedent and Mr. Bliss. Mr. Bliss apologized, which calmed the decedent, who later apologized for his conduct.

At approximately 1:20 A.M., the decedent excused himself as he was going upstairs to bed. Miss Lemmon at this time made a statement, "He is going to shoot himself." Shortly, they heard a dresser drawer being opened upstairs, and Miss Lemmon commented, "He is getting the gun out now, and he is going to shoot himself." Moments later a shot was heard and Miss Lemmon asked Mr. Bliss to go upstairs and see what happened.

Mr. Bliss entered the upstairs bedroom and observed the decedent lying nude on his back, across the bed. There was a large amount of blood on his body and head. He went back downstairs and told the rest of the guests what he had observed.

Mr. Bliss then called the LAPD and on their arrival, took them upstairs to the bedroom. There was a .30-caliber German Luger lying on the floor between the decedent's feet. The bullet had passed through the head and had lodged in the ceiling of the room. The shell casing was found on the bed under the decedent's body. The bathrobe was laying on the foot of the bed. No notes or messages giving reasons for his actions were found. Witnesses present stated he was quite despondent about not being able to get the type of acting work that he wanted. The guests were instructed to leave the premises and the residence was sealed by the Coroner's Representatives.

There was nothing in any class at the police academy that could have prepared Detective Sergeant Johnson for the way he felt in the Reeves house that night. He had been called to the scene of more than a few suicides; they were always miserable affairs. He remembered one, in a hotel room, when the room itself seemed to smell of failure and desperation, almost as if someone had swung a censer across the bed. An old-time actor had blown his brains out on his own monogrammed satin pillow. But this was different. For one thing, there were people around. Most suicides, in Johnson's experience, were private acts. Not even in Hollywood would someone want an audience when they decide to shoot themselves. And what were those fresh bruises doing on Reeves's forehead and chest, like faint inkblots? Johnson stared at the bedsheets for a long time. They looked pulled apart, stuck to Reeves's back, like someone had pinned them there. They looked, well . . . like a cape. If Reeves had sat up in bed and shot himself, why did the bedsheets look like they had just gone a few rounds with Rocky Marciano? When Officer Korby discovered the bullet hole in George's ceiling, that told Sergeant Johnson something. If George had shot himself while sitting up in bed, which is what it looked like from the position of the body sprawled out on the edge of the bed, his legs hanging off the side, then what was that bullet hole doing in the ceiling? He would have had to have blown the side of his head off to be holding the gun at the kind of angle it would take for the bullet to end up lodged in the ceiling. But Sergeant Johnson knew that bullets do strange things when they pass through bone and flesh and take a man's life. It wasn't the "decedent" that bothered him so much as the living, breathing "witnesses" downstairs—they gave him the willies. They all seemed too certain about what had happened. It was as if they were actors in a school play, struggling to remain in character and remember their lines. For example, Johnson thought it more than a little weird that they all started to talk about how George couldn't find any work after *Superman*—how depressed he'd been lately at his lack of prospects. Especially Miss Lemmon and Mr. Bliss. They all seemed more concerned with getting out of the house than with consoling one another. And they were very drunk.

Almost anything, Sergeant Johnson told his fellow officer, could

Sam Kashner & Nancy Schoenberger

have happened in that house. George's kitchen counter had looked like a distillery, and most of the bottles were empty. Sergeant Johnson was beginning to feel that he could use a drink himself as he waited for the coroner's office to send somebody over to Superman's house, where the Man of Steel was now cold as ice.

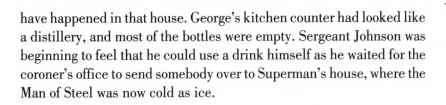

2

HELEN AND GEORGE

Who was he, this American stranger who became Superman? This Iowa-born, California-raised man with three names? George Brewer-Bessolo-Reeves and Superman had a lot in common, at least at the beginning. Both had more than one father, and both were told that their real fathers had died. Superman never knew his father, Jor-El, master inventor late of the planet Krypton; Helen Lescher left George's father shortly after their hasty marriage.

Soon after becoming pregnant with George in the spring of 1913, nineteen-year-old Helen married the man she had been seeing—a twenty-four-year-old druggist named Don C. Brewer—in a hurried ceremony. Helen and Don Brewer rented a small, white frame house in Woolstock, Iowa. The now-elderly daughter of the house's original owners remembers Helen Brewer as "finicky" and "demanding," complaining about the wallpaper the owners had put up in the house. She hocked her mother-in-law's jewelry to furnish the simple dwelling as if it were the abode of a Middle Eastern princess. She also insisted on washing George's dirty diapers in the kitchen sink and hanging them up to drip-dry over Don's sandwiches, going so far, remembers one relative, as to thrust a monstrous ball of George's dirty diapers under the startled young druggist's nose. She made him smell it, as if it were a bouquet of roses. It was clear from the outset who was the important male in the Brewer household. Soon after George's birth on January 5, 1914, the marriage collapsed.

So the young mother and son left Woolstock, Iowa, and bounced around for a while, moving near her parents in Ashland, Kentucky, for a time, before drifting west to California and settling in Pasadena, at that time a sleepy suburb of Los Angeles. Helen lied to George about his date of birth in order to cover up the fact that he was conceived out of wedlock, celebrating George's birthday in April instead of January. However, when George was old enough to understand, she told her boy a far greater lie: that his father had committed suicide by shooting himself in the head.

Helen soon set her sights on Frank Bessolo, a member of a well-to-do family from the wine country of northern California. This was during Prohibition, when the only people prospering besides the bootleggers were those who produced wine for the Catholic church, which is how the Bessolo family stayed in business. Helen and Frank married, and Frank adopted George in 1927, giving him the name that Jack Warner would later take away from him in 1939 during the filming of *Gone With the Wind.* George became very close to his adoptive father, which should have pleased Helen, but it had the unfortunate effect of exacerbating her possessiveness. Frank and George became inseparable, spending hours in the kitchen together concocting fabulous feasts—one of Frank's favorite pastimes—and Helen's jealousy of the close bond between her husband and her son grew. After eight years of marriage, Helen left Frank: There was no room in Helen's life for any man but George, whose acting career she would later follow with intense anxiety. Helen got a generous settlement from Frank Bessolo and moved back to Pasadena, where she bought a spacious and attractive house on Michigan Avenue, and could live happily with her son without competition from anyone else. George was hurt by the loss of the only father he had ever known, but Helen didn't concern herself with that. In fact, she forbade the boy even to mention his fondness for his adoptive father, and eventually she wouldn't allow Frank Bessolo's name to be spoken in her house. Perhaps she feared that Frank's infatuation with his adopted son was "unhealthy," and she was, after all, saving George's love for herself.

As George grew into a strapping young man, bigger and more solidly built than his school chums, Helen took to introducing him as her handsome brother instead of her son. She became known in her exclusive neighborhood as an eccentric, the kind of woman who would call the police whenever the kids in the neighborhood walked across her lawn. In one of George's school reports, a tactful teacher noted that "Mrs. Bessolo is something of an exotic."

At Pasadena Junior College where Reeves was a student, he developed an enthusiasm for boxing. He was good at it; he could have been a contender. A Pasadena sportswriter by the name of Mannie Pineta once sparred with Reeves and described him as "the greatest ring prospect in 1932 . . ." Another sparring partner who outweighed and outclassed George in the ring wasn't so complimentary, however. He said that George "wasn't a cream puff but he didn't have the killer instinct you need to be a great fighter." It's possible that George was drawn to the sweet science as a way to escape Helen's possessiveness. It was the one activity of George's that she severely disapproved of. Boxing served a dual purpose: It gave him back some control in his life, and it was a place where he could act out the rage he felt toward his domineering mother, to punch through the skein of lies she was weaving for him.

When George entered the Golden Gloves competition as a six-foot-two, one-hundred-ninety-five-pound light heavyweight, Helen was appalled by her son's willingness to hurt himself and mar his good looks. "At the last minute, his mother wouldn't let him fight. She was afraid he'd get banged up and ruin his acting career," Pineta remembered. So Helen allegedly paid a retired boxer to beat up her son before he set foot into the ring. George Bessolo gave up—*no mas!*—and decided to become an actor.

So George entered manhood after losing two fathers and caving in to his mother's wishes—not an auspicious beginning for the Man of Steel.

George trained as an actor at The Pasadena Community Playhouse (which later became the famed Pasadena Playhouse, training ground for a slew of successful actors, including Victor Mature, Robert Preston, and Dustin Hoffman). The Playhouse occupied a tiled, Spanish-style building, a duplicate of a Tucson, Arizona, theater, and it became George's refuge. George spent hours in the courtyard, absorbing the atmosphere and ingratiating himself with the students and directors, and with the Playhouse's majordomo, Gilmor Brown, an exquisitely well-mannered, pipe-smoking gay man who kept the Playhouse together, body and soul. Brown was the Tyrone Guthrie of Pasadena; Mature and Preston were two of his leading actors around the time George was there. Everyone liked George Bessolo—this big, friendly young man who played Spanish songs on the guitar. George met a young Hispanic acting student named Natividad Vacio—"Nati"—and the two became lifelong friends. Nati, with his courtly manners and good looks, had even charmed Helen.

George became Gilmor Brown's secretary. Brown, too, was mad about the boy, inviting his secretary over for dinner and taking some of "the boys" to Europe and to the London theatre for a holiday. Some people have speculated on whether George was gay or bisexual. This would have been a good beginning for any bisexuality to flourish, or simply for rumors of bisexuality to flourish, since those who knew Gilmor Brown assumed his inner circle were all gay men. Given George's lack of a strong father and his difficult relationship with his eccentric, domineering mother, George certainly fit the cliché, though no man has ever come forward to claim the distinction of being George Reeves's lover.

When Reeves started appearing onstage in productions at The Pasadena Community Playhouse, Helen began sending him telegrams after each opening night with intimate messages signed "All my love, Helen." Long before George's violent death, Helen had already created a kind of shrine to her living son, complete with flickering votive candles. Once he launched his acting career, she plastered her walls with his 8-x-10 glossies. Later on, she would prefer the photos in which George appeared with famous actors and actresses: Alan Ladd, Claudette Colbert, Rita Hayworth, Marlene Dietrich, Merle Oberon. Their reflected glory made George's star shine more brightly.

George made his movie debut in 1939 as Stuart Tartleton, one of the red-haired, Yankee-hating young gentlemen known as the Tarleton twins in David O. Selznick's epic soap opera *Gone With the Wind.* In that big panoramic opening scene, Scarlett O'Hara holds court under the spreading oaks of Tara while Brent and Stuart Tarleton flirt with her and discuss rumors of war. George's scenes were shot early in the production, when George Cukor was still directing the film. But there were problems that first day. George's makeup and hair dyed red looked comical on film, and they were never able to get it quite right.

On September 22, 1940, Bessolo—now Reeves, thanks to Jack Warner's seigneurial interest in how the credits would look on his film—eloped with a young actress named Ellanora Needles whom he'd met at The Pasadena Community Playhouse. (He had asked Gilmor Brown to introduce him to the fetching acting student, which Brown did, reluctantly.) Helen actually seemed to approve of Ellanora, and the two women got along well. Maybe Helen saw something of herself in the slim, dark-haired woman. Or perhaps she was relieved that this marriage proved her son's masculinity. Curiously, three of the most important women in George's life would have similar names: Helen, Ellanora, and Leonore, the last two being variations of the name "Helen," she whose face launched a thousand ships. (The cover of Action Comics's June 1949 Issue No. 133 announces "Can You Blame Lois Lane For Being Jealous When The Man of Steel Teams Up With The World's Most Perfect Girl?"—who happens to be named Helen.)

Reeves and his young bride were married just as the war in Europe was breaking out. The young couple soon began planning for a life in the theatre. Romantic theatrical couples like the Lunts and the Oliviers were icons for Ellanora and George. Their days were filled with auditions and gatherings with other young actors, but the long nights were another matter entirely. George was plagued by nightmares: Hardly a week would go by when he would not be awakened by the same dream. It wouldn't leave him. Once he'd dreamed it, sleep was impossible. Better to pour himself a drink and sit by the window watching Ellanora sleep. She would probably ask him in the morning why he had roamed about the small apartment until dawn. It was always the same terrible dream: It looked like a man but he couldn't see his face. It was as if the face were covered by wire mesh, as if he were looking at you from behind a screen door. The figure had a gun. George was afraid, begging him to leave him alone. The man just laughed and fired the gun once into George's face. That's when George would yell out in his sleep. That's what always woke him up: his own calling out in the night.

By 1943, George had enlisted in the Army and was assigned to the Theatrical Unit, where he served for the duration of World War II. Just before joining up, however, George had his greatest acting opportunity yet: He was signed by director Mark Sandrich to appear opposite Claudette Colbert in *So Proudly We Hail,* a wartime drama about nurses serving in Baatan in the South Pacific. Sandrich was taken with George Reeves and promised that as soon as the war was over, he would make George into a bona fide movie star.

But there was trouble brewing in paradise: If George already had reason to resent his mother's meddling, he would soon have proof of her cruelty. Toward the end of the war, Reeves was stationed in New York City, where the brilliant playwright and director Moss Hart cast him in the role of Lieutenant Thompson in the stage play *Winged Victory.* (He would later appear in the film version of this dramatic musical about the Air Corps.) Ellanora Needles was also given a part in the large cast. The play toured throughout the country, its patriotic themes stirring audiences. After one particular performance, however, George was approached backstage by a middle-aged man who introduced himself as Don Brewer, George's father.

The sight of this melancholy looking midwesterner bearing strange news was staggering to George. An army buddy remembered that he nearly passed out. George realized what an enormous lie his mother had told him—that his real father had committed suicide—and he refused to speak to Helen for the next several years. But his anger was not cleansing. Reeves's career and his marriage both took a nosedive, and in 1949, he and Ellanora divorced.

Ellanora had left him for another man, a well-to-do attorney named Edward Rose. She was tired of the insecure life of an actor, and it no longer looked like Reeves and Needles were going to become Lunt and Fontanne. George did appear in one film during his stint in the army— a V.D. training film which was a rather unpleasant black-and-white biology lesson and cautionary tale called *Sex Hygiene*. And whatever momentum his career had as a result of *Gone With the Wind* and *So Proudly We Hail*, the work he was offered after the war gave him little hope of stardom. The major film actors—Jimmy Stewart, Clark Gable, even Ronald Reagan—were quickly rebuilding their careers, but Reeves couldn't seem to regain his footing. The greatest blow to George's ambitions was his discovery after the war that Mark Sandrich had died.

The first time Jack Larson—who was to play Jimmy Olsen, cub reporter—met George Reeves, Reeves was dressed in his Superman suit. "We sat and talked a bit on the set of *The Adventures of Superman*," Larson remembered. "At that point, he had complimented me on a film I had done, *Fighter Squadron*, for Raoul Walsh, whom George had regarded as a great director. And I said I'd always remembered him in *So Proudly We Hail* with Claudette Colbert. He said, 'If Mark Sandrich hadn't died young, I wouldn't be sitting here in this monkey suit today.'"

The nadir of George's career was appearing in a 1948 Jungle Jim picture with an aging Johnny Weissmuller, called *Jungle Goddess*. "No matter how bad these features were," wrote film historian and writer Jan Alan Henderson, "they could not have prepared George for *The Adventures of Sir Galahad* [in 1949], considered one of the worst serials offered to the kiddie matinee crowd." The sets were from second-rate Westerns gussied up to resemble Arthurian England. Excalibur was clearly cardboard, and the enchanted forest was Hopalong Cassidy's old ranch. This had to have been a bitter pill for Reeves, who believed that

his detour in the armed forces had waylaid his career despite *Gone With the Wind, So Proudly We Hail,* and a small part in *Blood and Sand* in 1942. He should have been a movie star—he was trained to be a leading man on film—but the war did him in.

Meanwhile, Helen Bessolo perfected that shrine to her son, lighting candles under the glossy headshots sent over from the Warner Bros.' publicity department. If it was meant to be some kind of voodoo ensuring that her son would never leave her for the glamorous life of a movie star, it worked. If the shrine was the acting out of some unspoken premonition of a death foretold, well, that was appropriate, too.

• • •

George Reeves and Jack Larson were hoping that no one but a handful of kids would ever see *The Adventures of Superman.* In the early days of television, a TV series was an elephants' graveyard for film actors. Television started out as a live medium, but Hopalong Cassidy—William Boyd—changed all that. Boyd had bought up all of his forty-minute, Saturday matinee "programmers" and was able to distribute them to independent television stations, and they became the biggest sensation in the country after Milton Berle. "Hoppy" was on the cover of *Time* and he was absolutely the biggest kiddie star in the world. American youth were carrying Hopalong Cassidy lunch boxes to school with them and counting the long hours until the end of the school day on their Hoppy wristwatches. With the tremendous success of these early series, the TV geniuses realized that they could depart from live shows and work with film on television, so they began with *I Love Lucy,* the original *Life of Riley,* and *The Adventures of Superman.*

Superman had debuted on the cover of the first issue of Action Comics (a spinoff of Detective Comics) in June of 1938. The action hero was dreamed up one sleepless night in 1934 by Jerry Siegel, a skinny Jewish teenager attending Cleveland's Glenville High School. Siegel got his friend Joe Schuster, also a Jewish boy and the son of a Cleveland tailor, to create the drawings that would embody Siegel's fever dream—a dream inspired, some say, by his hopeless crush on Lois Amster, the class beauty who served as the inspiration for Lois Lane.

Detective Comics originally had balked at buying the comic strip from the two boys and paid them only $130 for the rights to their creation. By the time Reeves was donning his blue tights, the popular comic hero had appeared in two hundred fifty newspapers and had launched thirteen years of radio shows and two movie serials. Science-fiction writer Harlan Ellison has observed that there are only five fictive characters known worldwide: Tarzan, Sherlock Holmes, Mickey Mouse, Robin Hood, and Superman. All would eventually find their way in the new medium, beginning with Superman.

Jack Larson's response to being offered the role of Jimmy Olsen, Superman's pal, was typical of the attitude serious actors had about appearing in a TV serial made for children. "I was offered the part of Jimmy Olsen on the *Superman* show," remembered the eternally youthful actor, "and I had reservations about it. I said, 'I don't know if I want to do this.' They sat me down and they said, 'Kid, you're confused. You want to get to New York? That's good, but you don't have the money to go to New York. This is twenty-six weeks' work. It's money, and nobody will ever see the show.' They told me George Reeves had done something called *Sir Galahad* just to pick up money . . . They said, 'Take the money and run,' so I did it."

More than two hundred actors were being considered for the role of Superman. Producer and writer Robert Maxwell and director Tommy Carr scoped out the bodybuilders along Muscle Beach in Venice, California, and interviewed agents and actors in the Culver City studio where *The Adventures of Superman* would be filmed. But when George Reeves was ushered in by his agent, they knew Superman had walked into the room: It was the jaw—inviting and reassuring as a front porch. When Maxwell offered Reeves the job, Reeves talked it over with Nati Vacio, his friend from The Pasadena Community Playhouse. George was worried about accepting the role—after thirteen years as an actor in the movies, had it really come down to running around in longjohns? But then, maybe no one really would see the show, except for a bunch of kids with TV sets, so no harm would be done.

Phyllis Coates, a slim, auburn-haired young actress, was picked to be Lois Lane. When she first met George Reeves on the set of *The Adventures of Superman,* he invited the young actress to his trailer for a drink, to toast her being cast as Superman's inquisitive girlfriend and ace reporter for the *Daily Planet.* At the time, Phyllis Coates was broke and absolutely grateful to have a job, so she was taken aback by George's toast: "Here's to the bottom of the barrel, babe!"

The Adventures of Superman began filming in 1951 but was not broadcast until February 9, 1953. New York audiences first saw the show in April, when it premiered on WABC, a minor network at the time.

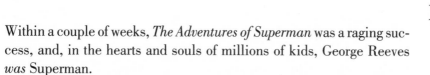

Within a couple of weeks, *The Adventures of Superman* was a raging success, and, in the hearts and souls of millions of kids, George Reeves *was* Superman.

The show's immediate success was no less bewildering to other members of the cast, especially Jack Larson, who had finally reached New York and was living in a little garden apartment on East 83rd Street near the Metropolitan Museum of Art. Six weeks into the show's run, Larson met a friend at a greasy spoon named Yankee Doodle's on Madison Avenue. "We were at a table," Larson remembered, "and I suddenly became aware of a crowd outside. It turns out that kids from a local school across the street had discovered 'Jimmy Olsen' eating breakfast at this place with its big windows. They were standing on each other's shoulders against the plate-glass windows to see 'Jimmy.' The police came in and said I was creating a hazard. By now there were hundreds of kids in the streets because they had been let out for lunch. It turned into such a scene that the police hustled me around the corner into the Metropolitan Museum. I stayed in the Met until I could come out. It was a mad scene and it stung me." Larson would later compare that incident to the scene in Tennessee Williams's *Suddenly Last Summer* in which Sebastian is cannibalized by street urchins on the beach at Rio Lobos.

It soon became clear that the harm was done—irrevocably, unarguably—after all. In 1951—the year Montgomery Clift made *A Place in the Sun* and Marlon Brando made *A Streetcar Named Desire,* George Reeves starred in the feature film *The Adventures of Superman and the Mole Men.*

However, in 1953, Reeves had another chance at film stardom: He was cast in an important film, Fred Zinnemann's roiling melodrama based on *From Here to Eternity,* James Jones's war novel about the Japanese attack on Pearl Harbor. This was the film that rescued Frank Sinatra's career from an accelerating downhill slide. The famous scene of a stalwart Burt Lancaster and a seething Deborah Kerr rolling around in the Hawaiian surf became the stuff of dreams—and was parodied on Sid Caesar's *Show of Shows* as "From Here to Maternity." The film won an Academy Award that year, as did the screenplay and cinematography. Zinnemann, Sinatra, and Donna Reed (very much before her apotheosis as TV's domestic goddess on *The Donna Reed Show*) also won Academy Awards for their work in the film. George Reeves was cast as Sergeant Stark in the picture.

According to Jack Larson, *From Here to Eternity* broke Reeves's heart. Larson attended the film's sneak preview, which was the most highly anticipated preview that year in Hollywood, to see George and his friend Monty Clift on the screen. This was Reeves's most important film role in ten years, since *So Proudly We Hail,* and several members of the crew of *The Adventures of Superman* were in the audience as well.

But when Reeves first appeared onscreen, the audience went wild and started to yell "Superman!" The studio executives, who were disdainful of television and never watched it, didn't know what the fuss was all about. Once they discovered the reason for the audience's excitement, an executive decision was made to cut George's role of Sergeant Stark from the film. Fred Zinnemann later insisted that George was never cut for that reason, but the decision was made. What clinched it were the audience members' preview cards that read "It's great to see Superman in the movie!" and "What a thrill. You put Superman in 'From Here to Eternity'!" Those who knew and worked with George who were at the preview that night were heartsick at the audience's reaction. They knew all too well what it meant.

Rancho Notorious and *The Blue Gardenia* were two films George Reeves made for his friend and neighbor, the great German director Fritz Lang, before *The Adventures of Superman* ever appeared on the air. (The films were released by RKO in 1952 and 1953.) Lang, who made his reputation in Germany with the film *Metropolis,* cast George as Wilson in *Rancho Notorious,* a "sleazy, womanizing braggart" hiding out with other lowlifes in a safe house run by Marlene Dietrich. George grew a mustache for his role in *The Blue Gardenia.* Nati Vacio remembered that Lang loved George as a son, and he often joined George and Nati for barbecues in George's backyard. Reeves—twice left fatherless—seemed to appeal to older men in that way. Despite Lang's efforts, however, neither film revived interest in Reeves as a serious screen actor.

George Reeves's last grasp at a significant film role was in a Walt Disney movie, appearing as a pioneer in a wagon train filled with Mouseketeers: Doreen, Tommy, Cubby, and Karen. The film's director, William Beaudine, who already felt saddled with Mouseketeers in the cast, ordered the makeup department to give Superman full face whiskers and a broad-brimmed hat. The film was released in 1956 as *Westward Ho, The Wagons.*

By now all the casting directors in Hollywood knew that Superman's secret identity was the actor George Reeves; after *Westward Ho,* Reeves

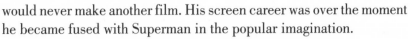

would never make another film. His screen career was over the moment he became fused with Superman in the popular imagination.

There was an added burden as well: What his millions of fans did not know was that George Reeves's private life had entered a new realm that had to be kept separate from the myth of Superman. Writing in the *Los Angeles Mirror* the summer that production first began on the show, radio and TV editor Hal Humphrey predicted, "Reeves will have to live the good, clean life of a scoutmaster." But by 1951, Superman had already met the girl with the million-dollar legs.

Hollywood Kryptonite

3

THE WOMAN WHO OWNED SUPERMAN

If you look closely at the 1936 movie about the impresario Florenz Ziegfeld's life, *The Great Ziegfeld*—the one with William Powell—you can see Toni Mannix in an elaborate Ziegfeld tableaux, floating by among the new and ancient beauties. It was said that King Farouk had been in love with her, but that was a long time ago. Toni told Jack Larson in George's dressing room what a knockout she once was. "I used to come down that stairway [in the Ziegfeld Follies]—I was beautiful, with feathers up my ass and tassles on my titties."

Toni began her affair with George Reeves around 1950, the year George's divorce from Ellanora became final. George had been hurt by Ellanora's abandonment of him, coming soon after the discovery of his mother's treachery; he always spoke of his mother and his ex-wife in a grudging, bitter way. By the time George was being suited for his padded Superman costume, Toni was a familiar fixture on the set of *The Adventures of Superman.*

"She brought George his lunch every day on the set," recalled one member of the cast. "I would hear George say, 'Well, it's about time for my olive.' He was hungry for his olive, and Toni would arrive with a shaker of martinis, and some days you didn't get a lot of work done after lunch."

It was clear that Toni was smitten, but that didn't keep her from indulging in other sexual encounters. After all, wasn't she the wife of the most powerful guy at MGM after L. B. Mayer himself? Why not take advantage of all that clout? Eddie was her insurance policy against rejection. Stewart Granger, the tall, aristocratic British actor with the chiseled profile, encountered Toni in 1950, around the time she began her affair with George Reeves. Granger had just been brought to MGM to film *King Solomon's Mines,* the adventure epic in which he appears as Allan Quatermain, a kind of cross between Tarzan, Jungle Jim, and Marlow from Joseph Conrad's *Heart of Darkness.* Granger described that encounter in his 1981 autobiography, *Sparks Fly Upward.*

According to Granger, Mrs. Mannix already had "quite a reputation" in Hollywood. One night his costar and friend Deborah Kerr arranged a dinner date for Granger and Toni, "my boss, the bouncer's wife," in Granger's words. The handsome, six-foot-two actor asked his leading lady if Eddie Mannix would object to his going out with Toni, and Deborah Kerr assured him it wouldn't be a problem. Because Granger recently had been put under contract by MGM, Toni "just wanted to meet me to pass judgment on this new MGM acquisition."

They met at a Hollywood restaurant called Don the Beachcomber's, which happened to be George Reeves's favorite, where he and Ellanora had gone on their first date. The restaurant was Polynesian in theme, complete with waterfalls and waiters in leopard skins serving flaming drinks in scooped-out pineapples. If Toni was worried that she might run into George, she didn't show it. Granger sat next to Toni, "a very luscious lady of a certain age," while they sipped their exotic rum punches. "We all sucked away at each other's drink and after about three rounds were feeling no pain . . ." The English actor suddenly became aware of a hand groping away at his zipper. He looked around, amazed that Toni was deftly handling her chopsticks and chatting away brightly with Deborah while her other hand firmly squeezed Granger's crotch. He caught Deborah's eye and they both started giggling—apparently Deborah, who knew of Toni's reputation, thought this might happen.

There's an unsettling coda to Granger's encounter with Toni. After their interesting meal, Granger begged Deborah Kerr to drop him off first at the Beverly Hills Hotel, before taking Toni Mannix back to her mansion. "I politely wished the groper goodnight . . . and let myself into my bungalow and locked the door as I had a suspicion the night's games had not come to an end. . . . I was right."

Shortly thereafter, Toni knocked on Granger's bungalow door, and, worried that she might rouse the whole hotel, Granger unlocked it.

"All right, let's take up where we left off," Toni said as she staggered into the bungalow and began to take off her clothes.

"Left off what?" He held her arms to keep her from undressing.

"What's the matter, kid, can't you get it up?"

Sam Kashner & Nancy Schoenberger

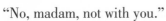

"No, madam, not with you."

"Fucking pansy!" she shouted. With that, Toni left the bungalow and stormed out into the night. What's interesting about this unflattering tale is how quickly Toni accused the handsome film actor of being gay. Was this her usual response to men who couldn't—wouldn't—have sex with her? And did she always react with such violence whenever she felt rejected by men she desired? George Reeves would discover for himself Toni's capacity for rage.

Granger went to bed that night convinced that Toni would return to her gated mansion and tell Eddie that he had tried to rape her. "Luckily," Granger later wrote in his autobiography, "I heard no more." What Granger didn't know was that Eddie Mannix kept himself occupied with a beautiful Japanese mistress and was tolerant of his wife's sexual adventures. Theirs was a complicated relationship, which began with the little-known fact that Eddie Mannix and Toni Lanier were never legally married.

"They were common law all the way," according to Sydney Guilaroff, MGM's chief hairstylist since the 1930s. Guilaroff was one of the key people who transformed Julia Turner into Lana; like hairstylists and beauticians everywhere, Guilaroff was privy to the gossip of his clients. Before lowering the cone of silence over the dyed-and-pincurled heads of his beauties, he took their confessions. One of the dark roots behind Toni Mannix's high-society pose was the fact that she was a common-law wife.

And Eddie's secret liaison also posed problems. It was not such a good idea for an executive of one of the major movie studios to have a Japanese woman for a girlfriend. Japanese-Americans had just recently been let out of internment, and the post–World War II climate was not one of happy multiculturalism. This was thirty years before the first sushi bars would crop up in Hollywood. The socially prominent ex-thug had to keep up appearances, and that meant Toni on his arm and his Japanese mistress behind closed doors. So Toni and Eddie made all the rounds together, even showing up once at The Pasadena Playhouse when George was appearing there. Bette Shayne, the widow of Robert Shayne, popular stage-trained actor who played Inspector Henderson in *The Adventures of Superman,* said that the four of them often traveled together. Eddie and Toni would sit in the first-class cabin, with George and Eddie's mistress seated in tourist class. Once they reached their destination, the two couples would regroup.

But Eddie had not always been so tolerant of the women in his life.

In 1937, Eddie's first wife, Bernice, sued him for divorce, charging "cruelty and infidelity." She accused her husband of "kicking and beating her so violently" that he broke a vertebra in her back, and of "associating with other women when he told her he was attending prize fights." The first Mrs. Mannix sought $4,000 a month in alimony and half of their community property, amounting to $1 million.

But Eddie was lucky. A few months after Bernice sued for divorce, a man named Al Wertheimer who ran a gambling joint in the desert just south of Palm Springs offered Bernice Mannix a ride home. After a long night at the gaming tables, Bernice accepted. Wertheimer's car went off the road, turning over a few times in the desert sand. The accident left him a cripple, but Bernice wasn't so fortunate. Her death threw the studio into a tailspin, for a few days anyway. Death is the one thing that throws Hollywood for a loop.

There's a private investigator who used to work with the Las Vegas police in the 1930s and 1940s who was convinced that Bernice Mannix's accident was no accident. There were two sets of tire marks running parallel in the desert sand, he wrote in a report prepared for the Highway Patrol. It was very easily observed, even in moonlight. "You could see a kind of racing stripe on the side of the car, which was where the paint had been sheared off by the close proximity of the other car," the one that pursued Bernice Mannix.

A head-and-shoulders photograph of Bernice accompanied her obituary on November 20, 1937. She looks Irish, like her husband. Thin, penciled-in eyebrows, as was the fashion; soft blond curls framing the face of an attractive, game gal. Not a beauty like Toni Mannix—her neck is short and her shoulders are fleshy—but nice. Wearing lots of expensive jewelry. Something a little grim, a little clenched about the smile. She knew what it was like to live with Eddie Mannix.

Two years before Bernice's "accident," Eddie had gotten involved with a showgirl named Mary Imogene Robertson who used the stage name Mary Nolan in the two films she made at MGM. Like Toni, she was also a hard drinker, a notorious kind of girl, the kind Eddie liked. One who spoke his language, which consisted of a lot of one-syllable words with hard consonants. Except Mary Nolan filed a complaint against Eddie Mannix with the Culver City Police Department, charging him with assault. Apparently Eddie just liked to beat up women. Nolan filed a $500,000 suit for assault against "Edward J. Mannix, v.p. and general manager of Metro's Coast Studios." Eddie dodged that one, too, by having his attorney claim that no summons had been served upon his client. But Mary Nolan's attorney finally slapped the paper on Mannix at the Sherry-Netherland Hotel in New York, after months of trying to track him down. The court gave Mannix twenty days to file an answer to the charges or cough up the $500,000 in damages. Nolan had lots of evidence: *Variety* reported that Mary Nolan detailed "numerous occasions on which Mannix is alleged to have beaten her. Actress specifies one instance when she had to be removed to a hospital."

But before those twenty days expired, a detective showed up at Nolan's doorstep, telling her that he had evidence that she was dealing in narcotics. The information, according to one source, was true, but it had come from Eddie Mannix. The detective made Mary Nolan an offer she couldn't refuse: leave town and the matter will be dropped. A studio car was idling at curbside, waiting to take Mary Imogene Robertson/Mary Nolan back to Broadway. That's just the kind of guy Eddie Mannix was.

The only person Eddie Mannix seemed to fear was Toni Lanier Mannix. She was certainly more unpredictable than Eddie, always a dangerous trait. Mickey Cohen once said that Toni Mannix was the only person he met in Hollywood who had any balls. Toni was a quick study, and she learned from her husband that the best way to win someone's loyalty was to find out what his or her weakness was and to cater to it. She saw how her husband ran his studio, how it never hurt to be feared, all the more after Bernice had her little accident in the desert. Jack Larson, though only a nineteen-year-old kid when he met Toni Mannix, noticed how she knew the ways of the motion picture industry. She knew how the movie business worked; not the numbers crunching, but the interpersonal stuff that really made the wheels turn in 1950s Hollywood.

Unlike her husband, Toni didn't have to read George's mail to know how he liked to live. He didn't just want to *be* a movie star, he wanted to live like one as well. But it was a bill that George Reeves couldn't pay, at least not as the star of a kid's television show. So Toni offered to give George the down payment for a small, Cape Cod–style house on a narrow stretch of Benedict Canyon leading up into the Hollywood Hills. She decorated the house and filled it with a lot of beautiful pine and maple furniture, marble lamps, and a good reproduction of a Rembrandt, which George hung over the fireplace. She even brought over from the Mannix estate a silver service and presented George with a silver ladle, with which the couple would serve up the Shrimp Newberg

Toni lovingly prepared for George and his guests, friends like Phyllis Coates, Jack Larson, Bob and Bette Shayne. The house quickly became the center of George and Toni's life together. In the early years of their relationship, George and Toni would do a lot of entertaining in that house: barbecues in the tiny backyard, mostly, followed by George getting out his guitar and singing a few Spanish songs to his assembled guests. And there was always a lot of booze. "They were very much comfortably married," Bette Shayne observed. "They meshed well together, and all the times I was with them they were very happy. I hear that they had their problems off and on, but they certainly didn't display it when they were having parties."

So Toni applied Eddie's methods to her relationship with George. That was in part the reason for the house at 1579 Benedict Canyon that George and Toni picked out together and Toni bought for George with Eddie's money. Eddie was even invited over for a housewarming. In the beginning, it was terribly civilized, like something out of a French movie. But it was all about control. If Toni controlled George's purse strings, she controlled George.

Phyllis Coates got to know Toni when the older woman took her for steam baths and massages at a spa on La Cienega. Toni had figured out that another way to hold on to George was to befriend the cast of *Superman* and get them on her side. Phyllis remembered that Toni "had so much money, was terribly regal. . . . She had the money to be extravagant, and she was a generous lady. . . . The bottom line is that Toni paid for everything when we did those first shows. She owned George's house, his car, everything. It was all in her name. . . . He used to call her 'Mother' and 'Mama Toni.' "

They certainly did look good together, especially when George wasn't filming *Superman* and he allowed his slicked-back, dyed hair to revert to its prematurely white color. George looked particularly handsome with a leonine head full of white hair framing his strong face. Toni loved that—it made them look more like a couple and less like a youthful mother with her handsome son, or like Helen Bessolo passing herself off as George's sister.

Sydney Guilaroff remembered that Toni seldom visited the MGM studios, rarely dropping in on her husband, Eddie. But she would pay social calls on certain members of the MGM "family," what she referred to as "going shopping." She'd drop in at their sumptuous homes and rarely left empty-handed. Usually all she had to do was to admire an

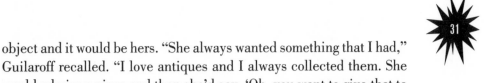

object and it would be hers. "She always wanted something that I had," Guilaroff recalled. "I love antiques and I always collected them. She would admire a piece and then she'd say, 'Oh, you want to give that to me, Sydney?' 'What do you mean?' I said. I told her, 'I bought them because I liked them, and I'm keeping them, Toni.' She never gave *me* anything that I can recall."

• • •

The early 1950s were a time of fear, not just for Eddie Mannix but for most of the moguls who ruled their studio kingdoms. Television was the culprit: It was the genie they couldn't get back into the bottle. The studios were in deep trouble, because millions of people had stopped going to the movies. By the end of World War II, there were only 6,500 television sets in the country, most of them in barrooms. But by 1948, "the number of sets had climbed past one million," wrote film historian Otto Friedrich in *City of Nets;* "It would quadruple in 1949, then triple in 1950 to more than 11 million." Milton Berle became "Mr. Television" on Tuesday night's *Texaco Star Theater;* Texaco begat the *Kraft Television Theatre,* which begat the *Philco Playhouse* and the *General Electric Theater,* which would soon be presided over by Ronald Reagan. What was visible on this piece of talking furniture was not "the vital thinking man's blockbusters that Darryl Zanuck had said the postwar audience would want, but it was all available in the living room or bar, and most important of all, it was free."

If the health of the movie industry was bad in the early 1950s, Eddie J. Mannix's health was even worse. For Eddie, who once awed bartenders with how much he could smoke and drink, his health had deteriorated to the point where a full day's work was out of the question. He had emphysema and angina, which were both getting worse. The pains in his chest terrified him. Now he needed Toni, to get him his medicine, to practice her brand of wifely solicitude whenever she was in the mood for it. He didn't want to end up alone in his mansion with his servants wiping the drool from his chin as he was hauled up and down in the new elevator they installed, from the bedroom to the living room, if you could call that living. These days Eddie, if he worked at all, was called on mostly to fire people. MGM, the largest and wealthiest studio in Hollywood, was suffering grievously in the early 1950s. What the studios had to do now was to drop everybody on contract in order to shrink their huge overhead: Errol Flynn, Humphrey Bogart,

Bette Davis—everybody. They cleared the decks. They didn't want to pay those high salaries for forty weeks out of the year. They didn't know how they were going to make films anymore.

The studios developed an absolute iron-curtain mentality against television people. They had tried to make a film with Milton Berle—it didn't succeed. They tried to do a film with Liberace—it didn't succeed either. So if you were in television, they didn't want you in films. And that was that.

Thus *The Adventures of Superman* and other early television shows became a refuge for out-of-work film actors, especially for some of the great character actors of the 1930s and 1940s. The character actors flourished, while actors trained to be movie stars had a harder time adjusting. The style of acting was changing, too, in the early 1950s. "George was a good actor," Larson believed, "although sometimes you couldn't tell what he was saying because he talked so fast. Acting has changed, though. . . . It was changing then. I came into the 1950s with a kind of naturalism that other people on the show weren't doing. Something was going on in the '50s, and I had done enough acting in live television that I was aware of it. But George had not moved into it. He was still doing Warner Bros. or Paramount performing. It was a different kind of training. He was a movie star, really—he'd had all the preparation and training to be a movie star. But he was trapped on that small screen. He was a movie star, acting in a box, on a kiddie show, in a piece of furniture."

Whether he liked it or not, the role of Superman belonged to George Reeves. A fellow actor told him that he could play Superman for the rest of his life. Unfortunately for George, he was right.

• • •

It's hard to figure out George Reeves. An affable fellow. A nice guy. He seemed like such a suburbanite in his white shorts among the patio furniture of the house Toni bought for them. The harder you look for what happened to Reeves that bloody June night in 1959, the more he seems to recede, to disappear from his own life. Superman really seems to have succeeded in swallowing up the actor who played him. George's friend and weight trainer Gene La Belle noticed that Reeves covered up his disappointment about having to play the Man of Steel by clowning around on the set, making fun of the characters and dialogue. "Low-ass Lane" was his appellation for the reporter who worshiped

Superman but had little patience for Clark Kent's passivity and apparent cowardice. Whenever the word "blue" appeared in George's script, he would say "blow." He was campy about the costume he had to wear. When Superman had to rescue Jimmy, it was particularly hard for Larson not to laugh. He would be tied up in a chair with a bomb at his feet, trying to get in the mood to be terrified. George would come around the corner of the set and blow him kisses. He'd say, "Don't worry, Junior, Superboy is going to save you."

In the early days of the show, Reeves was very athletic. Si Simonson, the show's special-effects man, would put mattresses behind the camera and Reeves would make a running jump off a diving board, taking off over the camera, doing a tuck and roll, and landing on the mattresses.

Someone once observed that the reason George Reeves was such a good Superman was that he didn't seem neurotic about having superpowers. He was, if anything, amused by them. That's why he seems so good-natured about having those gangsters pump their futile bullets into him. Like Nabokov's villain Quilty in *Lolita,* Humbert Humbert's bullets slamming into his chest are like tiny injections of energy. Of course, the number of cocktails George imbibed on the set added to his air of relaxed amusement.

It's been suggested that Reeves played Superman more as a symbolic figure than flesh-and-blood in the first twenty-four episodes of *The Adventures of Superman.* He's a living icon who "does his work and vanishes abruptly," and is described in one early segment as "an avenging angel sweeping all before him." But playing Clark Kent was another matter. George refused to play the reporter as a bumbling cipher. Even in the later part of the series' run, when the writers tried for sweeter story lines and played up the comedy, George went out of his way to show Clark Kent as capable and strong. So it really was just a pair of glasses and a suit that differentiated Clark Kent from Superman.

In the early episodes George was strapped into a harness and hoisted up with piano wire. The wire rubbing against the metal rigging snapped one day and Reeves—all 200 pounds of him—went crashing to the stage floor twelve feet below. At first Phyllis Coates and a few stagehands couldn't stop laughing. George gave them a murderous look and became very angry with Coates. "Rightly so," the actress said. "He could have been killed." Near misses like that were always hushed up—a shroud of secrecy surrounded the set and the cast was told the accident was strictly confidential. "After all," Robert Maxwell, the show's first producer, said, "we couldn't tell the world the great Superman had crash-landed on the movie lot."

Reeves's fall could have easily crippled, if not killed, a lesser athlete. What is significant is how National Comics felt it had to protect the reputation of their Superman investment and the illusion that George Reeves *was* Superman. That night—the night of George's fall—he and Toni drove up into the hills and sat in the backseat of Toni's Cadillac with a bottle of hooch and watched the sun come up. Toni arranged for George to see her physician, who took a page out of Dr. Max "Feelgood" Jacobson's book and gave George an injection that banished most of his pain but kept him up for three days. Later that same doctor would be called on to help Toni sleep in the weeks following George's death.

In another incident, a breakaway door banged George up pretty badly. Not since Helen Bessolo hired that ex–Golden Gloves champ to give her son an object lesson in mother love did Reeves ache in so many different places. The first season was backbreaking work. But at 4:00 P.M. on the button, regular as Kant, George Reeves would open up the bar on the set. To get to know George, Phyllis said, you had to drink with him. "I could always tell when George had had a couple. He would get bloated, and one eye would droop a little."

Now no one seems to have liked George Reeves more than Jack Larson did. A rapport developed between Superman and the young stage actor who played Superman's pal over the course of the series' original six-year run. The only bone of contention the two men had was over the issue of George's drinking. Toni Mannix would bring a shaker of martinis to George on the *Superman* set. He would drink so much during the day that by the afternoon he just couldn't hold up his end. As a result, the cast couldn't break for lunch until late in the afternoon. George would go and sleep it off, and then come back and say, "Okay, kids, now let's do it." He didn't want to be blamed for holding up the production. The day players would get sent home, and the rest of the cast would try to pick up the scenes. Which of course meant that Larson and the other lead players often had to work late into the night. Finally, Larson confronted Reeves about the effect his drinking was having on everyone's schedule.

"George," he said, "I don't care if you drink and walk off the set. Do it, and enjoy yourself. But don't come back. Otherwise, I have to work late. Just stay off the set."

Sam Kashner & Nancy Schoenberger

One night when they did work very late, George felt bad about it and took Larson to Trader Vic's to apologize. He promised it wouldn't happen again. "Well, it did," Larson recalled.

Larson had an interesting life away from the *Superman* set. From Christopher Isherwood, to Monty Clift, to Leslie Caron, Larson was becoming part of a circle of celebrated writers and actors whose artistic reputations stood in stark contrast to the more commercial glamour of Hollywood. Off the set, Larson and his pal Leslie Caron always dressed in black.

To make up to Jack, whom he called "Junior," George would invite him out. "Come on, Junior. You have to eat with us." Toni would be outside waiting in her pink car with the top down.

Larson didn't disapprove of Toni and George's romance. "I loved being with George," Jack Larson recalled, "but when he wanted to go out it meant belting a few before sitting down to eat, and that meant getting home after eleven. I wanted to go home and memorize my lines for the next day." George, apparently, had it easier than most in this regard. "He read his sides and had it down in a single reading," Jack said. Of course, this wasn't *Long Day's Journey Into Night*, but Reeves was a quick study.

No one in George's circle—not his trainer Gene La Belle, nor the makeup man Harry Thomas, nor Phyllis Coates, who got to know George by drinking with him—will say that George was an alcoholic. But George was spiking his orange juice at seven o'clock in the morning. His drinking interfered with his work and disrupted the schedules of his fellow actors. Only Jack Larson has gone on record as saying that, whether George shot himself or not, he was doing a pretty good job of killing himself with booze. Certainly alcoholism can be a factor in depression, can cloud judgment, can push someone over the edge. But in 1954, if you weren't Ray Milland in *The Lost Weekend,* you weren't an alcoholic. And it was considered bad sport to intervene.

Reeves's drinking would lead a lot of his friends to believe that he was indeed capable of destroying himself. But Reeves was probably a high-functioning alcoholic. Incredibly, the high alcohol content found in Reeves's blood at the time of his death—.27 percent—was not so unusual for him. He had for a long time been able to drink heavily and still appear in control. "Drinking gave George an enormous amount of pleasure," remembered one friend. "It also gave him courage."

4

SUPERMAN AGONISTES

It's easy to miss the two-bedroom house halfway up Benedict Canyon, wedged into the side of the mountain just a few feet off the narrow road that snakes through the arid California hills. It's a smallish house, with the steep, slate roof of a Dutch Colonial, dark wood siding, and a pretty little row of birch trees that provide some protection and privacy from the nearby road. Little canyon breezes carry the scent of eucalyptus and pine resin. It looks more like the home of a schoolteacher, however, than the mansion of a television star, and maybe that's why Toni went out of her way to decorate the place with marble lamps and fine mahogany furniture. She allowed George to "live big," paying his liquor bills and buying him dinners at Chasen's and Scandia. The house looks like what it was: a cozy love nest, and in the early 1950s Toni and George bought it for $12,000.

With Toni's money, George could not only live big but hand out generous tips and loans to friends, because his major expenses were all taken care of.

"George was an easy touch for a hundred, anytime, day or night," remembers his longtime friend Nati Vacio. "He lost a lot of money in Hollywood by handing out thousands of dollars for which he was never repaid." He liked to call himself "Honest George, the People's Friend," and he had a soft spot in his heart for out-of-work actors. He'd tip the boy delivering bottles from the liquor store and tell him, "Here's a hundred—go out and make your first million, kid." Larson thought George probably loaned out as much as he earned on *Superman,* which was $2,500 per week for thirteen weeks at the height of his earning power.

George and Toni's bedroom was on the top floor, under the pitched roof: a small room with a low, beamed ceiling. Though the only window is in the adjacent bathroom, they must have heard cars creeping by at night, speeding up on the flat stretch of road directly in front of their house and braking suddenly to take the curve just past it, heading higher up into the hills. After sundown, the headlights of passing cars must have raked the walls of the living room, like a searchlight sweeping the dark.

All three downstairs rooms open onto the brick patio and backyard, which George and Toni planted with rows of pink and white impatiens. The grass is a heavenly green. The yard stops abruptly at the side of the mountain, which is fenced off and covered with brambles. On the bricked patio George placed a metal table with a large umbrella and a few patio chairs that looked more like flowered kitchen chairs dragged out into the open air. Here he liked to work out, practicing his judo moves and lifting weights, wearing white bathing trunks as he soaked up the California sun. It was easy to slip in and out of that house from the backyard, and George would sometimes be surprised when one of his friends suddenly appeared in the living room or in the little den off to the side.

Reeves's Benedict Canyon neighborhood has a strange and violent history. Less than a mile from George's house was the former Melcher home on Cielo Drive—now torn down—where the notorious Manson Family murders took place. Jean Harlow's husband Paul Bern died of a gunshot wound in a Benedict Canyon house not far from George's residence, a probable murder by a mysterious woman in black, who happened to be Bern's discarded common-law wife.

Other residents have testified to the problems of living on that particular stretch of road. "First, there's the inherent problem of living in a canyon," explained Michael Selsman, a former agent and producer who at one time lived two doors away from the Reeves house. "Before you buy a house in a canyon, you should look at where it is in relationship to the sun for all four seasons. Because on this particular curve, every house is in the shade from October 15 through March 15, which means that the sun only hits the yellow line down the middle of the road during those months. It might have been eighty degrees in December and January, but in the house it would be forty. You'd have the fire going and the heat going six months out of the year. . . ."

There were other problems as well. Benedict Canyon Road north of Sunset Boulevard is just on the periphery of the Beverly Hills Police precinct, so residents can't always count on the Beverly Hills Police answering their calls for help. The Los Angeles Police Department usually will show up a lot faster—though not always. And the roads that wind through the Hollywood Hills can be treacherous. In the 1960s, on the stretch of road directly in front of the Reeves house, a popular actor named Jim Stacey lost an arm and a leg in a motorcycle accident. "He got hit by a car with no lights on," according to Michael Selsman. His passenger, a young woman to whom Stacey had offered a lift, "got cut in half." She was lying on the roadway for nearly an hour until they could get an ambulance, because that stretch of road is outside of the Beverly Hills' police jurisdiction, so they wouldn't come—that's a common problem in that area. Stacey's leg was found on the roof of a house down the street."

Nonetheless, the house was a sanctuary from the increasing humiliations Reeves had to endure as Superman.

The first year of the show, National Comics arranged for the Superman costume to go on display at Chicago's Marshall Fields in the children's department during the Christmas season, with a muscle man hired to wear the red-and-blue outfit. An eyewitness told a local reporter that "some kid showed up who had already bought a drawing set where you have those compasses. When no one was watching him, he hit the Superman guy in the rear with the pointed end of his compass. It was a real wound." Reeves read the account of that incident and began to worry about his well-being. He didn't think any child was crazy enough to shoot him with a gun, but he often said that "it only takes one BB to take out your eye." He just didn't like appearing outside the studio dressed as Superman. So, as an accommodation to Reeves, all the location shooting was done in the studio, because "it worried him that someone in the crowd would do something, and he would be hurt," recalled a member of the crew.

Kellogg's, the show's first sponsor, sent Reeves on personal appearance tours in 1955, on behalf of the National Safety Council. Reports of children injuring themselves were cropping up in the news: Superman fans jumping off the garage roof in capes fashioned from bath towels or, even worse, in store-bought Superman costumes! Reeves buzzed around the country, visiting children's hospitals and giving talks about the dangers of thinking you could fly.

But those whirlwind tours were exhausting for the Man of Steel. First of all, Reeves had never adjusted to the fact that his masses of fans were all children. In an effort to salvage a shred of his actor's dignity, he insisted on signing his own name instead of "Superman"—surely a confusing disappointment for most of the show's diminutive autograph-seekers.

Reeves didn't just dislike making those appearances. He'd become terrified of making them. The first time Reeves made a personal appearance dressed in full regalia as Superman, the impossible happened. A child approached the actor brandishing a gun. Ironically, the child had hijacked his dad's Luger, a souvenir from World War II. The boy had wanted to own a bullet that had been flattened by bouncing off Superman's chest. Reeves managed to talk the youngster into handing over the weapon by explaining that someone else might get hurt when the bullet bounced off Superman.

In one backbreaking promotional stunt, Reeves accepted the "challenge" of Hess's Department Store to take over the job of every Hess employee—all 1,600 of them. George found himself running elevators, driving store trucks, wrapping gifts, and selling appliances—all in costume. He ended his day in the toy department, where he skinned his knee in a collision with a tricycle.

After this Augean stables stunt at Hess's, the show's producers dreamed up the idea for a cross-country tour for Reeves, Noel Neill (who replaced Phyllis Coates as Lois Lane in the show's second year), and Nati Vacio. George also arranged for Gene La Belle to join the troupe and appear onstage as Mr. Kryptonite in wrestling matches with Superman. (Or "Mr. Kraptonite," as George affectionately called him.) Nati Vacio, who often accompanied his friend on the guitar as the two men sang Spanish songs, arranged for a trio of musicians to appear at the end of the show.

Noel Neill was the first out onstage. Gene, dressed as Mr. Kryptonite, would pretend to attack Lois, whose screams summon Superman. Reeves leaps onto the stage and throws Gene around on a rubber mat. The second half of the show featured George Reeves dressed in his street clothes playing the guitar with Nati while Noel Neill and the backup musicians sang "Celito Lindo." Except for the music, the kids loved it. When George made his appearance onstage as Superman, there wasn't a dry seat in the house.

It was fun the first couple of times they did it, but the routine got stale mighty fast. At one appearance at a theater in Inglewood, California, a pint-size fan in the front row yelled out, "You bum—let's see you fly!" Unnerved, George quickly left the stage. Special-effects man Si Simonson remembered that George was so demoralized by the incident that he didn't show up for work the next day.

Being Superman all the time was exhausting. The other actors could just go home after a day's shoot and be themselves. But Superman was so popular that, for George, there was no escaping the role. The show, which preceded the Monday installment of Walt Disney's *Mickey Mouse Club*, had become a true phenomenon. One rating service reported that it was watched by 91 percent of all households with children under twelve. He was their hero. In April of 1955, when George made a personal appearance at the Broadway Department Store in downtown Los Angeles, 15,000 children were waiting for him. Later that same day, at another department store in Crenshaw, California, 20,000 Superman fans greeted him.

Walter Ames, writing in the *Los Angeles Times,* described Reeves's travails as Superman: "He has been kicked in the shins, slugged in the back and subjected to other such tricks by his admirers to test his endurance." At first George blamed the Superman costume, complete with its "S" insignia and that red cape billowing in the artificial breeze of the studio's Vorado fan. Soon he refused to make public appearances dressed as Superman. Reeves phoned his agent: "The costume stays home!" He even went so far as to try to prevent the sale of Superman costumes during Halloween. But, by then, *The Adventures of Superman* was a juggernaut that couldn't be stopped, and the marketing possibilities were endless.

It was hard to feel like Superman in that costume, with twenty pounds of foam rubber muscles under the wool. The countless retakes when the rubber muscles didn't quite look the way they should. His breaking out in a rash across his back as they readjusted the padding. And those lights they used when they were filming in color, burning the Man of Steel from his shoulders to his forearms. The weight of the suit itself restricted his movements. Even his boots were hand-me-downs. They were Kirk Alyn's boots, the first Superman of the old Columbia movie serials. Some frugal costumer took them out of storage at Western Costume and had them "surgically altered" for George. When he was finally given a new pair of boots, they put three-inch lifts in the heels to make him look even taller.

Occasionally Reeves got so disgusted with the costume that he wouldn't even bother to take it off before leaving the studio. With all that rubber and sponge padding, Reeves could lose ten pounds of water weight after filming on sweltering days under hot lights. He would walk through the studio buildings in costume, soaking wet and disgusted, lighting up one of his cigarettes and holding it disdainfully at the end of a long, black cigarette holder.

From 1951 to 1957, 104 episodes of *The Adventures of Superman* were made, in addition to the pilot film, *Superman and the Mole Men.* Plans were developed for at least two more feature films, but it's likely that National Comics scuttled the idea. Why jeopardize the Superman franchise and by risking a box-office failure? It's too bad, really, because it might at least have made Reeves feel like a movie star, the thing he was so close to becoming before the war came along, before *Superman* flickered into all those living rooms, draining George Reeves's soul in the process.

There were days when he simply couldn't live up to the image of being the Number One Citizen of America's Youth. Reeves blew up one time at director Harry Gerstad, when Gerstad told him he had invited a neighbor's kid and her parents onto the set to meet Superman on her birthday.

"In the first place," Reeves told Gerstad, "I'm sick of beating my brains out for moppets. In the second place, you know how I feel about having kids on the set. And in the third place, I'm not going to entertain kids when I'm working."

But the child and her parents were already there, standing in the shadows, waiting. Reeves walked over to the little girl. Something must have softened him, because he beamed from ear to ear and knelt down in front of her. He said, "Your name is Miriam, and I love you." He leaned forward and kissed her on the cheek.

Little Miriam wet her pants.

Basically, George was bored silly by the role. Throughout the run of the series, the only change in the character was, in the words of TV critic Allen Asherman, that Reeves "quickened Superman's movements . . . for these new segments [of the show]."

Reeves went on location in his Superman outfit one last time when the ABC network executives asked him, as a publicity stunt, if they could televise Superman hooking up the coaxial cable that would unite the network from New York to Los Angeles. It came as a big surprise to George, however, that he was going to have to go up to the top of the mountain where the transmitter was located.

Sam Kashner & Nancy Schoenberger

The cameras were set up and waiting, but they had neglected to provide a dressing room or anyplace for George to change into his costume. So he decided at the last minute to change in his studio dressing room and wear the cape and tights to the site.

By now it was hard for Reeves to get in and out of costume without help. In the three years since the show began, his waistline had thickened to the point where he first had to put on a corset underneath the rubber muscles. But Reeves couldn't see a way to wriggle out of his commitment to the network, so he went into his dressing room, wedged his way into his hairshirt, and got drunk.

"They had a limousine and a crew to take him up to the mountain," Jack Larson recalled, "and George was absolutely pissed in the dressing room. He used to be particularly funny when he'd drink. He liked to smoke cigarettes in a long cigarette holder. He held the cigarette very elegantly, leaning back in his cape and tights. I was standing outside the soundstage when George came out, and he was doing this thing with his cape, throwing it around, making curlicues in the air. I thought, 'How is this going to work out?' because he was definitely drunk. But he was very daring, and he pulled himself together to do this. It was very funny."

During the run of the show, the whole cast made only one big public appearance together, a benefit for Naval Relief in Memphis, Tennessee. All were present: corpulent, courtly John Hamilton, the revered character actor who played *Daily Planet* editor Perry White; Noel Neill, the cinch-waisted, sharp-tongued reporter Lois Lane; Jack Larson, renamed "Junior" on the set; and distinguished-looking Robert Shayne, who played Inspector Henderson.

Once the cast landed in Memphis, it was discovered that the theater would be segregated. Reeves was the first to arrive, but he refused to perform when he realized that the legions of black children who had waited all day in the rain were relegated to the back of the theater. Though Reeves was politically conservative, he had a strong sense of justice and he acted upon it, persuading the rest of the cast to boycott the performance. They all agreed, deciding just to sign autographs instead. So they set up shop in a big room where thousands of kids lined up with their mothers to receive signed photographs from their heroes.

Toward the end of that long day in Memphis, George became disgruntled. One mother who approached with her child must have sensed George's fatigue. "What's the matter, Mr. Reeves, don't you like children?" she asked.

"I love them. Appetizing little things. I have one for lunch every day."

Later on, when a little boy asked him at the air base, "How do you fly?" George answered, "They just know how to touch me in the right place."

"There were a lot of little girls," recalled a participant in the afternoon's events. "I remember George saying, when their mothers weren't there, 'Hello, you little ovary clanker! And what is your name?' George was just amusing himself."

His exhaustion notwithstanding, Reeves really did feel a sense of obligation to his millions of tiny fans, however. When producer Whitney Ellsworth's young daughter was stricken with myasthenia gravis, the degenerative muscle disease, George and Toni lent their support to the Myasthenia Gravis Foundation, which the Ellsworths founded in 1952.

"He had a lot of Superman's fine qualities, among them gentleness and kindliness," Ellsworth daughter Pat recalled. "The strongest man in the world, Superman, came to the aid of one of the weakest people in the world—me."

• • •

During the years of estrangement from her son, Helen Bessolo moved to Galesburg, Illinois, to be closer to her family. It was from Galesburg that she began pointing the bony finger of indignation at George for his relationship with Mrs. Eddie Mannix. Reeves had only recently begun speaking to his mother again. Perhaps his relationship with "Mama Toni" had, for a while, at least, made him feel protected from Helen's ability to hurt him. His own testiness around the children who worshiped him could well have been rooted in his anger toward his mother and her years of dissembling about the past. But Helen, a devout Catholic, chose to renew her relationship with her son by disapproving of his affair with Toni. Helen kept up her friendship with Ellanora, frequently calling her on the phone, the younger woman commiserating with the jilted mother.

Whenever Helen Bessolo was confronted with a fact of life she didn't like, her reaction was to willfully ignore it and reinvent another reality in its place—one she could live with. Early on, she convinced herself that Toni hadn't bought the house at 1579 Benedict Canyon but that George had built it himself. On the back of photographs of George and Toni, Helen would write little descriptive captions for posterity: "George

Sam Kashner & Nancy Schoenberger

Reeves and an unidentified woman." She had, of course, met Toni on several occasions and knew very well who she was.

• • •

Art Weissman was in his late thirties when he became George Reeves's personal manager. Weissman was the West Coast editor of *TV World* magazine when he first met George in the early 1950s. His publisher had sent Weissman to interview him on the set of *The Adventures of Superman* and to get the actor to pose for a photograph. According to Weissman, *TV World* had received over 40,000 letters asking to know more about "the man behind the costume," but when Weissman presented his credentials to the show's producer and asked for an interview with Reeves, Ellsworth turned him down.

"The producer," recalled Weissman, "seemed disappointed that he had to turn down the interview on George's behalf, but explained that he was under orders to do so. 'He hates too much attention, and that's rare for any actor. How about one of the other cast members?' " But Weissman was determined to speak to Reeves, and so he walked from the producer's plush office to Stage Seven of the Independent Studio that had once been the home of Charlie Chaplin's films.

Weissman walked right by Reeves and onto the soundstage, where he met Noel Neill, who was looking for George herself. "I didn't recognize . . . George Reeves," Weissman remembered, "because he wasn't wearing his Clark Kent hat or glasses, or his brilliant red flying cape—he was a hatless, gray-suited guy sitting on a railing."

Noel told Weissman, "George stepped outside for a few minutes. He's sunning himself. I'll get him for you." Weissman then heard her call out, "George, it's Toni. She sounded upset or I wouldn't have called you."

George picked up the phone and spoke so softly that Weissman couldn't make out the conversation. " 'Okay,' I finally managed to hear him say. 'I'll be there as soon as we wrap up shooting at five-ish.' He paused for a few seconds after he had replaced the phone as though he might be reflecting upon the conversation."

Weissman told Reeves that he was assigned to get some personal impressions for his magazine. George shook his head. "My personal self is my private business. I'm not interested in public consumption of stuff about me."

"Well, aren't there any personal causes or charities that interest you, because if there are, you can make it possible for them to get exposure. . . ."

George agreed to that. The two men arranged to meet later at Scandia, one of George's favorite restaurants on the Sunset Strip, and eventually Reeves invited Weissman to become his personal manager. Meanwhile, they arranged the interview and photo shoot for *TV World* to be held at the elementary school where George's good friend Nati Vacio now worked as a teacher. The interview took place in an empty classroom dominated by a wall-length mural of Superman.

Weissman would later testify that George "wasn't too ambitious about pursuing his career. That was one of the bones of contention we used to have, that you have to work at your career. . . . He'd say, 'You take care of business for me, and I'll take care of the acting.' " George liked to spend his free time away from Los Angeles, Weissman remembered, usually in New York, Florida, or Hawaii, three of his favorite vacation spots between production schedules.

Then there were the charities: After mass on Sundays, Toni and George would visit the local children's hospitals. All that sadness and suffering seemed to heighten Toni's desire for George, as if George were the last connection she would ever have to life itself. After making love on Sunday nights, they would visualize the life they would have once Eddie died. After all, his health was deteriorating rapidly—she swore she could see death in his eyes and in the grayish cast to his skin.

● ● ●

In the beginning, the cast of *The Adventures of Superman* felt like pioneers. One of the show's directors, Tommy Carr, was considered a first-rate director of action sequences. Orson Welles's old crew worked on the show in its infancy—"We basically had the sound crew from *Citizen Kane,*" a cast member recalled.

There were days when Reeves did enjoy his fame and good fortune, when he was just grateful to be working when a lot of gifted actors were at home waiting for the phone to ring. He started to write poetry, to sit outside on his patio, trying to clear his head and remember a time not too long ago, really, when his youth was like a key that fit every lock. But the present did not live up to that feeling. The price of George's fame was Superman, a role that refused to let him go, that seemed to be eating him alive.

"It was a very unhappy situation," Noel Neill would later explain, "and I felt particularly bad for George, who was supposed to have been

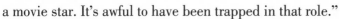

a movie star. It's awful to have been trapped in that role."

Reeves wasn't the only one who felt straitjacketed by his role. "I began to have bad experiences about being typed," Larson recalled. "They always wanted you on live television, but when there was no more live television, they didn't want you around anymore . . . producers and directors don't want you because you're too cheap to be in their fine productions."

It was Robert Shayne—Inspector Henderson—who first recognized that while he and other cast members could go home after shooting each episode and be themselves, George couldn't do that. "He was Superman in too many people's minds all the time." It was as if the country was suffering from a mass hallucination that George was really Superman, and George himself was the only sane man left.

By 1957, forty-three-year-old Reeves was beginning to have some trouble with his eyes, and so he insisted on replacing the empty tortoiseshell eyeglasses he wore as Clark Kent with his own personal prescription. But the cameraman found it maddening to shoot around the annoying light that was reflected off George's glasses.

Maybe George's eyes were playing tricks on him in other ways. One Saturday morning when George was lifting weights on his backyard patio with his trainer Gene La Belle, they heard the familiar sound of Toni's key in the front door and her footsteps as she headed to the back of the house and let herself out into the dazzling sunlight. George, prone on the bench with the sweat dripping into his eyes, suddenly thought he was seeing his mother.

"He called her 'Mama' sometimes," La Belle remembered, "but this time, judging from the look on his face, he thought his mother had walked through the door. I think it bothered him."

You could see it in the photographs. Within just a few years of their initial meeting, Toni Mannix had gone from being a sexually vibrant, extraordinarily attractive woman to "something very matronly," remembered Phyllis Coates.

George had tried his whole adult life to be free of Helen, and now here she was, walking right back into his life. "Toni was very much a mother figure to him," observed Jim Beaver, the actor and writer who has spent many years researching the life of George Reeves. "My feeling is that George Reeves liked that in women, until they started *looking* like his mother. . . . You didn't see it at first, but there was actually a close physical similarity between Toni and Helen."

But it was too late to do anything about it. Toni owned him—the house, the car, the big bills that allowed him to live like a movie star. He was trapped in a kiddie show that was eating away at his viability as an actor; he had gotten used to a life that *Superman* couldn't support, especially with the shabby contracts National Comics foisted on cast and crew, according to Jack Larson. "Every fifty-dollar raise I got was a nightmare. It was like pulling teeth," Larson recalled. "But we never discussed these things. It used to be in the old days, you never discussed money, and you didn't discuss your feelings, and you didn't discuss your part, you just went on. It was a kind of noblesse oblige with actors. So, there were no complaints, and I didn't know how George felt, and I don't think he knew how I felt. We were both very depressed, but we never discussed it. It was the 1950s, and you just learned to go on."

5

WHOM THE ANGELS CALL LEONORE

There's a dark-haired, dark-eyed woman sitting in a Havana nightclub in Cuba. She is far from home, but she is at home in this milieu. Havana in 1953 is filled to overflowing with gangsters, racketeers on vacation, hard guys dodging official-looking pieces of paper with their names on them. It will be six long years before Fidel and his men come down from the mountains to drive Fulgencio Batista from power. The woman is sitting, laughing, watching a sex performer on stage who calls himself Superman. He is Hispanic, a dark Cuban with an ugly face and an eleven-inch penis, which he seems able to turn into a piece of lumber at will. Part of the act has him whistling to a couple of parakeets who alight on his distended member. When in its recumbent state, "Superman" goes into the audience and wraps it around the neck of a woman sitting ringside, as if it were a strand of pearls, or one of those minks with the head still attached—the kind with the glass eyes sewn into the skull.

Her name is Leonore Lemmon and she is laughing. This is her first encounter with a man named Superman.

Leonore Lemmon wore the reddest lipstick in New York. They even named a shade of lipstick after her—"Lemmon Red." It didn't stick. At eighteen years of age she was a co-respondent in the Paterno divorce case. Joseph Paterno, Jr., was heir to a real estate fortune calculated to be worth about $63 million. "Café society first became aware that it had a problem child on its hands," wrote reporter Charles Robbins in *American Weekly* when Beverly Parker Paterno named the teenage Leonore, the daughter of a prosperous Broadway ticket broker, "as one of the chief reasons why she and her husband weren't being seen in the same bistros anymore." Robbins covered Leonore Lemmon in the press the way certain reporters were assigned to cover the German Anschluss or the Spanish Civil War. Leonore claimed that she and the real estate multimillionaire were just in business together—*business delecti*—even when a Paterno butler testified that he saw Leonore in Paterno's bed. Leonore showed neither qualms nor sympathy for Mrs. Paterno; "Just think!" she's quoted as saying. "Here I am, only eighteen, and already named a co-respondent." But Leonore's real claim to fame in the early 1940s was for being the youngest woman thrown out of the swanky Stork Club for punching out another glamour girl. She was finally barred from the Stork Club *and* the El Morroco—no mean feat.

Robbins remembered one night after Leonore was readmitted to the Stork Club, after some arm-twisting by her ticket-broker daddy, when she nearly immolated a nightclub photographer. It seems that a young woman often made the rounds of the Stork Club, stopping at each table to ask if any of the happy couples wanted to take home a remembrance of their night out (seeing that otherwise many of the couples wouldn't have had any recollection the morning after). When the young woman in question approached Leonore Lemmon's table, she was permitted to snap a flashbulb photo of Leonore and her date. The only problem was that when the high-heeled photographer returned with the photos, Leonore was out of the picture and a completely unsuspecting woman on the other side of Leonore's date was pictured instead.

Leonore Lemmon was fuming. She took her cigarette and let it smolder at the edge of the photographer's short, crinoline skirt. Robbins remembered that the unsuspecting young woman would have gone up like a Christmas pine in February if someone hadn't thrown a bucket of champagne ice over her. The headlines were averted, mostly as a favor to Leonore's father, who had a business to run, and a very lucrative one at that. He certainly couldn't spend all his time putting out Leonore's fires, but he often tried.

In the newspapers and magazines of the early 1940s, Leonore Lemmon was often depicted in photographs as a long-limbed, raven-haired young beauty. Her photograph was once juxtaposed with the drawing of a raven gripping the back of her couch and holding a lemon in its beak. In fact, Poe's poem "The Raven," with its lines about "the rare and radiant maiden whom the angels named Lenore / nameless here for ever more" got a lot of play in the columns whenever they were covering Leonore Lemmon. She was certainly not "nameless," however.

There would be a second divorce case naming Leonore that same year. She liked honeymoons—breaking them up as well as going on them.

Probably as much to get away from her parents—who were a little afraid of her—as to shock society and have a good time, "Lem" up and married Jacob Webb, the great-great-grandson of Commodore Vanderbilt. The press called their hasty romance and quickie nuptials a "comic-strip marriage." He was as unconventional as Leonore—a Vanderbilt with no money but a lot of tattoos.

There's a photograph of Jacob L. "Jakie" Webb and his bride taken in Charleston, South Carolina, shortly after their elopement on September 29, 1941. The caption reads "Society Newlyweds . . . Both were widely known for their New York night life 'activities.' The elopement created universal surprise in café society circles. He was reported engaged to Vivian Stokes, Newport debutante at the time." But he doesn't look too much like a Vanderbilt in this photograph. Although still in his early twenties, he already looks dissipated. His eyes have the kind of mushy, red-rimmed look you see in serious drinkers. He appears bashful and a little surprised at himself; Leonore, on the other hand, is staring at the photographer with clear, cool eyes and a sense of determination. Her tapered fingers end in bloodred nails; her long legs are elegantly crossed at the knees *and* the ankle, the way they teach you in charm school. Black, open-toed, high, high heels. She still manages to look doe-eyed and very pretty, but there's a steely strength underneath.

The honeymooning couple went bouncing around the nightclub circuit "like a couple of berserk rubber balls," wrote one reporter who tried to keep up with Webb and his wife. In one club, as amusement for the paying customers, they paused long enough to reenact their wedding vows with the maitre d' serving as justice of the peace and the rest of the nightclub as their witnesses.

With all of his tattoos, Webb would have felt at home on one of the South Sea Islands. Leonore liked the spectacle of battleships, flags, eagles, even a straight poker hand, embroidering a man's chest. "I used to drop a quarter in his mouth and the eagle on his chest would light up and play 'The Star Spangled Banner,' " Leonore told the newspapers. But within a few weeks of that elopement, Jake was busted for financing his honeymoon with bad checks.

"Where are you going?" Leonore asked her husband when a bunch of men with fedoras showed up to escort Jakie downtown.

"Out to get some tickets for the World Series."

It was raining. He ducked out. He never came back. He had been brought up on charges of cashing $120 worth of rubber checks. When a friend lent him $200 for bail, Webb skipped, and Leonore Lemmon blotted her lipstick on the hotel bill before going home to mother.

There's another photograph. This one is dated October 8, 1941, and is captioned "Oh Where Is My Wandering Jakie, Sighs Leonore." The photograph was taken at her mother's home at 38 East 85th Street. Leonore is dressed like a good girl in linen slacks and tailored blouse, with the sporty addition of a man's tie serving as her belt. She stares pensively out the window, her long, dark hair curling nicely along her shoulders. The photo caption continues: "Jakie, great, great grandson of the original Commodore Vanderbilt, had disappeared. 'If and when I get out of this mess, I am going to marry a bricklayer who has never been in a nightclub.'"

She did see Jake Webb again, after the fedora boys took him away and he allowed the army to catch up with him. He went AWOL—twice—and on one of those unscheduled trips he caught up with his wife and asked her why her name kept popping up in all those divorce cases he read about in the gossip columns.

Leonore pretended to pout. "Can't people go 'pfft' without me? Maybe not. Maybe they don't disappear unless you help them a little."

After Armistice Day, 1945, Leonore Lemmon started her own private little war against her husband Jakie Webb, divorcing him as soon as the war was over. Jake Webb was hard to track down, but Leonore kept the process servers busy. Jake had fled to New Jersey to escape her divorce papers. He once crowed to her over the phone, "I got Dutch Schultz's lawyer."

"But Jake, Dutch Schultz is dead."

"So what? He didn't die in jail, did he?"

There would be another wedding. In this one she wore a long black veil. Leonore Lemmon and Robert "Hamish" Menzies, a Scottish nightclub entertainer, were married in London in 1951 and moved back to New York that summer. Three years later that marriage soured. This time it was Leonore who complained that Menzies drank too much, frequently beat her up, and taunted her with allusions to his other women. Once Leonore claimed that on returning unexpectedly to their hotel suite, she found a strange woman asleep in their connubial bed.

According to a lawyer familiar with the case in New York, however,

Leonore merely described the way in which *she* mistreated Hamish but reversed who did what to whom. She filed for divorce, asking $400 per week in alimony. But the judge in the case threw out Leonore's motion in the spring of 1954, concluding that Menzies's hasty retreat to Cleveland put him outside of the court's jurisdiction.

Leonore had tried to reinvent herself as the adoring wife of an up-and-coming entertainer. "It's too bad," wrote gossip columnist Leonard Lyons. "They were divorced just at the time she could have used him—when she started a nightclub singing career."

"I wasn't too demanding," she said of both of her marriages. "I believe a husband ought to be in love with his wife all the time, except three hours a day when he's watching a beautiful actress onstage or while he's with another girl."

Leonore tried to parlay her notoriety as the wayward bride of a Vanderbilt into a theatrical career. She made her nightclub debut at the Beachcomber, where she sang a couple of novelty numbers, "I Was Simply a Deb Caught in a Web" and "Jake's a Fake," sung with a knowing look and a wink. But she saved her best performances for Jake Webb's mother, who told her son before he skipped town, "It's good to know that Leonore's going to settle down." And she was on her best behavior in Saratoga, New York, where she spent one summer following the horses and making sure she always came in first. Whitney heiress Liz Whitney named a horse after her, or so she said.

She tried to act stunned and hurt when the wife of bandleader Charlie Barnett mentioned her in a separation suit. "I can't think of anything sillier than Mrs. Barnett's mentioning me in a separation suit for being seen around too often with Charlie," she told the press. "Mr. Barnett is a great musician, and I shall continue to enjoy his music—unless boogie-woogie with a musician is grounds for a divorce."

She was a handsome woman with a brooch where her heart should have been, a cigarette always burning down between her exquisite fingers. She liked to sit with her legs tucked under her. She favored big black feathery hats—anything to make that first knockout impression—and her legs were as long as the autobahn. Her eyebrows were drawn on her by her beautician, a man named Dante. Superman—always attracted to women with the initials "L.L."—would meet his match in Leonore Lemmon.

She tried acting, for a while, anyway. But it was a full-time job just being Leonore Lemmon, and by the mid-1950s it was getting harder and harder to play it right. The nightclub scenes that were her forte were dying out. With those bloodred fingernails, she clung to the tablecloths of New York, Miami, Chicago, and—briefly—Los Angeles. She would hang on until all the table settings got pulled down with her. At thirty-five, she was still a knockout in artificial light. That had to be worth something.

It was said that she knew a lot of gangsters. For Leonore, power like that was a bath in asses' milk—it kept you beautiful and young. When Leonore and some of the girls would meet mobster Frank Costello for lunch, they would each find a hundred-dollar bill under their plates. Sweet Frank. What was it Oscar Levant used to say about him? "Frank Costello gets as sentimental as a Chopin nocturne."

Leonore used to like to paint. Big canvases of little birds. Oil paintings of birds, only instead of their bird heads she would paint the faces of her friends onto the little feathered bodies. A cardinal in all its reddened splendor with the face of Jake Webb. Or Frank Costello smiling, having just alighted on a branch. Maybe one day she'd meet someone who really could fly. Take her places she'd never been. A view of the El Morocco as seen from the air, above the cigarette smoke and the sounds of Charlie Barnett's band—above all that dirty air, where she could become something new, someone without a past. In the aquarium of her nightclub world, Leonore Lemmon was like an octopus stuck to the glass.

• • •

In the early 1940s, Leonore Lemmon was much in the public eye. "She's become a household word," wrote one reporter. "She is the signal for an explosion." In the press Leonore Lemmon offered herself up as a self-styled waif who can't for the life of her understand what all the fuss is about, why everything seems to go to hell in a handbasket when she enters a room. "I'm the little girl who wasn't even there," Lemmon told Charles Robbins in an attempt to explain the Affaire Paterno. After first denying her charges, Charlie Barnett did nothing to stop his wife when she traveled to Reno, Nevada, for a divorce. But there was something willfully naive about Leonore Lemmon in the 1940s, even as a precocious socialite. She would often suggest marriage to men she barely knew, as a way to control them and to test the boundaries. Or perhaps simply to assuage some vestigial, Puritan nerve ending that still twitched somewhere in her subconscious, as if, despite all her bed-hopping, she'd really just planned to settle down all along. She also showed a troubling tendency to put the most simplistic, reductive gloss on everything that ever happened to her in her life. "She was obviously a smart woman, but chose, like a lot of women, to play dumb. It's how they thought they had to act to survive," recalled one of Leonore's golfing buddies.

Golf was a sport she would become particularly avid about throughout the 1950s. She was fond of quoting President Eisenhower's doctor on the subject: "It's a walk with interruptions, I know," she'd say, "but I love it. Babe taught me. I learned from the best." Babe was her friend Mildred Didrickson, perhaps the greatest woman athlete of modern times. (Didrickson, who was born in Port Arthur, Texas, won two Olympic events in 1932: the javelin and the 80-meter hurdles. But her greatest fame came as a golfer when she captured the U.S. Open in 1948, 1950, and then again in 1954.) Leonore Lemmon certainly went right to the top if she needed anything. She had allowed her father to teach her at least that much. "Bunk with a swimmer if you're going to be on the *Titanic*," Arthur K. Lemmon used to tell his daughter. As she got older, she repeated his advice like a mantra.

• • •

Despite America's fondness for the 1950s, our nostalgia for *luxe* touches of fur, "Toni" home perms, Buddy Holly, the four-door station wagon, and the polka-dotted chemise, it was also a time of fear, paranoia, cover-ups, and shame. A real-life test for George "Superman" Reeves and the extended family that made up the cast and crew of *The Adventures of Superman* was the day the McCarthy-inspired industry blacklist came to Metropolis. For once, Reeves overcame the inertia of his usual passivity as he stood up for his friend and fellow actor, Robert Shayne.

One ordinary day in the first year of the show, a pair of dark-suited FBI men appeared at the studio. In front of the entire cast and crew, they arrested Shayne, handcuffed him, and dragged him off the set.

Shayne, who had worked as a journalist in Washington, D.C., before launching his distinguished Broadway stage career, was a great favorite in his role of Inspector Henderson. Now he was being called up by the House Committee on Un-American Activities. George Reeves was furious. He grabbed one of the FBI men by the lapels and threatened to knock him off of his feet. "My God, what are you doing?" he demanded.

They were quick to read him the riot act.

"But this man is a wonderful family man—he works for all of us, for causes! He's in the Screen Actors Guild!" George said, unintentionally making it worse for his friend and fellow actor. Actors and writers who worked for "causes" were always suspect in the eyes of tall, even-featured men in dark suits. Shayne's political work on behalf of actors, going back to the 1930s, was partly responsible for his being under suspicion as a member of the Communist Party. Now dignified, kindly "Inspector Henderson" was facing the potential ruin of his career.

Kellogg's, the show's sponsor, wanted to cut bait and run by sacrificing Shayne. "Get him off or we're not going to sponsor you," they told Whitney Ellsworth.

"Are you kidding?" Ellsworth asked the cornflakes executives. "Our show wouldn't be anything without the inspector. No way!" So Kellogg's backed down, but at least they insisted that of all the show's cast members, Shayne be prohibited from making commercials for Kellogg's.

Reeves, who was a Republican and—in Jack Larson's words—"unkind about Adlai Stevenson," was terrifically supportive of his friend and colleague. Throughout the 1950s, it would be dangerous to come to the defense of a friend so charged—as in *The Invasion of the Body Snatchers,* the 1956 sci-fi parable of McCarthyism, mere proximity could finish you off. Eventually certain members of the House Committee "apologized all over the place," remembers Bette Shayne, "and Senator Jackson worked two years trying to get Bob off that list. He said, 'Bob, you never should have been called, not in a million years.' "

None of the actors Shayne had tried to help through his activism in the 1940s and 1950s could save him now. His presence on a fact-finding committee studying the question of residuals for actors working in television did him no good. Ronald Reagan, as president of the Screen Actors Guild, had vetoed residuals, striking a blow against actors like George Reeves, Bob Shayne, Jack Larson, Phyllis Coates, and Noel Neill. "None of the people in *Superman* ever got residuals," explained Bette Shayne. "Rather, the cast received residuals for only six telecasts—just six showings. That was it. Every one of them would have been millionaires if it hadn't been for Ronnie Reagan's veto. So George wound up relying on Toni Mannix and his mother's inheritance to make ends meet, John Hamilton [Perry White] lived in a small, run-down apartment house on Vine Street with his young son. Bob and I really suffered. . . . But that was in the 1950s, and Reagan said, 'No.' After

1960, a new president of the Guild finally let it go through. It was too late, then. But think of poor George Reeves, what he could've gotten for *Superman.* It breaks the heart."

It wasn't just out of a sense of loyalty that George stood up for Bob Shayne, but genuine affection for the dignified, stage-trained actor. The Shaynes had had a steadying influence on Reeves and were often present at the casual dinner parties Toni and George gave at the Benedict Canyon house. When Leonore Lemmon entered the picture and put an end to that friendship, however, George would find himself alone and adrift, heading toward disaster.

• • •

People were beginning to talk. American youth's foremost role model for manhood didn't even have a girlfriend, at least as far as the public was concerned. There's a publicity photo of George Reeves in black tie escorting the fetching and immensely popular skating star Sonja Henie to the premier of *The Egyptian.* The date must have been arranged by the sponsors of *The Adventures of Superman* to quell any theories about why George Reeves wasn't married or involved with anyone he could be photographed with. His relationship with Toni was an open secret in Hollywood, but not across America. For many, his involvement with a much older woman fueled rumors of Reeves's homosexuality. In Hollywood in the 1950s, the biggest career-killer next to being a Commie was being an avowed homosexual. This was the era of the studio date: James Dean paired with Ursula Andress, Rock Hudson in an arranged marriage with an agent's secretary. Everyone in the entertainment business knew about Rock Hudson, but the secret was kept from the rest of the country. It was easier for actors and studios to keep their secrets back then, because of the tougher libel laws in the 1950s. When the flamboyant pianist Liberace was called a "marshmallow" in the English tabloids, that was enough for a lawsuit. Liberace knew that the implications of such a charge would virtually end his career—just ask Johnny Ray—so he took *The Daily Mirror* to court and won £8,000, about $22,400. The high court jury decided that the word used by columnist William N. Connor—"marshmallow"—implied the pianist was homosexual, and they decided in the entertainer's favor. Upon leaving the courtroom, Liberace announced to a cheering crowd of women fans that he was "delighted that his reputation had been vindicated."

• • •

George and Toni often talked about what life was going to be like after they were married, though by 1956, they were no closer to that goal. However, they decided to buy property together and began planning their dream house. They chose a site at the top of Laurel Canyon and often drove up there just to look it over, opening a bottle of wine and making a toast to their beautiful future. They would drive there together in George's custom-made Alvis, which Toni had bought for him. (The Alvis was a handmade, English automobile produced from the 1920s through the late 1960s, touted as "a gentleman's car," not quite as expensive as a Rolls or a Bentley but a cut above a Cadillac. Toni had ordered the car made with an extra-long steering column to accommodate her tall amour.)

On those idyllic afternoons at the top of Laurel Canyon, it didn't even seem as if their future was bought and paid for with Eddie's money, because they both knew nothing was going to happen until Eddie gave up the ghost. Divorce, as it had always been, was still out of the question. Even if Toni and George were not Catholic, Eddie wasn't about to see his wife make her love nest with a strapping younger man, condemning him to the twilight of being cared for by hired servants. After his first heart attack in 1954 came long nights of thinking about the soul, about being in a state of grace. After all the things he'd done in his life, a divorce wasn't going to help him enter the gates of heaven. He and Toni had an agreement, but it would only go so far. After all, Bernice never got that divorce she wanted either.

By the end of 1956, George and Toni's trips to their parcel of land became less frequent. Toni was beginning to show the strain that comes of having an ailing husband. By then, Eddie Mannix had stepped down as studio manager of MGM, though he would remain on the board of directors and keep an office on the lot. "Poor Eddie had to work at staying alive," recalls Phyllis Coates. He would visit the studio several times a week, though by 1957 he was confined to his wheelchair. But there were those who said that Eddie overdid it—that he wasn't as feeble as he appeared and that he had found a new way to terrorize and control, this time from the sickroom.

Although his doctors had warned him to take it easy, Mannix ignored this advice for as long as he could, going to the racetrack every week and betting heavily, refusing to stop smoking. He told one friend, "If I

Sam Kashner & Nancy Schoenberger

58

have to cut out everything, I don't want to go on living." He was the kind of guy who actually boasted about how many angina attacks he had. "I've had at least seven coronaries and fifty anginas," he bragged, blowing a smoke ring as big as a Christmas wreath from his fat cigar.

The strain of waiting for her husband to die was taking its toll on Toni. In public she was always elegant and gracious, but privately, the slightest thing would set her off. When George replaced one of her tasteful reproductions with a painting he had brought back from a trip to New York, Toni demanded to know why she wasn't consulted. And she had begun to put on a little weight. The bright sundresses and hats that once looked so becoming on her began to seem almost silly on her slightly thickening frame, as if she were trying too hard to look like a young girl. "She began showing up at garden parties looking like Bo Peep," an acquaintance remembers.

But George had other worries. *The Adventures of Superman*—now on the air for five years although it had been in production for seven—had become an ordeal. The show was no longer just a job, it had become a new American religion with Reeves as its symbol. He still longed to return to the big screen, which is where Mark Sandrich once told him he really belonged. But Sandrich had been dead for more than ten years now, and things had not worked out as Reeves had planned. There was even talk of a Superman movie. At least it would give him a chance to break out of that box, a last chance for a different kind of fame.

6

THE PHANTOM ZONE

When asked why he thought the figure of Superman immediately captured the imagination of millions of young viewers, Jack Larson pointed out that Superman was the first creature from another planet who is entirely good instead of entirely evil. Fifteen years before *The Adventures of Superman* aired on television, Orson Welles's radio broadcast of H. G. Wells's *War of the Worlds* caused a national panic over the belief that Martians had landed in New Jersey and were colonizing America. The 1951 films *The Day the Earth Stood Still* and *The Thing (From Another World)* further stoked our national paranoia regarding space invaders—followed by a plethora of end-of-the-world scenarios, on film and television, playing on our most basic brand of xenophobia. In 1953, the film *The War of the Worlds* capitalized on our collective horror of invaders, as weird aliens from outer space do indeed take over America, only to be felled by the least among us—viral microorganisms. *I Married a Monster from Outer Space* and *The Blob* were two notable additions to this genre in 1958.

"With 'Superman,' " says Larson, "it was a first. He's the first *hero* from outer space. Otherwise there are all these monsters. But Superman takes poor little threatened creatures, like Jimmy Olsen, up in his arms and saves them. It's wonderful for children—they love to see that."

It didn't take the sponsor of *The Adventures of Superman* long to realize who their audience was. The first twenty-four episodes of the show were "taut little exercises in TV film noir," wrote TV critic Allan Asherman, which were probably the result of Robert Maxwell's previous involvement with the "Superman" radio series, and the writers' penchant for pulp fiction. In these early episodes, Reeves's Superman is more of an avenging angel, a symbol who appears, dispatches the crooks, then vanishes. But when Whitney Ellsworth was brought in to replace Bob Maxwell after the first season, the tone of the series changed. (It was, in fact, thought that Maxwell was dismissed because his shows were too violent.) Maxwell and his coproducer Bernard Luber did indeed film some disturbing images for what would turn out to be a children's show: a dead dog in "The Deserted Village" and, in another episode, a grandmother in a wheelchair being pushed down a ramp. "They created a pretty tough show," observed *Superman* chronicler Michael Hyde. ". . . The first producers wanted Superman to appeal to adult viewers as well as children. Most markets carried it at eight-thirty in the evening, hardly the ideal time for a viewership of five-year-olds."

The later segments under Ellsworth's supervision, now clearly aimed at younger viewers, featured "Runyonesque gangsters and whimsical plots" with Reeves acting more as a straight man to the comic shenanigans of Jimmy Olsen and the various guest gangsters.

Despite his growing distaste for the role, Reeves was perfect for the part. Allan Asherman noted that "Reeves never talked down to the children. . . . The more Superman admonished [Jimmy and Lois] and shared his secrets with the viewers, smiling and winking at the end of each adventure, the more kids regarded George Reeves's Superman as their friend."

Whit Ellsworth's steering of the series toward comedy and away from film noir was also, perhaps, a reaction to the fallout from the 1953 publication of an influential anti–comic book diatribe called *Seduction of the Innocent,* written by New York psychiatrist Dr. Fredric Wertham. Not content simply to attack the violence and sadism in popular crime and horror comics, Dr. Wertham went so far as to attack "Superman" before a legislative committee, arguing that the Jerry Siegel–Joe Shuster creation stemmed from Nietzschean concepts of the Superman ("We should, I suppose, be thankful that [Superman's S] is not an SS"). Nothing, of course, could be farther from the truth, and the TV show, taking its cue from the beautiful Paramount-Fleischer cartoons made in the early 1940s, presented Superman as heroically American. The opening of *The Adventures of Superman* follows closely the stylized introduction to the Max and Dave Fleischer cartoons: Superman topping the world, the American flag flapping in the solar wind, while galaxies twinkle in deep space all around him. Can there be a purer expression

Sam Kashner & Nancy Schoenberger

of post–World War II boosterism, as America claimed its ascendancy in what would become known as the American century? Reeves's Superman was the embodiment of America as friendly watchdog, the protective father making the world safe for democracy. While millions of *real* fathers were spending increasing hours away from home in the strict division of labor known as the nuclear family, millions of children were being raised by a surrogate father who possessed not only superhuman strength, but a playful twinkle in the eye. No wonder America's youth fell in love with Superman. World War II had left as its legacy a belief that young boys, especially, should not be "mollycoddled" but raised sternly, given military buzz cuts at the age of three, with any sign of weakness soundly discouraged. Here was a father figure whose strength and toughness were unassailable, but whose relationship to Jimmy Olsen—really young enough to be Superman's son as portrayed by Larson—was as lighthearted as it was paternalistic. Superman's moral lessons to Jimmy and Lois at the end of each episode were softened by the appearance of Clark Kent, whose self-effacing modesty undercut Superman's absolute power. As Asherman has observed, "Reeves's Superman and [Clark] Kent also conveyed the magnetism and determination of 'Captain Video,' the patriotism of 'Captain Midnight,' the good manners of 'The Lone Ranger' and the fatherly attitude of 'Hopalong Cassidy.' " Jim Nolt, a retired schoolteacher and editor of a fan magazine devoted to George Reeves called *The Adventures Continue,* remembers that his father, an alcoholic, was not around much when he was growing up. As a kid he adored Superman and wore his bath towel–cum–cape all over the family farm, acting out favorite episodes. "I think it was George Reeves's influence—not entirely but partly— that persuaded me to become a teacher. When I work with children, I can feel myself talking to children the way George did."

Another chronicler of George Reeves and *The Adventures of Superman,* the actor and writer Jim Beaver, has observed that what made Reeves so likable in the part was a certain naturalness on camera and immense charm. "Acting was mainly a fun way to make a living for George . . . it was a lark to him." However, by 1955, after four years of appearing in *Superman,* the role had ceased to be much fun, and George was feeling not just compromised but trapped.

Toward the end of 1956, Reeves filmed a guest appearance on *I Love Lucy* that would air in January of 1957 and would prove to the world just how inextricably Reeves and *Superman* were bound together.

At first George didn't want to do it. Special-effects man Si Simonson recalled that George was reluctant to do the show without Simonson along to work out the stunts. *I Love Lucy*'s directors agreed to hire Simonson to work out the particulars of George's appearance, especially Superman's trademark landing and take-off, which have always been what convinced generations of kids that Superman did indeed fly.

The show's writers prepared a story: Superman making a surprise appearance at little Ricky's birthday party just in time to save Lucy, masquerading as the caped one, who is perched on the ledge of her apartment building with a legion of city pigeons. The episode opens with little Ricky wearing a Superman shirt and cape, sitting on the couch in the Ricardo living room watching *The Adventures of Superman* on television. "Can Superman come to my birthday party?" he begs.

The fun of the episode is when Superman *does* appear, by crashing through the Ricardos' breakfast nook. It's a particularly stunning entrance, and when he goes out on the ledge to rescue poor Lucy, his six-foot-two frame dwarfs her (though Lucille Ball was tall enough herself to choose to appear in most scenes with Desi Arnaz wearing flats). But the single most interesting thing about Reeves's appearance on the show is that he went uncredited. His name simply did not appear. The credits just read "Superman"—no trace of George Reeves anywhere.

"What I don't understand," Simonson said, "is why George didn't get billed." No one seems to have a good explanation as to why George Reeves's name was kept off the crawl of credits at the end of the show. Did the folks at Desilu think they were doing him a favor, keeping the illusion of Superman alive?

Another friend of George's saw a marked change in the actor after his uncredited appearance on *I Love Lucy*. "After that, 'Superman' was no longer a challenge to him. He was a very good actor who had possibilities beyond what he did. I know he enjoyed the role, but he used to remark 'Here I am, wasting my life.' "

George was beginning to feel desperate. He was interviewed a few times about the direction of his career, and now he didn't hold back: "It's like Hopalong Cassidy trying to get an acting job in white tie and tails," he said on more than one occasion.

• • •

As far as Toni Mannix was concerned, Helen Bessolo was a challenge. And Toni was a challenge to Helen, too. George's mother certainly knew about her son's relationship with the married wife of MGM's vice pres-

Sam Kashner & Nancy Schoenberger

ident, but she didn't have to approve of it. Helen was planning to visit George over Christmas. The two were back on speaking terms, but Helen knew she had to be on her best behavior around her son—he could be so temperamental! George had promised her a trip to Catalina Island—a boat ride, and some other surprises. It sounded as if he wanted to make up for the years of estrangement that followed his discovery that his father was still alive.

Maybe it was because she had recently inherited a lot of money. By 1956, Helen Bessolo was worth $1 million, thanks to shares in a pharmaceutical company left to her by her father. Helen could now afford to be generous with George, but, as with everything else in her life, her random acts of kindness came with all sorts of emotional strings attached.

George, at first, refused Helen's offers of money. Not because he didn't need her help, but probably because it was already enough of a humiliation to have Toni paying most of the bills. He didn't need two "Mamas." So Helen Bessolo took the train to Los Angeles to visit her son. She had always hated to fly, and now that she was in rather delicate health, she felt that traveling by rail was easier. In truth, the trip was far more exhausting by train than it would have been on a prop plane from the middle of the country. But Helen liked to be seen as a martyr. She liked to be fussed over, worried about, catered to, especially by her famous son who was such a hit on the television.

Secretly, Helen was rather disappointed in George. He hadn't become the same kind of star as the boys he knew at The Pasadena Playhouse, like Robert Preston and Victor Mature. "Preston was one of the biggest things to hit this town," actor Fred Crane remembers. Crane had appeared with George as the other Tarleton twin in *Gone With the Wind,* and the two men had maintained their friendship through the 1950s. Of course, George "knew better than anyone that he hadn't achieved that level of success," said Crane. He didn't need Helen to remind him. Helen had always hoped her son would become as respected as Victor Mature—he of the manly bosom.

Helen's trip to Los Angeles to visit George and meet Toni was, by all accounts, a disaster. At first, George tried to keep the two women apart, but when Toni insisted on meeting Helen, George decided that Catalina Island would be the best place for it. Perhaps the bracing sea breeze and shining blue vistas would distract the two women, born rivals, and put them on their best behavior.

Toni showed up inappropriately dressed to the nines, in a little out-fit called a "Tea Timer" that consisted of white satin capri pants teamed with a flowered satin frock coat with a Mandarin collar. The frock coat was cinched at the waist and then belled out below, exposing the snug pants. White "wedgie" shoes completed the outfit, which made her dangerously unstable on the boat. It was a cocktail outfit, really, meant to show Helen that she still had something George's mother could never give him.

Toni had invited one of her girlfriends along on the trip, a red-haired former script girl named Constance Shirley. "The trip was an unmitigated disaster," Constance recalled. The first thing Toni tried to do was get Mrs. Bessolo drunk, but Mrs. Bessolo didn't drink, at least not then. But Toni did, and it wasn't pretty. "She hung all over George, as if she was trying to remind Mrs. Bessolo who the important woman in George's life really was." At one point, Helen said she didn't feel well and wanted to lie down. She had some medicine to take, and Toni offered to get her some water. "She told me later," Constance said, "that the water came from the commode. It was a very tense trip."

Two years later, Helen would deny ever knowing anything about George's relationship with Toni and would feign surprise that George and "a married Catholic woman" could have ever become so close.

It wasn't easy for Toni, either. Toni was a member of Hollywood royalty, not because her husband was beloved but because he was powerful and had been around for a long time. Toni had official studio dinners and other social engagements to attend to—such as the MGM wives' organization that sponsored a tag sale every year, taking up a collection of last year's discarded fashions and selling them to raise money for charities. The name "Mannix" opened many of the electronic gates in Beverly Hills and Bel-Air, and Toni was not about to throw all that away, not even for Superman. Simply for Toni to be promenading on the deck of a boat with George and his mother was to set herself up for a certain amount of ridicule, but she was, after all, still in love with "the boy." Not even a possessive old woman like Helen Bessolo would change her mind about that.

As for Helen, despite any disappointments she might have harbored about the direction of George's career, she still reveled in her son's fame. She still loved him in a possessive and desperate way, the way that a lot of parents have of seeing their child as a reflection of themselves. Helen lived through George "Superman" Reeves, and she

Sam Kashner & Nancy Schoenberger

couldn't accept his relationship with a married woman. She had a sense of foreboding about it—she felt instinctively that George was headed for some terrible fate as long as he stayed with that woman. She lit the candles in the shrine she had made to her son and prayed for deliverance of his soul.

• • •

In 1956, George wrote his will. There wasn't a lot to be seigneurial about: the house and the Alvis and about $25,000 in savings. He wasn't getting rich being Superman. The contract negotiations with National Comics were always a battle royale. The contracts were designed to make it virtually impossible for George and the other cast members to get any other work. "I loved acting and I thought I was getting real good," Jack Larson recalled. "And George thought so, too. And I had opportunities I couldn't take due to the *Superman* thing." National Comics locked all of their players in a thirty-day option clause, so cast members could work elsewhere without their permission only for a thirty-day period, which made any sustained production, such as appearing in a Broadway or Off-Broadway play, impossible. This rule was in effect all year, whether the show was in production or not.

At the height of George's popularity as the Man of Steel, National Comics was paying him $2,500 per week while the show was in production. The breakneck shooting schedule—twenty-six episodes shot in thirteen weeks—meant that George was not getting paid the other thirty-nine weeks of the year. Robert Shayne in particular thought this an outrageous situation. Residuals, of course, were still a thing of the future.

Three years after the disastrous preview of *From Here to Eternity*, things had only gotten worse for George as an actor. The man who could "change the course of mighty rivers, bend steel in his bare hands"—but who, disguised as George Reeves, couldn't get a legitimate job offer—had too much time to brood over his situation. Once the thirteen weeks of work were over, George didn't see too much of his fellow actors on the series. But Larson knew what George was going through, because he was going through the same doldrums. "It's terrible to have your career taken away," he said.

In an effort to try to help his friend and only client find work, Art Weissman and George put together a promotional film in George's backyard. The two men cleared away the cast-iron table and umbrella

from the patio where George had presided over all those happy barbecues, and Weissman filmed George, dressed in a karate outfit, doing
what looks like a tumbling act on the lawn as he executes a number of
forward rolls and demonstrates his knowledge of judo. At the end, a
tuckered-out George goes over to the patio to wipe his brow and take a
drink of water. Fred Crane, one of the few people to whom they showed
the film, thought "the whole thing was a little desperate." It looks like
what any number of middle-aged suburbanites might have shot with
their first home-movie camera—you can even hear George saying, "Did
you get that, Art?" Why Weissman didn't hire professionals to put together something a little tonier for his client is a mystery, except for
the fact that Weissman wasn't really a professional manager himself.
He was a journalist manqué, really, maybe not a bad business manager,
but what did he know about marketing George, about rustling up some
real opportunities for him? George was just too nice a guy to tell Weissman to walk, so the two of them made this amateurish film meant to
show off George's talents and musculature, but revealing instead a
poorly lit, aging kiddie-show actor in decline.

• • •

The sight of George Reeves—Superman—sweaty, shirtless, and waist-
deep in a trench under the noonday sun—must have been a startling
sight. A member of the show's crew found out about George's moon-
lighting while out for a drive during a hiatus in production: "I was with
my family; we were going up north for a few days, for a camping trip,
and my daughter notices Superman digging a ditch, with a handker-
chief on his head. I pulled over to see for myself. It was George all right."
Reeves was actually spending his spare time digging ditches for chump
change.

There are a number of ways of looking at this extraordinary sideline
of Reeves's. Some felt that George's offering to dig ditches for friends
and neighbors who were putting in septic tanks was simply a way for
the aging actor to stay in shape. But the fact that he was paid $100 for
each trench he dug didn't hurt—George was always in need of money.
It's nice to have someone pay your bills and give you the down payment on a house and buy you a car, but what about spending money for
all those big tips George liked to hand out? Now, in his early forties,
George had found himself having to struggle for money like he'd never
had to struggle before.

Sam Kashner & Nancy Schoenberger

Larson was a close observer of the changes in George and Toni's relationship during this stressful period. Jack remembered Toni, in the early days of the show as still beautiful. "She looked great. She was much more beautiful than George was handsome. George drank and let himself go a little bit. He got a little paunchy. He was definitely in corsets and padding when we finished the series. It was uncomfortable for him to get the waist tightened, and the shoulders. . . ."

In September of 1957, the cast was reunited for the beginning of the show's sixth season. George noticed during the script conferences that the stories were much less violent and seemed to be geared to even younger audiences. "The change was made," Gary Grossman wrote in *Superman, From Serial to Cereal*, "to weather the criticism of the fifties, pacifying the vocal antagonists who spoke of Superman and vigilante justice in the same breath. . . . Superman dealt in his last episodes with bumbling villains, two-bit con men, and frazzled reporters." In the new season, it became increasingly difficult to figure out how to make the scenes look interesting. Low-key performances deteriorated into somnambulistic experiences. "Tired, overweight, and bored" were the words most often used to describe George on the show.

Reeves, however, found a way to make that last year bearable, even challenging: For three episodes at least, he became the eighth director of *The Adventures of Superman*.

Reeves joined the Director's Guild in April of 1957. "We all pitched in real hard to make these good shows for George," Larson recalled. "And he was very concerned and excited. Noel and I thought George had a real future as a director, that he'd segue and direct other television."

George's first episode as director was essentially a vehicle for Nati Vacio, who plays a Mexican policeman. "The Brainy Burro"—episode #102—takes place in a sleepy Mexican village. Perry White receives a cable from Lois, who has just learned about the existence of a burro with psychic powers. Clark Kent is sent south of the border to investigate. Carmelita the Donkey psychically intuits Clark's real identity, and Superman and the beast actually make a pact to keep his identity a secret. "Two of the shows [George directed] were very good," Jack Larson said. "One of them is not a good show." "The Brainy Burro"—even for most *Superman* fans—was the clinker.

Episode #103, "The Perils of Superman," was an attempt to create an old serial-style cliff-hanger, with Superman rescuing Jimmy and Lois from a quick succession of near disasters, including old standbys of being tied to a railroad track and being fed into a buzz saw at a lumber mill. The original touch to this episode is the introduction of a clutch of bad guys all wearing featureless leaden masks. Their sci-fi, oversized heads give the villains a truly spooky presence, as if Lois and Jimmy and Clark have stumbled into a postapocalyptic city full of faceless cyborgs. Superman chronicler Gary Grossman has pointed out that Reeves's own performance in this and the other two episodes he directed perked up considerably. "The pride of directing a good solid script brings out the best in Reeves," wrote Grossman.

Better still is the final episode, "All That Glitters," one of the best shows of the entire sixth season. In this story, Jimmy and Lois are given a chance to fly. In a storyline closer to original comic book conceits, a dose of "positive K" (kryptonite, of course) isolated by eccentric Professor Pepperwinkle turns Lois and Jimmy into superbeings like Superman. Noel Neill remembered what fun it was actually to be made to fly: "Si Simonson fashioned molding to both our bodies and George suspended us above the set. It was great. Absolutely fantastic! For once it looked as if our fantasies were acted out."

As Grossman has observed, the final words of dialogue of this last episode were poignantly significant. Jimmy Olsen, stars in his eyes, pipes up, "Golly, Mr. Kent, you'll *never* know how wonderful it is to be like Superman."

"No, Jimmy," George Reeves answers. "I guess I never will."

Those are the last words Reeves would ever speak on-camera.

• • •

The 104 episodes had been backbreaking work. George had hung from cables, worn padded muscles, and sweated through heavy woolen costumes. He had to wear a red cape for seven years. After the last episode was wrapped, George went home and set fire to his Superman costume. It was a strange ritual, one that he performed at the end of each season. First he'd cut out the "S" emblem and keep it for a friend as a souvenir, then he'd take the costume home, pour gasoline on it, and strike a match. Once he performed this ritual in the parking lot behind Musso & Frank's, the cavernous old eatery on Hollywood Boulevard. He'd watch it burn with a big hole in the chest where the "S" used to be, the whole thing blackening like an eclipse.

George walked off the set that day—November 27, 1957—con-

Sam Kashner & Nancy Schoenberger

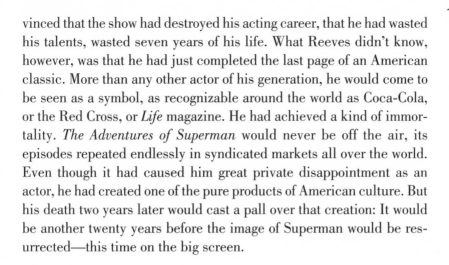

vinced that the show had destroyed his acting career, that he had wasted his talents, wasted seven years of his life. What Reeves didn't know, however, was that he had just completed the last page of an American classic. More than any other actor of his generation, he would come to be seen as a symbol, as recognizable around the world as Coca-Cola, or the Red Cross, or *Life* magazine. He had achieved a kind of immortality. *The Adventures of Superman* would never be off the air, its episodes repeated endlessly in syndicated markets all over the world. Even though it had caused him great private disappointment as an actor, he had created one of the pure products of American culture. But his death two years later would cast a pall over that creation: It would be another twenty years before the image of Superman would be resurrected—this time on the big screen.

7

COLD CHICKEN AND WARM CHAMPAGNE

Phyllis Coates, the first Lois Lane on *The Adventures of Superman,* had in many ways remained closer to George than other members of the cast who stayed with the show throughout its original six-year run. She was glad to learn that George's plans now included directing and that he was going to leave *Superman* after the 1957 season closed in November. The last time she visited George on the set, Phyllis was appearing in *I Was a Teenage Frankenstein,* which was being filmed at the same studio. (The production of *The Adventures of Superman* had moved to ZIV Studios the previous year.)

Things hadn't gone so well for Phyllis in terms of her own acting career after leaving *Superman.* Reeves actually had tried to get his original costar to return to the series after she left, but she wasn't interested. Ellsworth had even offered to double her salary, but Phyllis had already made up her mind to appear in another TV series. Unfortunately, her new show had barely lasted a season.

Phyllis arrived at the studio for an early morning call and ran into George, who invited her over to his dressing room for a cup of coffee. It was oddly similar to their first meeting in 1951, at the show's inception, when Reeves toasted their new venture with "Here's to the bottom of the barrel, Babe!" Only this time, George had begun his drinking at 7:00 A.M., having laced his coffee with a generous slug of brandy. Phyllis, who knew George could handle a lot of liquor, nevertheless was surprised and a little alarmed.

"I'm directing now, Gypsy," he told her as he nursed his coffee and offered to set Phyllis up with one. "I feel great—it's just what the doctor ordered! And don't think I'm going to forget my old friends, either!"

73

George took another sip of his brandy-laced coffee and told Phyllis there would be a part for her in his first production, whatever and whenever that might be. Phyllis left happy for George, feeling that he just might have found a second act to his career; if she was concerned that his drinking might have gotten out of hand, she didn't say anything to him about it.

Reeves's interest in directing had a psychological component, as well. For the first time in his theatrical career, he could exercise control over the material he was given to work with. While directing television in the 1950s didn't offer tremendous opportunities for creativity—"it was more like directing traffic," Jack Larson once said—it still offered George a larger measure of autonomy and control than he had ever had as an actor.

From November of 1957 through the fall of 1958, Reeves and Art Weissman tried to hustle acting work with the home movie Weissman had made. At one point Reeves entertained a proposal to portray Dick Tracy—he certainly had the jawline for it—but he decided against doing another television series. One pop icon per lifetime is enough, and besides, he was serious about turning his attentions to directing.

George had always had plans in the back of his mind to produce his own television series and feature films. As early as 1954 he'd formed a production company, George Reeves Enterprises, and the following year he'd bought *The Deserter,* a novel by Lowell Barrington, intending to produce a feature that he would star in. Though nothing ever came of these earlier projects, it showed that Reeves didn't just see himself as an actor. Reeves looked for new properties. He was especially interested in science fiction, feeling that his experience on *Superman* had given him valuable know-how in the special-effects department.

In the summer of 1958, George found a property he liked for a science-fiction feature. Phyllis Coates remembers that one of the major studios was going to put up the money. George stopped by to make good his promise to cast Phyllis in his first production, and he offered to give her a copy of the script.

"No, George. You keep the script. I'm moving and it will just get lost in the move. When I get settled, call me and we'll get together and go over the script."

"I'm through with the acting bull," George told her enthusiastically. "I'm moving on to directing."

Toni was as pleased as George about his new prospects, even though there had been a visible strain in their relationship over the past year. George was the only cast member of *The Adventures of Superman* who had worked out a way to get limited residuals for the show, so he wasn't entirely dependent on Toni's money, but his income was drastically reduced once production of the series was over. George was increasingly irritable around Toni, and that just seemed to make Toni all the more possessive.

Though the sixth season of *The Adventures of Superman* was wrapped up, Reeves still had obligations to publicize the show. National Comics sent him on a cross-country tour in October of 1958, which brought him, sans Toni, to New York. This time, though, he spent more time talking about himself and his future than *The Adventures of Superman.* His excitement over his new directing career is revealed in an interview he gave for the *New York Post.* Bob Thomas, the reporter and author of a number of Hollywood biographies, wrote that "Superman is looking for a place to land." Thomas's portrayal of Reeves is more sympathetic, less tongue-in-cheek, than the actor's usual treatment in the press. "After 26 years of acting," Thomas wrote, "and a screen career of 21 years, George Reeves was beginning to understand why he wasn't offered acting jobs—simply because he was Superman." Reeves explained how the dearth of jobs "drove him behind the camera." In a revealing slip of the tongue, Reeves said, "I took over as director on the last thirteen Superman segments that we made last fall. I did it as a sort of a chance, but I was surprised to find out how much I knew . . . I suppose you ought to absorb some knowledge after being in this business as long as I have. Now I am enthusiastic about doing more. I am forming a production company and we plan to make a couple of science fiction pictures. The trick stuff should come easy. We've done everything imaginable in the Superman series."

Was it a copy editor's mistake, did Thomas mishear George, or did George purposely mislead Thomas when he said he had directed thirteen—not three—episodes of *Superman?* Or was it George's unconscious mind assigning an unlucky number as a kind of jinx to his directorial debut?

Whatever the explanation, the tone of this interview is clearly optimistic. Reeves told Thomas he was going to be writing as well as producing movies. "And if things ever get dull," he added with self-deprecating humor, "I can always go on a personal appearance tour. I'm great when they want to open something to attract kids. This summer I may go to Japan." Reeves had, in fact, just received a fan letter from Japan's Emperor Hirohito. He now had the prospect of producing and directing a science-fiction feature; if George was nursing a suicidal depression, he was giving a good imitation of a man with a lot to live for.

• • •

George had always loved New York. While in the army and just after the war, he had appeared on numerous live television dramas broadcast from the city, including *Kraft Television Theatre* and *Fireside Theatre.* He loved the town's nightlife, and one evening in October of 1958 in the middle of his New York junket, George found himself sitting alone at the popular nightclub Toots Shor's. A few tables away a striking woman in a feathery black hat was leaning over to let her escort for the evening light her cigarette. A friend of Leonore's caught sight of Reeves sitting by himself. He called the maitre d' to his table and inquired if the handsome man sitting alone was, indeed, the actor who played Superman on TV. Yes, indeed it was. So the friend went over to Leonore's table and asked her if she'd like to meet Superman.

"Superman!" Leonore exclaimed. "You mean that dirty man in Cuba who does a sex act? Are you out of your mind? You're going to introduce me to that dirty person from Cuba?" The Cuban "Superman" had made an impression on Leonore, with his candelabra of parakeets and his ugly mug. She shuddered.

"No," her friend insisted. "This is the *real* Superman." Leonore glanced over at George's table to assure herself that the man sitting alone in black tie was not that notorious Cuban. She must have liked what she saw, because she arranged through her friend to meet George later that night, after putting in an appearance at a dinner party she had promised to attend.

George was staying at the Gotham Hotel. Leonore left her dinner party early and picked up half a capon and a bottle of champagne on her way over to the Gotham. She took the elevator up to his suite and knocked on the door.

"Here you are!" she said when he opened the door. "Look what I've brought you: warm champagne and a cold chicken!" George let the voluptuous woman with hair the color of burnt cinnamon into his suite.

• • •

It had been sixteen long years since Leonore Lemmon had made headlines as the teenage terror of the Stork Club and the most incendiary member of café society. Her parents had not only given up on Leonore; by the end of the war they finally sent her abroad. After two busted-up marriages and lots and lots of newsprint, she had burned too many bridges between New York and Bridgehampton. They had no choice but to put some distance between her and the rest of New York, before she ruined all of their reputations.

Europe—and in particular, London—in the late 1940s and early 1950s was where Leonore reinvented herself. In England, Arthur Lemmon's reckless daughter learned to create a more respectable persona for herself. Where once she had been a wild, sexually voracious debutante, she now became a sophisticated woman of the world. Her "comic-strip" marriage to a Vanderbilt and her father's money helped pave her way through London society. Those English nobs found her breezy and iconoclastic, appreciated her ribald stories, her refreshingly frank American manners. After all, the 1950s was the American decade. The American ego was in pretty good shape throughout the postwar years, and in England especially, Americans were all the rage.

Dr. Philip Terman, a dentist and sometime saxophone player in New York, got to know Leonore when she moved back to the city. "I know she spent the Second World War in England, where she met lots of people," he recalled. "She was the darling of society's 400, and she got that way as a result of acquiring a lot of sophistication in England." Leonore was befriended by the Duke and Duchess of Windsor and members of the Churchill family. She had become a wonderful raconteur. "She could be spellbinding," according to Terman. "Dropping all these names. She knew all these people and had these stories. Whereas people do the name-dropping thing for impact, she did not. When she mentioned somebody that she knew, she really knew them! She did all that stuff." She knew Stavros Niarchos, the Greek shipping magnate and rival of Aristotle Onassis; she went with Churchill's son; she was James Roosevelt's girlfriend; she was rumored to have been one of Joe Kennedy's lovers. "She was at the party, she took the plane, she was on the boat."

Terman remembered Leonore's lusty voice. Henny Youngman had been booked at the Beachcomber the night Leonore had made her singing debut. The old raconteur remembered her as having a good voice, knowing her material and having her arrangements all prepared, but she ultimately wasn't interested enough to forge a real singing career. "She was gorgeous," according to Henny Youngman. "I really liked her."

But by 1958 Leonore's doelike look had hardened. Where once she had been smoldering vulnerability, she now had a polished veneer, a harder face, a more practiced manner. She knew her power over men, the poor darlings. She still had a tremendous vivacity. "She was very sharp—she had a fierce intelligence, superb wit, and original style," Terman remembered. Her wit and intelligence appealed to George, who once upon a time thought of himself as something of an aesthete, reading George Bernard Shaw, whom he had met once in London, and pursuing a serious interest in music. Didn't Fritz Lang think of George as a son? George had even gotten to know the expatriate Hollywood composer Dmitri Tiomkin, and the two had once collaborated on an oratorio. If only those millions of munchkin fans had known that about Superman! Even Toni, who was queen of her social sphere, didn't share George's appreciation of music and literature. In short, George was bowled over. Here was a woman with Toni's looks and style, far richer connections, and fifteen years younger. Maybe at last he had found a reason to bolt.

So George and Leonore started going around together, even taking short trips to other famous watering holes—in Miami and Palm Beach, for instance. In the first photograph that began to circulate of George and "Lem" at a Florida nightclub, George's adoration of Leonore is palpable in the harsh light of a nightclub photographer's flash. They are dressed up and dining out in a glamorous Palm Beach club, and he's beaming down at her. He's doting on her; he's smitten; he's the cat who ate the canary. She's looking down, giving nothing away, no hint that she knows she's the adored one. She gazes almost demurely into her wineglass, her hair pulled back from her face in dramatic fashion. The lineaments of her face and arch of her eyebrows reveal the intelligence and sophistication that Philip Terman described. Reeves is in love, or giving a good imitation of it. Why, then, doesn't she return his amorous glance? She looks down, avoiding his eyes.

One thing that hadn't changed in all those years since Leonore had been the hellion of the nightclub scene was her temper, her inability to countenance being crossed. "If she got mad, she would just proceed to let you have it," Terman recalled. "She had a violent temper. She'd battle her way through a meal if she chose. She could rape you with some of her angers."

If Terman was convinced that Leonore had done all the things she said she had done and had met all the people she claimed to have met, there were others who considered her a fabricator. Peter Levinson, a longtime friend of Leonore's in the years following George's death, said he'd always heard that "Leonore made up a lot of things." She was like Helen Bessolo in that respect, maybe better at it. The more skeptical of her friends would try to check up on her stories. Sometimes they'd find out she had been telling the truth after all. Levinson would ask, "Is it true what she said?" and her friends would say, "Oh, yeah. It's the real thing." Like Helen, truth and fantasy were woven into the same fabric, and it was getting impossible to separate the threads.

What all her friends could agree on, however, was Leonore's sexual boldness. "She'd just walk up to somebody and throw herself at him," Terman remembered. "And given her high sexuality, it was easy for her to make an entrance."

As far as George was concerned, Lem seemed to have it all. None of George's friends remember him as missing Toni during his hiatus in New York. Too bad; all of George's buddies thought of Toni as the one who had real class and Leonore as the abrasive sex tiger of New York. "Let's face it," said a friend of George, "they were both broads!" Toni married a crude guy who made tons of money. She could afford nice things. She could get involved in charities. Leonore married a dissipated aristocrat who had no money. She supported herself off and on throughout her life, and when she wasn't supporting herself, men supported her. She liked being married. "People who get married more than once in their life really like it," Terman has observed. Leonore had a reputation going back to the 1940s for asking men she hardly knew to marry her.

Like Toni, Leonore loved luxurious things and always found a way to have them. She was also artistic and enjoyed the company of musicians—just ask Charlie Barnett's wife. Leonore had once entertained the idea of writing her memoirs. She painted (albeit weird little bird pictures with human heads). She sang. Would she have been a feminist had she been born thirty years later? She was, compared to Donna Reed and Dale Evans, independent, daring, and aggressive. She was a great talker. She was an adventuress. She got George to promise her that they'd go to Africa and to Spain. She was sexually liberated—maybe *too* liberated, some would say. By the time George Reeves left New York to go back home to Hollywood, Leonore had completely taken over his life. For George, sleeping beside Lem was like lying down next to the third rail—exciting, dangerous, maybe even deadly.

Yet his Edenic weeks with Leonore couldn't go on forever. It was time to go back home, to deal with Toni, to somehow break the news to her that their "luv affahr" was finally over.

• • •

And so George returned home to tell Toni that he had met someone in New York. But George was an honorable man, and at first he thought it would be wrong to tell Toni about Leonore in the house they had shared for almost ten years. On the other hand, if there was going to be a scene, it would be worse in a public place. And the telephone—that's a coward's instrument. It didn't really matter, however—Toni could tell there was something wrong. On one of those winter days when the canyon is in shade and as cold as an icebox, George mixed a few cocktails, sat Toni down on the couch, and then he told her. It was easy to do, as long as he didn't have to think about their shared past. Toni had a way of throwing her head back and looking up at the ceiling. Constance Shirley remembered it as "very Isadora Duncan." She would do that whenever she was angry and trying to hold back, trying not to cry or throw a fit. But the ceiling didn't hold any answers: just the dark, heavy, exposed beams in the little love nest she had given George the down payment for.

But Toni's real reaction, back home at El Retiro Drive with her wheezing husband, was venomous. "She was shaking like a leaf when she told me what happened," her friend Constance remembered. "She said that she threatened to expose George as a pansy, that she knew he'd had affairs with men and she would make sure everyone knew about it. She kept asking me how this could be, that she had given George everything. Everything! The last dregs of her youth. She kept saying that, 'the last dregs of my youth.' She said that if it ever got around that George slept with men, that he was a faggot, he could become a national joke. I don't think she believed a word of what she was saying, but she was so stunned and so hurt . . . so she started making things up and threatening him. Just to get back at him."

The news of George's breakup with Toni hit their small circle of friends like a tidal wave. Jack Larson remembered that it was, oddly enough, at John Hamilton's funeral that George began talking to everyone about his new lady love. It was a sad occasion: The white-haired, burly actor who had seemed born to play Perry White had died of a heart attack, his condition exacerbated no doubt by years of solitary drinking. He had been a B actor all his life, really, always playing a judge or a cop or a lawyer, ending up in the elephants' graveyard of early television, and not making a very good living at that. He had been perfect as the curmudgeonly editor with a kind heart, whom Jimmy Olsen was forever infuriating by calling "Chief." Born in 1886, Hamilton had witnessed enormous changes in the entertainment industry. The younger cast members always called him "Mr. Hamilton," and Jack Larson especially idolized the older actor, impressed by his long history in theater and movies. At least he went out having acquired a whole new generation of fans—had he lived long enough, he might have ended up making the rounds of Superman conventions and signing autographs for legions of admirers. Bette Shayne remembered the last time she saw him alive was at a barbecue that George and Toni had held at the house. She remembered that "all of a sudden, he just fell over, in the middle of a sentence." George had to take Hamilton home to his apartment on Vine Street, near the famous Hollywood Ranch Market, because he had passed out after a few drinks. George undressed him and put him to bed, which was by now a familiar ritual with Hamilton whenever he drank. "He was such a sweet man, and ever the gentleman," Bette said. "He kept court at The Brown Derby nearly every night, at the bar. He was a quiet alcoholic; he would drink, then call a cab and go home." His death was the first shadow to fall across the "family" that made up *The Adventures of Superman.* George's abandonment of Toni would be the next.

All the cast and crew showed up for the funeral: Bob and Bette Shayne were there, Whitney Ellsworth and his family, Tommy Carr, Si Simonson, Noel Neill. Larson remembered that George seemed changed. "He was excited," Larson said, "but at the same time not quite sure, as if he was trying to convince himself that this was the greatest thing since sliced bread."

George tried to contain his buoyant optimism among the sad faces and dark glasses at graveside. He leaned over to Jack as they lowered the old actor's body into the grave and whispered, "I've met someone new and we're talking about getting married."

"George, are you sure?" Larson whispered back. "How can it be that you'd leave Toni? You've been together for so long."

"It's all over with Toni and me," George said. "It's all over. Leonore makes me feel like a boy again," he added with a grin.

Larson could only shake his head. He instinctively felt that George was making a big mistake, but he assumed that he had given up on ever marrying Toni. Maybe Eddie had had a change of heart, or his doctors had. Maybe George thought there was no future for him with Toni. Larson believed that when Eddie died, Toni and George would have married, and George would have been a very rich man. "It would have been a very different ending," Larson has said.

Larson later observed—years after it was indeed all over—that Toni Mannix's life was ruined by the breakup with George. "Absolutely ruined." Tiny fissures started appearing all over her famous veneer. She became obsessed with George and "that horrible woman," her faux English accent falling away whenever she started to rant about the two of them sleeping together in *her* house. All those beautifully rolled Rs, the gentility she had worked so hard to acquire, dropped away like last year's autumn leaves. "That slut—that pig—is sleeping in my bed!" she'd say. "How could he let that whore into my bed? I can't believe he belted me with that brunette, just when we were going to have everything our way!" She took her travails to Phyllis Coates and to Bette Shayne, trying to enlist their help in "getting the boy back." She complained bitterly at all hours of the night that Leonore "had bewitched George with her cunt."

"Ordinarily I would never hear language like that from Toni," Bette Shayne recalls, "but these were not ordinary times."

MGM beauty stylist Sydney Guilaroff witnessed this bifurcation of Toni's personality. "She had a beautiful house—immaculate," he said, "and I was over at her house on several occasions. There's a marvelous kitchen she had that was more like a sitting room and kitchen combined. She lived there most of the time and would invite me over. . . . I saw a man there at one time. She had rearranged the living room, and he was there when I came over. As I recall, he was very handsome, but a little on the tough side. He didn't have any sort of refinement at all."

Toni invited Guilaroff into her living room but she kept the handsome stranger hidden away in the kitchen.

"How is it you let him in your living room when you never let me in the living room?" the stranger pouted.

"Well, he's a gentleman and you're not," was Toni's answer.

Guilaroff found that embarrassing and didn't stay long. "That annoyed Toni," he recalled, "and I never saw her again."

No one was more surprised by the breakup than the Shaynes. Theirs had been a happy, December–June romance and marriage, and perhaps they saw themselves reflected in George and Toni's cozy domesticity. Bette Shayne told Jan Henderson, a chronicler of George Reeves and *The Adventures of Superman,* about the day she and her husband attended a barbecue at George and Toni's Benedict Canyon home. "George enthused about buying a lot farther up the canyon. He and Toni were going to build their dream house. Bob was very excited for them. He kept saying, 'Great, that's great.' "

The day George returned from New York he ran into the Shaynes at ZIV Studios. George was happy, bubbling over with goodwill and enthusiasm.

"Bob, this is the year for me," he told Inspector Henderson. "I'm going to be directing a lot of pictures. I've got another picture outside *Superman.* And guess what? I'm getting married!"

George saw Bette sitting in the Shaynes' car and strolled over and gave her a little kiss. He mentioned Leonore Lemmon, but Bette had no idea who she was.

"Oh, well, I brought her back from New York with me."

Bette was shocked. She gazed back at Reeves with a blank look on her face.

"That's all right, Bette. Bob will tell you. I won't bother to explain because everybody knows who Leonore is!"

"But what about Toni?"

"Well, it's over. No more Toni."

Bette wanted to ask about the house and the new property they had recently bought, about all of his plans with Toni, but she didn't say anything. She was too surprised to speak.

Toni, meanwhile, continued to carry a torch for George. She refused to believe that her love affair had come to an end. She felt that this was some temporary insanity on George's part, a product of the pressures of being Superman all the time, as Bob Shayne had once observed.

Phyllis Coates was now living in Beverly Hills. Toni used this proximity in her attempts to get George to come back to her. "She used to call me constantly the days and weeks after the breakup," Phyllis said. "She would tell me, 'Please, go over and talk some sense into the boy! This is crazy! That tramp! That slut!' She would carry on about Leonore. She absolutely went into a rage. I kept saying 'Toni, he's a big boy.' " But Toni kept after Phyllis, urging her to "do George the favor of talking him out of Leonore."

"She wanted to cut his throat," Phyllis remembered. "She asked to see me once and she wanted me to hold him down while she cut his throat. The two of us climbing all over this Superman to pin him down and kill him! So I told Toni, 'You can't kill something you love.' She was obsessed with it."

Constance Shirley was another friend Toni tried to press into service to talk some sense into "the boy." "She wanted me to speak to George like a Dutch uncle. Well," Constance recalled, "I went to the studio. I didn't know that the show had wrapped for the season. A lot of the things were there, the sets, some of the costumes. The place was lousy with quiet. I called George up and was going to ask him to meet me, but a woman answered the phone, and it was a scary voice. I didn't know what to say. I just knew it was all over for Toni, at that point."

8

THE PERILS OF SUPERMAN

There was nothing George loved more than Sam, his one-eyed schnauzer. George had admired the breed ever since he and Helen had lived with Frank Bessolo. Frank's schnauzer was a lot like Sam, and it used to follow Frank and young George around the kitchen where man and boy happily prepared elaborate meals. Sam was often the only other being George would take with him on sailing trips—just George and the dog with the salt-and-pepper whiskers. Or the two of them would play out in the tiny backyard, or Sam would curl up at his master's feet on the bricked patio while George sat on the glider and strummed his guitar, a neighbor boy peeking around the corner to catch a glimpse of Superman at home.

George didn't have the heart to leave Sam alone in the house when he went out to do errands, so he took the dog along with him wherever he went. Sam, like all dogs, loved to sit in the passenger's seat next to George while they tooled around Beverly Hills and West Hollywood, or went farther up into the canyon. "Sam's not a Superman fan," George liked to tell his friends. "He's a George Reeves fan." With that George would pick up the small dog and bury his face in Sam's bushy whiskers.

One January day in 1959, George made one of his runs to town and dashed into a store on North Vine Street in Hollywood, while Sam the Schnauzer waited in the passenger seat of George's Jaguar XK140. (The Alvis had been damaged not long ago by a freakish accident with a lumber truck and had been replaced by the sporty new car.) George had just gone in to pick up an electric razor he had had repaired. When he returned to his car, Sam was gone.

George panicked. He managed to locate a policeman and was told to file a complaint with the nearest station house; otherwise, nothing could be done to help him locate his missing schnauzer. Frantic, George told the desk sergeant that Sam had lost an eye in an automobile accident and was under constant medical care. He described his beloved dog and asked that he be called as soon as anyone heard anything about his whereabouts. He was worried that the dog might become disoriented, and, with only one eye, he could easily walk into oncoming traffic.

George was devastated. He spent the day driving all around North Hollywood. In an attempt to help his friend, Art Weissman asked the *Los Angeles Herald* to run a story and description of Sam and a place to contact George if the dog were located. To protect George's privacy, he gave his business address: "In care of Superman, Inc., 7324 Santa Monica Boulevard." But the truth was that Toni Mannix had snatched the dog from the open car when George had ducked into the building on Vine Street. Toni had begun following George, and had tailed him that morning when he left the house. She had gone over to the car and scooped up the schnauzer, who of course knew her and went willingly. She tossed him into the back of her Cadillac and sped off before George even left the building.

"I knew something was wrong," Toni's friend Constance said, "because I spoke to Toni over the telephone after the breakup and I heard a dog barking. I knew that the Mannixes no longer kept a dog, and with Eddie's health and all, they weren't about to get one. So I asked Toni where the barking was coming from, and did she buy a dog? She was caught up short and said something like it was the neighbor's dog. I nearly gasped, because just then I knew what she had done. She pinched George's dog. I don't want to think what she did with it. The dog was old—twelve years or something—but George wouldn't dream of putting him to sleep. I don't think George ever saw his dog again after that."

Constance resented Toni's attempts to put them in the middle of her "terrible quarrel" with George. "I didn't want to be part of a campaign to talk George into going back to Toni," Constance said. "In the first place, it was unseemly. 'Why would you want him back?' I asked her. And in the second place, she'd never forgive him even if he did return. It would forever hang over both their heads."

But her friends' persuasions did nothing to assuage her anger. Toni turned to her husband's colleague at MGM, Howard Strickling, and ac-

Sam Kashner & Nancy Schoenberger

cused him of being a traitor when he refused to get involved. "She wanted me to wage a publicity campaign to win him back," Strickling told his friend and fellow MGM executive Sam Marx. "She thought we could get George to come back to her the way you get people to come into the theater for a picture they're not sure about."

Unable to stir the pot any further, with her friends unwilling to speak to George on her behalf, Toni was left alone to fume in her mansion alongside her ailing husband, who was retreating even farther into sickness. The two would sometimes scream at each other down the long corridors while the servants went about their business, pretending not to hear them.

Maybe Toni snatched George's dog to have something of his she could curl up with in bed at night. Something that when all this craziness was over, and he came back to his senses, she could then reward him. In her algebra of need, she could return Sam to George when George returned to her. Or maybe as things got worse, Toni felt that she had nothing to lose, and she did what would have been unthinkable just a few short weeks ago: She had Sam put to sleep. She could pretend that it was Leonore Lemmon—"the whore of Babylon"—she was "putting to sleep." She had, according to Phyllis Coates, become crazy on the issue of Leonore. "She really turned a corner somewhere."

• • •

Meanwhile, Eddie Mannix was having his own problems. It seems as if the worse things got at the studio, the sicker he felt. And to add to the Bulldog's worries, his wife seemed to be going off the deep end. A protégé of Strickling's from the publicity department recalled that Strickling had once told him about Eddie Mannix's reaction to George's bust-up with his wife. "He was outraged, and hurt on Toni's behalf." George had gone out of his way to upset the apple cart that had been doing a good business on the same corner for ten years. Everyone had been content with the arrangement, everyone except George, apparently. For a guy like Eddie, if you insult his wife, you've insulted him. And Eddie never forgot an insult.

There's been speculation about whether Helen Bessolo—who had never liked Toni and had never warmed up to the fact that George was long involved with a much older, married woman—had a hand in George's breakup with Toni. Had Helen somehow persuaded her son to look elsewhere, under the promise of inheriting her hefty fortune upon her death? Had she threatened to leave George out of her will if he stayed with Toni, or did she dangle a sizable chunk of cash over his head for his more immediate needs? It was obvious to all concerned that Helen and Toni disliked each other—Helen would cross Toni's name off any photographs of Toni and George that fell into her hands. The last time George had seen his mother was in 1958, just before leaving for New York. He had stopped by on his way to the East Coast, in part to help her out after a mysterious fire had destroyed part of her home on The Public Square in Galesburg, Illinois. It's possible he had been considering breaking up with Toni at that point, and Helen may have added some additional pressure.

"I remember Toni at home one day looking up at the ceiling," Constance Shirley said, "like she had a way of doing, and asking out loud, 'Is it money? The boy knows I gave him whatever he asked for. He can have whatever he needs. . . .' "

By the spring of 1959, George had begun to play a dangerous game. He was mixing a volatile cocktail by accepting Helen's money and still allowing Toni to pay some of his expenses. Toni must have felt she still had a stake in the game by paying some of George's big bills. She still hoped he would return to her, though she bitterly complained to friends that she would never have him back. Toni had become addicted to the sense of power and control she once had over George—it was the only thing she lived for now—that, and waiting for Eddie to die. She still needed some kind of connection to her "boy."

George had spent most of his adult life refusing to accept money from his mother. "He often sent back money Helen would send him," remembers a Bessolo relative. "Of course, Helen wouldn't take 'no' for an answer and she'd send it back. But things must've gotten tougher for George in 1959, because he'd stopped sending it back. I guess that was when *Superman* ended and he really needed the money. I don't think he made very much in residuals."

It's true. George's career—both acting and directing—was moribund in the long months following the end of the 1957 season. He had been optimistic about producing and directing new properties, but backing for the science-fiction feature he'd bought the rights to never came through, and Phyllis never got her copy of that script.

Now George needed every cent Helen could send him. "I know that

Sam Kashner & Nancy Schoenberger

in the last months," Jack Larson recalled, "he was living pretty high. I was out of the country at the time, but I remember that Toni told me when I got back that she was getting George's bills from restaurants like Scandia for $900 for a single month. And believe me, that was a lot of money in those days."

In compiling material for a biography of Reeves, Jim Beaver managed to collect George's liquor bills from the last months of his life. "He was running up tremendous tabs from the liquor store," Beaver noted. "Sometimes $600 for a single bill . . . they were delivering it by the case." Between Leonore Lemmon's penchant for living high and George's increasing desperation over the turn his career had taken, George was drinking more and more by the spring of 1959.

In fact, palpable changes were occurring in George's personality, attributable to a number of factors. Depression caught up with him once the realization sank in that his acting career was truly over. Typecasting—and changes in acting styles ushered in by the "Method" and exemplified by Monty Clift, Marlon Brando, and James Dean—had ensured the end of George Reeves's old style of studio leading-man acting. George might have gotten himself another television series, like the aborted *Dick Tracy,* but he was shut out of the more interesting work available in Hollywood at the time. In 1959, Tony Curtis and Jack Lemmon dressed up in drag and starred in *Some Like It Hot;* deeply closeted Rock Hudson was the biggest box office star of 1959, followed by Cary Grant and Jimmy Stewart; even Glenn Ford was one of the top-ten box office draws, as was Frank Sinatra. Sinatra! His career had been saved by Fred Zinnemann and Monty Clift when they put him in *From Here to Eternity,* the very film that rang the death knell of George's career. The previous year, Charlton Heston—another old-style, leading-man actor like George—had earned an Oscar for *Ben Hur.* That movie had won enough gold statuettes to open up a bowling alley. And Heston couldn't even take a fall like George!

Whereas the thought of directing still buoyed his spirits, "He paid a price for running around in a cape and tights," Jack Larson observed. "He did this year after year, and the casting people never forgot. They never forgive a success, you know. But he was very noble about his dilemma."

The price George paid showed up on the bills being sent to Toni from Scandia and from George's local liquor store. "He was drinking more than usual," Phyllis observed. "He had an enormous tolerance for alcohol. He could drink all day and never show the effects of it. So when he wasn't working, he could pace himself and just keep drinking. You'd never know it. He had the original hollow leg. I just don't know where he put it."

That accounts for the conflicting reports as to George's drinking habits. Constitutionally he was so capable of handling his liquor without showing any ill effects that even an ordinarily observant person like Bette Shayne could overlook the degree to which he imbibed.

"Contrary to what I heard," Bette has said, "I never saw George drunk, let's put it that way." Even Robert Shayne, who worked with George every day, never smelled liquor on George's breath. "I'd go in the trailer every morning," he told his wife, "and we'd do our lines together. I never saw him drunk." To this day Bette Shayne is convinced that George could not have imbibed as much as his reputation indicated. "I can't believe it because I never saw it," she said, "and I saw him a lot. And I never, ever, saw George, at any of those parties at the house with Toni, ever look or act drunk. If he had wild parties, then I wasn't in on them."

But George's liquor bills belied Bette and Robert Shayne's observations that he wasn't drinking heavily, at least in the spring of 1959. And if George's parties got wilder after he left Toni and took up with Leonore, then that was partly Leonore's influence, and, yes, Robert Shayne, who had once studied for the ministry, and Bette would not have been invited.

• • •

George proposed to Leonore Lemmon practically the moment he laid eyes on her in New York, at least if you believe what Leonore told Suzy Knickerbocker, the society gossip columnist who covered the busted marriages, raised-pinkie parties, and expensive mergers of Social Register types. Suzy wrote in her column that George had asked Leonore to marry him but that "Lem was in no hurry to get married." Of course, Leonore's modus operandi ever since the 1940s was to pop the question before it could be asked of her. According to Phil Terman, it got the preliminary stuff over with, and it gave Leonore the upper hand in the relationship, keeping the guy sufficiently boxed in. "Let's decide to get married," was the game, "and then we can go ahead and do whatever the hell we want." And now that Leonore hadn't worked since her brief career as a canary at the Beachcomber in the 1940s, and Daddy's

Sam Kashner & Nancy Schoenberger

money wasn't going to last forever, she now had to find out who was going to support her. "She had to get all her ducks lined up in a row," remembers Terman. So after telling Suzy, Earl Wilson, and Walter Winchell—"whom I know personally"—that George had proposed to her, Leonore Lemmon left New York for a city she would later claim to loathe: Los Angeles. She flew across the country as the "girl who was going to marry Superman." Lois Lane, you might as well start crying into your beer.

Leonore Lemmon did indeed hate Los Angeles. She hated it with a passion. "I don't know what you do out here," she'd complain, often and loudly, and she'd amuse her New York friends over the telephone by tearing into Beverly Hills society. Leonore had always loved Fifth Avenue, and in particular the tony department store Saks Fifth Avenue. "Every apartment I ever had, I always asked the landlord the same thing: 'Can you see Saks Fifth Avenue on a clear day?'"

Leonore would have other reasons to complain: She was used to New York City's pace and excitement, and everyone seemed to be sleep-walking in Los Angeles; she couldn't just roll out of bed and hail a taxi to the nearest watering hole in Hollywood, where there was a dearth of good restaurants and clubs in 1959; and she had already made a reputation for herself in the Big Apple, but on the West Coast nobody knew her. "I'm a New York gal," she insisted, but there she was, sitting on three suitcases on George's front steps, waiting for him to answer the door. Gene La Belle recalled that Leonore's appearance at George's was a bit of a shock. "George was head over heels for Leonore, but I think he was also intimidated by her aggressiveness. He was in shock that she actually came out here."

Leonore just didn't have any friends in Los Angeles, except for three "girlfriends" who were also transplants from New York's nightclub-and-society world. One of them was Gwen Dailey, "a dynamic gal" who was married to Irish actor and dancer Dan Dailey and who had previously been married to Donald O'Connor. "How can you be married to two Irish tap dancers in one lifetime?" Leonore often teased her friend. Then there was Henny Backus, the talented wife of the actor Jim Backus, who had a few years earlier appeared as James Dean's henpecked father in *Rebel Without a Cause* and would enchant baby boomers as the voice of Mr. Magoo and the unflappable millionaire Thurston Howell III on *Gilligan's Island.* Henny Backus had grown up in show business and knew everyone in New York, and though she had not been a close friend of Leonore's, she certainly remembered her—as a "wild, indulged party girl. Fun-loving. Crazy. You wouldn't dare give a party without her. She'd always give a party a lift." Leonore's third friend in Los Angeles was another transplanted New Yorker, none other than the notorious ex-madam Polly Adler.

Polly Adler ran one of the most popular and scandalous brothels in New York throughout the 1930s and 1940s. Producers, actors, musicians, judges, police chiefs, all manner of politicians and businessmen flocked to her after-hours house of prostitution, not just to buy the services of Polly's girls but to drink and socialize and be part of the best ongoing party in New York. Showgirls fresh from Broadway would drop in and stay to earn the price of a designer gown. It was considered sophisticated fun for men to take their dates to Polly's, who advertised her business with a discreet little business card depicting nothing but a parrot and a phone number.

"Polly's an old friend," Leonore would later say, "and I don't mean a professional friend." It would have been easy for Leonore to have been mistaken for one of "Polly's girls," since she liked to frequent the joint and no doubt wasn't above bedding down a visiting dignitary on occasion for a particularly pretty bauble. But she was too smart to make a regular habit of it. "God save us from Pearl Davis," Leonore used to say with her New York girlfriends, referring to Polly Adler by "her Sunday name."

"I knew her from Bob Benchley," Leonore admitted, referring to Robert Benchley, the alcoholic *New Yorker* humorist and creator of such inimitable film shorts as *How to Sleep* and *The Sex Life of the Polyp.* Leonore liked to visit Polly before the madam retired from the world's oldest profession and moved to California, where she attended one of the state colleges and actually earned her bachelor's degree. Leonore had always liked the atmosphere of Polly Adler's brothel, where Polly often served "a wonderful pot roast" for Lem and a few of her favorite girls and more illustrious customers. "She mothered her girls and the big important men who paid for their services," Leonore later reminisced. It was at Polly Adler's that Leonore learned Polly's unique brand of home economics. "We would speak of the guys who wanted girls, and Polly made sure those girls were put together! And let me tell you something. Many a lady in this town right now was groomed by 'Pearl Davis.' " Perhaps that was another reason Leonore felt like a fish out of water on the West Coast: She didn't know the players in Hollywood and Beverly Hills. She didn't know which snooty producer's wife had once been a working girl being taught which fork to use by shrewd, savvy Polly Adler.

The New York madam also had a genius for getting people out of scrapes. She would prove an invaluable ally to Leonore in the hours after George's body was discovered in that tiny upstairs bedroom.

And now Leonore's little black cocktail dresses were hanging in Clark Kent's closet. And even though she only knew three people in Los Angeles, she was determined to find occasions to wear those little black dresses.

• • •

Bette and Bob Shayne knew something was wrong when they suddenly stopped being invited to George's house for those "family-style get-togethers" on the weekend. "I think that's when the wild parties began," Bette recalled. "After he met Leonore, we didn't see him. Everything seemed to change when she came into his life."

This was becoming a common complaint among George's circle of friends, especially among the family of people involved with *The Adventures of Superman*. "George was such a social animal," Fred Crane would explain in later years. "He loved to have people around." From New Year's Day until June 16, 1959, George had what one observer referred to as "an open-house situation. People came and went. That was Leonore's influence." Once when Constance Shirley dropped in on the Benedict Canyon house, she saw a living room full of people, none of whom she recognized. "George may not have had any kind of relationship with any of them, either," she said. "None of George's old friends were there." Apparently Leonore was practically picking people up in the street, inviting strangers to stop by the house. Leonore instituted a policy of leaving the front porch light on to indicate that cocktail hour was in full sway and anybody could drop in, sort of like raising the flag on a yacht. Only sometimes she would forget to turn off the porch light and it would burn all night.

As much as George's friends loved him—old friends like Gene La Belle, Fred Crane, Phyllis Coates, Art Weissman—they just weren't around him very much in the winter and spring of 1959. And since *The Adventures of Superman* had wrapped with "All That Glitters" in 1957, it had been nearly two years since George had seen friends like Jack Larson, Noel Neill, and the Ellsworths. Except for running into Bob and

Bette Shayne at ZIV Studios, George hadn't seen them since the last barbecue he and Toni had presided over together, a couple of months earlier.

So there weren't any trusted friends around to help steer George back to safe harbor, just in case Leonore was leading him into dangerous waters. George's friends certainly didn't care for his new amour. Bette remembers hearing that Leonore "had a temper and was very wild," though she quickly adds that she never actually met Leonore. Jack Larson, traveling abroad in 1959, remembered how changed George had seemed at John Hamilton's funeral. "I could only think that he had made a terrible mistake. I thought it was a mess, a very unhappy situation. He certainly made a major mistake."

And then there were those friends like Phyllis Coates, who didn't want to get in the middle of Toni's despair and George's determination to forge a new life for himself.

And so George and Leonore continued their mad affair. With few prospects for work on George's horizon, the two had leisure enough to travel to their favorite spots: Miami and Palm Springs. Leonore was a golf enthusiast, and she got George hooked on the sport, so the two followed the golfing circuit for a while, often betting heavily on the games. They did a good amount of traveling together according to Constance Shirley, who had become a travel agent and was quietly handling some of the accommodations for their trips. "And George was rather consistently introducing Leonore as 'Mrs. Reeves.' I mean I registered them in hotels as 'Mr. and Mrs. Reeves.' "

While Leonore no doubt believed that traveling as Mrs. George Reeves was proof enough of George's intention to marry her, that was not necessarily the case. It was a different story in 1959, when George had to be as careful of his reputation as he was of Leonore's. The 1950s were more scandal-sensitive than the '40s, when Leonore relished all that salacious publicity. Even though *Superman* was ostensibly over, Reeves was still publicly identified as the Man of Steel, and his own innate sense of honor prevented him from flaunting his affair in the face of all those young believers out there in TV land. As media columnist Hal Humphreys had written in a typical description of George's public persona, "He's got to be a Boy Scout who knows how to fly and when to come down to earth." Well, George's flying days were not entirely over.

In the company of Leonore Lemmon, who had known Roosevelts

and Churchills and had danced with the Duke of Windsor, George began to care all over again that he had never achieved the status of a movie star. It had been so close, but had evaporated like water. In the early months of their affair, he wondered how much longer Leonore would stick around with an out-of-work star of a TV kiddie show.

There was another reason for George and Leonore's prolonged absences from the Benedict Canyon house: Toni Lanier Mannix. With the kidnapping of Sam the schnauzer, she had raised the stakes dangerously high in her war of nerves against her ex-lover.

One Sunday night that spring, George and Leonore were going to take in a movie after dinner when George saw Toni Mannix's car parked across the street from his house. George felt trapped, and a little scared. He decided to go outside and confront her. He was tired of skulking around, afraid to be seen by any of their old friends. He was going to tell Toni to leave him alone, that she was only making it worse, that she should stop driving everyone crazy. But as soon as George walked across the narrow road in front of his house, the woman in the car—it had to be Toni—took off like one of Werner von Braun's rockets. It nearly knocked him off his feet.

"I don't feel up to a movie tonight, babe," Reeves told Leonore. "Why don't you call up Gwen and have a gals' night out?" So Leonore called up Gwen Dailey, one of her few local friends. But before she left for the evening, she confronted George: "You've got to do something about that woman, or I'll take care of her myself." A few hours later, as if to apologize, Leonore called George from the theater. She and Gwen had gone to see a preview of a new James Stewart picture, a long one, called *Anatomy of a Murder.* The whole plot revolved around whether or not Lee Remick was wearing a girdle.

George was nursing a hangover and his head felt like a brick thrown through a window. He just couldn't believe that Toni was stalking him, determined to break up his love affair with Leonore, a woman who made him "feel like a boy again." When she wanted to be, Toni could be as sweet and charming as a thousand Avon ladies, but when crossed, she was a match for Eddie. If she was melodramatic before, now she was acting like Medea with an Oedipus complex.

Tonight would be an Ed Sullivan night for George, with dinner on a snack table in front of the TV. He had done the Sullivan show once. Had flown across country for it—a bumpy, horrible flight. He had been

Superman for about five years then, and people liked hearing him sing. But tonight even the chimps couldn't make him laugh like they used to. They just seemed like a bunch of monkeys pushing over the furniture. He even thought he saw one of them wearing a cape with fake jewels sewn into it. Its trainer had gotten the animal to fly over three chairs. Sometimes the world is a joke and you're the punch line. And no one, absolutely no one, is laughing.

• • •

Toni's efforts to win George back had failed. Her attempts to press their mutual friends into service to "talk sense into the boy" had also failed. By the spring of 1959 she had become desperate and insanely jealous of Leonore. "She wanted to drive George and Leonore crazy and to deprive them of whatever peace they could have," according to Phyllis Coates. And that's where Santiago comes in.

It seemed that whenever George picked up the phone, it went dead. It started just after the New Year, after Leonore had come to Los Angeles, having told Suzy Knickerbocker that Reeves had proposed to her. The phone would ring, and George would always leap to answer it in case it was Art Weissman with news of a job prospect. But instead there was no one on the other end: just an eerie quiet, and then a hangup. Sometimes the calls would start in the middle of the night, rousing George and Leonore from their sleep. Then it would come again at breakfast, that insistent ringing, and one of them would answer the phone and there would be nothing . . . no response on the other end of the line. It was beginning to unnerve them. George first asked certain people, such as Weissman, if he had been calling, but none of his friends admitted to being the phantom caller. Now the calls were coming day and night, twenty to thirty times every twenty-four hours. "Call and hang up. Call and hang up," Leonore would later explain. George changed his phone number three times, but within a day of each change, the calls started up again. "You didn't have to be a rocket scientist to figure out who was making those calls," Phyllis Coates observed. Through Eddie's connections, it would have been easy for Toni to get hold of the new number each time.

Bette Shayne, who knew immediately who was behind those phone calls, pitied poor Toni. "She was devastated. She was an obsessed woman who wanted to hear her lover's voice. She just wanted to hear his voice because she knew he'd never talk to her."

Later on, Jack Larson would come straight out and ask Toni Mannix if she had been making all those harassing phone calls to George. "She admitted to me that she was behind them, but she was clever," Larson recalled. "She didn't really make them herself. She got someone else to make them for her. She hired her groundskeeper, Santiago, to make the phone calls for her." Though she had kidnapped George's beloved schnauzer, Larson believed that Toni "was incapable of doing anything against George" himself.

So George started taking the phone off the hook and burying it in a drawer or under a pillow. Suspecting Toni all along, George felt he had no choice but to go to the police and file a complaint against her.

So George went to see Noel R. Slipsager, who was the deputy city attorney, toward the end of March of 1959. He told the D.A.'s office about his hunch that Toni Mannix was making 'round-the-clock phone calls that were driving him and his fiancée to distraction. Slipsager told George that he couldn't do much without proof positive, but on the basis of George's suspicions and "as a favor to Superman," his office would write to Mrs. Mannix on George's behalf.

"Kindly be advised," Slipsager wrote on official stationery, "that Mr. George Reeves . . . has complained to this office about telephone calls by you to his place of residence. In the event you pursue a course of conduct which harasses, annoys, and disturbs him, this office must consider a criminal complaint based on such action. Your cooperation in this matter would be most appreciated."

Within a week of receiving the district attorney's letter, a furious Toni Mannix filed her own complaint, saying that someone was phoning *her* up "at all hours of the night and day." And because Toni had her groundskeeper Santiago make the calls from his own abode, Slipsager's office informed George that the phone calls were definitely *not* coming from the Mannix estate.

If Toni was actually being harassed herself by constant phone calls, the culprit was probably Leonore, who loved a good brawl. But this was not going to be just a catfight in a nightclub lobby; this was the beginning of a deadly struggle. It was also the first time the whole mess had come to the attention of the authorities, and that troubled George, "the People's Friend," who was still Superman to tens of millions of fans, and who—if word ever got out—surely expected another kind of life from their hero.

Despite the politely threatening letter, the phone calls did not stop.

Slipsager told George one afternoon at the house that the calls were probably coming from someone in the Mannixes' employ. George figured it had to be Santiago, a sweet man, really, who worshiped Toni and would do anything for her. Leonore would later describe him as "a combination gardener and gofer." One day Leonore picked up the phone and said, "Okay, Santiago, you've got to stop this. How much, Santiago? How much is she paying you?" But if she was about to make a counteroffer, her plan failed, because there was no one on the line. "She was a crazy lady," Leonore would later say. "She wanted me dead."

• • •

George was beginning to be frightened. When he and Leonore were alone together, he would jump whenever the phone rang. Now only Leonore would answer it, sometimes yelling at Santiago, or calling Toni unspeakable names, or sometimes trying to sweet-talk Santiago into giving up this nonsense. But there was never any response: just the slight sound of breathing and then the phone being gently replaced. Soon George was unable to sleep. He became morose and irritable. A friend of Bette Shayne's who had been hired to do some electrical work in George's home remembered seeing him "loafing around the house, spending a lot of time stretched out on the couch, just looking at the ceiling." He seemed anxious and depressed. He was beginning to feel more like Job than Superman.

On the morning of April 9, 1959, George was driving his three-year-old Jaguar when he suddenly lost control of the car and hit a cement abutment on Benedict Canyon near Easton Drive, just a few minutes from his house. George smacked his head on the windshield, suffering a mild concussion and opening up a nasty gash on his forehead. He was able to extricate himself from the car on his own, but when several policemen arrived on the scene, George collapsed.

He was taken to Cedars of Lebanon Hospital, where his doctor kept him overnight for observation. They finally sent him home with twenty-seven stitches in his head and a pocketful of painkillers for the headaches that began as soon as he left the hospital.

When the story of Reeves's crack-up reached the newspapers and weekly magazines, the tone was typically snide. "They never forgive you a success," Larson had warned. Even in Los Angeles, George's hometown, where similar accidents on that stretch of the canyon had resulted in serious injury and death, the incident was treated in the press as a kind of joke. Again George had to read about himself as Superman and how he just didn't measure up, out of costume, when compared to his television alter ego. "The actor who delights viewers by soaring through space with the greatest of ease couldn't negotiate a turn in his sports car early yesterday, and wound up with a five-inch gash on his forehead. What's more, when police were questioning him . . . Superman fainted," reported the *Los Angeles Times*. *Newsweek,* which carried a story of the event eleven days later, was even more cruel: "Tooling down a terrestrial canyon near Hollywood . . . TV actor George Reeves, beloved to millions of kiddies as indestructible Superman . . . hit an oil slick and piled into a stone wall. . . . Climbing out of his crashed earth vehicle, Superman fainted."

When would it ever stop? George's head was killing him. His headaches were so severe that he was forced to sleep on the cold bathroom floor with a towel wrapped around his head to alleviate the pain. The accident also injured Reeves's wrist, although that pain was minor compared to his headaches. He could have been killed in Benedict Canyon, and they were all having a good laugh at his expense, comparing him to the Man of Steel.

While George was in the hospital, a mechanic checking his car made a shocking discovery. He would later tell the police officers—the ones who had shown up at the scene of the accident—that it was "a miracle George hadn't been killed and taken a few other people with him. Didn't George know that there wasn't enough brake fluid in the Jag to fill a cavity?"

9

ALONE IN THE WORLD IN BENEDICT CANYON

The discovery that the Jaguar's brake fluid had drained away made George wonder about the previous accident he'd had in Sherman Oaks in the custom-made Alvis. At the time he hadn't given it much thought. He had been so proud of that car, ever since he and Toni drove it out of Cavalier Motors right into Beverly Hills traffic, big smiles on their faces. A lumber truck had tailgated him one afternoon when he was driving alone down Ventura Boulevard and finally plowed right into the car's back fender. George had decided to sue the lumber company, though he'd felt badly for the young driver of the truck. Now he wondered if the two accidents were related, or was he just becoming paranoid? Is this what Toni had wanted all along, that he would lose Leonore and his sanity at the same time?

He went back to the deputy city attorney's office, but, again, Slipsager told Reeves that there wasn't much he could do. A policemen who happened to be in Slipsager's office at the time suggested that George start carrying a baseball bat in his car for protection. His secretary later said that the guys working for Slipsager were amused by the fact that "Superman was going to the police to complain that his life was in danger, and blaming it all on some woman . . . [it seemed] funny to them."

None of these troubles improved Leonore's volatile disposition, either. Gene La Belle vividly remembers Leonore's temper, and George's indulgence of her moods.

"I was working out with George one day," La Belle recalled. George used to pay his young friend and trainer $200 a session to come over to the house and help him get into shape. "We didn't like to be bothered when we worked out, but Leonore barged in and said to George, 'I want to talk to you.'"

"I'll be there in twenty minutes," George said.

"Now!"

"George had just bought Leonore a $1,500 antique lamp. Right in front of us, she picked it up and crashed it down into a thousand pieces. George didn't blink an eye. He gave a look that said, 'Women! You can't argue with 'em!' George used to tell me he'd give Leonore $100 bills to light her cigarettes with if she wanted it."

Though La Belle was a witness to George's devotion to Leonore, he was one of the circle of friends who never believed George truly planned to marry her. Jack Larson and Bette Shayne were of the same opinion. Both recalled that whenever the subject of marriage came up, George would say "You didn't hear that from me!" George's old friends chalked it up to a case of George being in the throes of "a midlife crisis."

Art Weissman in particular was convinced that George never intended to marry Leonore. But then, Weissman hated that ex–New York society dame, feeling that Leonore had come between him and George. He and George had been in close contact nearly every day until Leonore came on the scene; George had even made him the executor of his will. But as long as Leonore was living in the Benedict Canyon house, Weissman stayed away. "She and I obviously didn't approve of each other," Weissman later told Chuck Harter, a writer and film archivist who has written about Reeves and *The Adventures of Superman.* "He made a personal choice by inviting her as a house guest." Weissman would spread the rumor that marriage to Leonore had not been George's idea and that George was planning on calling the whole thing off.

Jim Beaver shared that opinion. "It strikes a lot of men in a combined front. It's not just one thing, it's not just 'I'll dump my wife and marry a younger girl.' I think George found himself forty-five years old and having to struggle the way he'd never had to struggle quite before."

Perhaps as a way to deal with his midlife crisis, at the age of forty-five Reeves agreed to undertake a series of publicity exhibition matches with the light heavyweight champion Archie Moore.

It wasn't as far-fetched as it sounded. After all, hadn't George once been a contender for the Golden Gloves during his college boxing days? That is, before Helen had him roughed up, to prevent him from permanently roughing up his face in the ring and ruining his chance for

Sam Kashner & Nancy Schoenberger

movie stardom. At forty-five and clearly not in the best shape of his life, George wasn't serious about becoming a professional boxer all over again. This was a publicity exhibition, a way of doing something he loved and reminding the world that he was still out there. But a number of his friends saw it as a desperate act.

Jack Larson was still in Europe when he heard that George was trying to get a job wrestling. "That sounded real bad to me," he recalled. For weeks, Leonore and her Los Angeles friend Gwen Dailey and Benedict Canyon neighbor Alfred "Rip" Van Ronkel watched as George increased his workouts on the backyard patio.

Rip Van Ronkel was a screenwriter who had had success in the 1930s adapting *Abie's Irish Rose* for radio. He was married to a very young, very pretty wife, Carol Van Ronkel. They were an interesting couple. Carol—nearly thirty years younger than her husband—reminded people of Carol Lynley, the dewy ingenue who would portray Jean Harlow in the movies.

Rip Van Ronkel had known Leonore in New York, though they weren't close friends. However, she discovered that she and Rip spoke the same language: Both sniffed distastefully at all the boobs in Southern California. But if Rip was New York personified, with his expensive Brooks Brothers' smoking jackets and cigarette holders, his morocco-bound volumes and Johnson's dictionary under glass in the living room, Carol seemed to have wandered down out of the Hollywood hills like a beautiful feral child. Theirs was a Professor Higgins–Eliza Doolittle romance. Carol felt safe with the dignified radio writer, like a girl who's fallen in love with her English professor.

Rip Van Ronkel was one of those who saw George's willingness to go on the road giving boxing demonstrations as the act of a desperate man. "It was a lousy thing, a carnival act, and it ruined his dignity," he said. Nonetheless, he and his wife helped George train, following George in their car as he ran on an unpaved stretch of road at the top of the canyon. The whole thing had been cooked up by Art Weissman to raise George's spirits, get him back into shape, and bring him a little publicity in his post-Superman slump.

Leonore herself had misgivings. She, too, thought it was beneath George's dignity to go on the road in his boxing shorts and have at it with Archie Moore. But when George told her he wanted to go ahead with it, she went along with his plans. The first exhibition match was scheduled for Wednesday night, June 17, in San Diego.

In May of 1959, National Comics decided to exercise its option on Reeves, Larson, Neill, and Shayne, bringing them back to ZIV Studios to shoot twenty-six more episodes of *The Adventures of Superman.* It was the last thing George had wanted to do: He thought he was finally finished with that role. He still hoped to find more work directing and even producing properties. "I'm through with all that acting bull," he had told Phyllis Coates. But the fact was he needed the money. He agreed to go back to filming twenty-six more episodes of crashing through Si Simonson's walls, twenty-six more shows lying on his stomach as they "matted" him flying over the mythical city of Metropolis, twenty-six of takeoffs and landings—grabbing a metal bar and swinging into the shot, or taking a tumble over the cameras from a springboard and landing on a mattress.

"People always say, 'Well, he was going to film twenty-six more Superman shows,'" Larson would later tell a Los Angeles journalist. "[But] it had no meaning to him. It didn't have much meaning to me. We weren't getting that much money." Reeves would give an interview to UPI reporter Henry Gris, confirming that he'd "just signed to appear in a seventh season of 'Superman'" and proclaiming his love for Leonore. It is in fact the first time he publicly states his intention of marrying her, despite the impression Larson and La Belle had that matrimony had been entirely Leonore's idea. He also confided that he was returning to the show only because Whit Ellsworth—whom George called "Dad"—promised him he would be permitted to direct several of the new episodes. With this renewed shot at directing, and a series of exhibition matches set up with the great Archie Moore, at last things seemed to be going his way.

"Scripts were ordered and the costumes were sent out to the cleaners," Noel Neill later told writer Gary Grossman, as cast and crew geared up for the new season. Noel saw George on the ZIV lot, "rarin' to go," passing the hours by playing cards. "He was in good spirits. We saw no sign of discontent on him at all." Bette had thought George was in great spirits when she had run into him a week earlier at ZIV. "He was very happy. He was very 'up' because everything was going very well for him. He said, 'Isn't it great that we're signing new contracts?' The Shaynes were excited, too, because Robert Shayne's new agreement with the show was going to give him more money and expand his role.

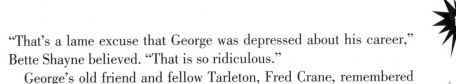

"That's a lame excuse that George was depressed about his career," Bette Shayne believed. "That is so ridiculous."

George's old friend and fellow Tarleton, Fred Crane, remembered running into George at a stoplight shortly after he'd signed his contract to do the new episodes of *Superman.*

"He was ebullient when I ran into him," Crane recalled. "He told me he was getting behind the camera instead of in front of it. . . . A director has to be good with people, and George fit that mold. This man had a future. When we met that day, George was enthusiastic and I was happy for him."

George had told his old friend, "You don't seem to have gained a pound over the years. I wish to Christ I had your physique!" Crane thought that Reeves had gotten "a little pudgy" and seemed like he might be on pills, either to lose weight or as a result of the Benedict Canyon Drive accident, but that he seemed happy. What he didn't know at the time was that within a week, George Reeves would be dead.

• • •

George's ebullience took a strange form. He had always been something of a prankster, and late one night, around 3:00 A.M., George called up Gene La Belle, waking him from a deep sleep. "Gene, help me!" he cried, and then the phone went dead.

La Belle, who had lost his own father at an early age and who worshiped George as a kind of father substitute, was thoroughly alarmed. He got up, got dressed, and drove the narrow road through the canyon, parking just up the street from George's. There were no cars on the stretch of road in front of 1579 Benedict Canyon at this hour of the night. It had been an especially hot summer so far, but at 3:00 A.M., the night air was cold. La Belle walked over to George's house, and just as he was about to ring the bell, he got the shock of his life.

"Suddenly two naked women jumped me!" La Belle remembered. Apparently, a drunken Leonore Lemmon and an equally inebriated girlfriend—probably Gwen Dailey—decided to play a prank on George's wrestling buddy, with George's help. They must have crouched in the bushes in the front of the house in order to waylay poor innocent Gene. George opened the door and burst out laughing. "He thought it was the funniest thing in the world!" La Belle remembers, but it was an eerie, unsettling prank, because the next time there was a late-night phone call, George would be the one who was naked, and his need for help would be genuine, not a prank.

• • •

If George had become unhinged by Santiago's incessant phone calls, convinced that his recent accident was an attempt on his life, he tried not to show it. He continued to spend lavishly on entertainment for himself and Leonore. His spirits had definitely improved since signing on for more *Superman* episodes, with Ellsworth's promise to let him direct. On Saturday, June 13, 1959, George and Leonore attended a party given by James and Wendy Miller. It was there that he met Dr. Paul Hanson, a general surgeon who headed the emergency room of St. Luke's Hospital in Pasadena. Dr. Hanson has never forgotten that evening, and he told writer Jan Henderson what transpired.

After dinner, Dr. Hanson's son and the handful of kids who were at the party talked Reeves and Hanson into putting on a westling match in the living room. Hanson, who was over six feet tall and weighed more than 200 pounds, was probably in better shape than George was at the time. "I could have lifted George over my head," he would recall many years later. The two men threw each other around the living room for a while, to the squealing delight of the kids gathered around. The circumstances were so innocuous—pushing the living-room furniture off to the side so these two, big, middle-aged men could roll around on the plush carpet while the kids in their short pants and clip-on ties rooted and yelled from the couch. Like a domesticated version of that scene from *Women in Love*—the movie—in which Alan Bates and Oliver Reed wrestle in the nude before a roaring fireplace: the homoerotic adventures of Superman in the suburbs! "I sustained no bruises," Hanson has said about that evening, "and I'm sure George had none, as well."

• • •

A few days before George's scheduled exhibition match with Archie Moore, Robert Condon had arrived in Los Angeles to accompany George to the match in connection with a book he was writing on the light heavyweight boxer. Bobby Condon, as he was known, was a New Yorker, the brother of novelist Richard Condon, who had scored a huge success with his Cold War novel *The Manchurian Candidate*. The book he was researching was going to be Archie Moore's autobiography, "as told to" Robert Condon. Reeves, generous as always, offered to put Bobby Condon up at his house, where he could stay in the little guest bedroom upstairs from the living room, a few feet away from George and Leonore's bedroom at the top of the stairs. Condon had told George that he might also write an article on George's new career, perhaps for *Esquire,* "the men's magazine" as it was touted at the time. Though there was no indication that Bobby Condon knew Leonore Lemmon, there was a curious connection between the two New Yorkers: Condon had ghost-written Polly Adler's autobiography, *A House is Not a Home,* published in 1953 by Rinehart and Company. And Polly and Leonore were good friends.

By now Leonore had gotten fairly chummy with Carol Van Ronkel, Rip's young wife. The Van Ronkels lived about a mile and a half away, so it was a convenient friendship. Leonore liked having them around. George and Rip would trade stories about the old days in New York during the war, when George was with the army's theatrical unit. Rip was crazy about his young wife. He loved watching her dance—hell, he loved watching her walk through a supermarket. After a few drinks, Carol would put a record on the hi-fi—maybe the Fleetwoods singing "Come Softly to Me"—and invite her scholarly looking husband to dance with her. But there must have been trouble in paradise, because their marriage would bust up the following year, in 1960, and that bust-up would no doubt have had a hand in Van Ronkel's death a few years later, on March 29, 1963.

But, according to Leonore Lemmon, during one of those hot June nights in 1959 when it seemed the sun would never go down, Carol suddenly developed a more than neighborly interest in Bobby Condon. Leonore didn't seem to be offended on Rip's behalf. She claimed she found them smooching in the dark little den just off the living room, with its own private entrance from the backyard. Never one to stand in the way of love or lust, she let it be known that if she and George happened to go out to dinner one night, leaving Bobby all alone in the house, no one would mind if Carol just happened to stop by to keep their house guest happy.

Leonore Lemon would later tell gossip columnist Earl Wilson that she and George planned to get married that Friday, June 19, two days after his exhibition match with the light heavyweight champion. "He said, 'I'm going to go two rounds with Archie Moore . . . so how about Friday?' I said, 'Friday is a good day. Anybody who goes two rounds with Archie Moore is my guy, so I'm your girl.' " To celebrate their hasty engagement, that weekend George filled up his Oldsmobile convertible—the car he had bought to replace the demolished Jaguar—with flowers and bottles of champagne and, in keeping with his "George, the People's Friend" image, hot dogs from Pink's, a popular hot-dog stand on North La Brea Avenue, not far from the old Chaplin studios. Leonore loved that. On Monday morning, George would purchase $4,000 worth of traveler's checks to take with them on their trip to Spain—money he had probably accepted from Helen Bessolo. George had told Gwen Daily that they were planning on staying in an old villa in Barcelona.

But several newspaper accounts later mentioned that Gwen Dailey, "the girl who married Irish tap dancers," gave Leonore some cash as well, because she planned to accompany the couple on their trip. That bit of information calls into question whether this trip was a honeymoon or just another pleasure jaunt for the couple. It also may have been work-related. In a retrospective article published years later in the *New York Post,* a journalist wrote that Reeves was "offered a featured part before the cameras in a film to be made in Spain," though the name of the film and its producers have never come to light. In any case, plans were made to leave for Spain at the end of the week.

Leonore dragged George to Scandia's on Sunday night for a late supper. She wanted to discuss the party she had planned for the following night, ostensibly to celebrate their engagement. Leonore hadn't heard from a number of the people she'd invited, so she tried tracking some of them down by phone between courses. One of the people she reached was her friend from New York who had been living for many years now in Bel-Air: Henny Backus. Leonore had tracked Henny down at Chasen's, where she was dining with her husband Jim Backus, Keenan Wynn and his wife, and Everett Sloane and his wife.

"Come on over to Scandia's," Leonore pleaded over the phone. "I want you to meet my fiancé."

Henny remembered the encounter: "Well, we went over to Scandia and met this big, handsome, charming guy. We didn't know who he was—we didn't really watch television, and that was a kid's show anyway. . . . But Leonore said to come over to the house afterward, so we did."

When Henny and Jim Backus went into the living room at 1579 Benedict Canyon, the first thing they heard was "a big, loud voice coming over what must have been the first answering machine in Los Angeles. The first I'd ever heard." George must have decided to put in the answering machine as a way of avoiding Santiago's harassing phone calls. He may have first gotten the idea after seeing Mike Hammer listening to his messages in the 1955 film *Kiss Me Deadly*. It was a big, clumsy, reel-to-reel tape recorder the size of a small house, hooked up to the telephone, but it worked.

"It was Toni Mannix, saying something like 'How dare you not be home! You're living in my house!' " Henny recalled. "George and Leonore just laughed. George, I think it was, picked up a guitar, and I remember I excused myself to go to the powder room. George said I'd have to go up through his bedroom to use the bathroom upstairs. As I did so, I noticed a gun lying on the dresser of his bedroom. I came back downstairs in a hurry and said quietly to Jim, 'We're leaving . . .' "

Leonore called Henny Backus the next morning, Monday, June 15, to remind her of the invitation to her little party planned for that night. But that same day, someone mentioned to Henny that she ought to get her long hair cut, so Henny called up her hairdresser and asked him to come by the house.

"All we could find that day were garden shears!" Henny recalls. "But those studio stylists—like Sydney Guilaroff—could do wonders, with garden shears or whatever! Anyway, Jim had to fly to New York that day, so I decided not to go to Leonore's party but to have dinner with Keenan Wynn and Everett Sloane and their wives again. The next day Jim called from New York and said, 'I'm so glad you didn't go to that party!' "

That same Monday, June 15, George was met by a new disappointment when he returned from running errands in preparation for their trip to Spain. He received a letter notifying him that one of the exhibition matches he'd set up—the one scheduled for July 3 in Pittsburgh—was canceled due to poor ticket sales. The response from *Superman* fans had been less than enthusiastic. Weissman showed up later at the house—an indication of how worried he was, since he avoided crossing paths with Leonore—to tell George that other midwestern cities had backed out as well, and the entire tour would have to be canceled. Ticket sales had been "so poor that local promoters were running scared."

"It was devastating," Leonore would later explain to the *Journal American*. "George thought, 'Here I am doing something I shouldn't be doing in the first place, and they don't want me.' " It was a crushing blow.

Rip Van Ronkel called up Monday morning to accept an invitation from Leonore to attend a little party planned for later that evening at the house. George uncharacteristically poured his heart out to Van Ronkel, telling him how disappointed he was to see the bookings for his wrestling exhibition dry up. Van Ronkel commiserated with him although he hadn't liked the idea to begin with.

George did another uncharacteristic thing in his preparations for the trip to Spain. He arranged to have the locks changed on his house. He must have been thinking of Toni, who still had her keys. After that accident in April, and the phone calls that kept coming, George didn't want Toni marching into the house in his absence. Besides Santiago's hang-up calls, Toni was still haranguing him over the phone—the answering machine was full of her invective. No, he would arrange to change all those locks so Toni—who God knows felt she had every right to that house—wouldn't waltz in there and do some real damage. What was the saying? "Hell hath no fury . . ."

Weissman would later admit that it was his idea to get George to change the locks—he saw those road accidents as attempts on George's life, and he was worried for his friend.

When the locksmith arrived on Monday afternoon, June 15, Leonore was busy checking the list of people she had impulsively invited to the house that night. She started calling up those who hadn't responded to her invitation.

But in the middle of her phone calling, the locksmith announced that he didn't have the right equipment to finish the job. The double doors at the back of the house leading to the patio needed a special lock. With half the job done, he said he would come back on Wednesday, and he left the original locks in place. Leonore waved him off and continued with her conversation, telling Gwen Dailey how happy George was now, "because he finally knew what he was doing and where he was going."

• • •

As it turned out, there wasn't much of a party going on at 1579 Benedict Canyon after all. Bobby Condon was there, and the Van Ronkels, and probably Gwen Dailey, but Leonore's last-minute plans for a get-together were so unproductive that she and George decided to go out

Sam Kashner & Nancy Schoenberger

to dinner, leaving Bobby Condon alone with the Van Ronkels, who left before George and Leonore returned that evening. According to Leonore's later testimony, they had all been drinking quite heavily, but then that was business as usual at the Benedict Canyon house. Leonore and George dined at Scandia's and returned shortly before midnight. This was two nights before George's scheduled match with Archie Moore, so maybe that's why George went to bed early, taking his lady love with him, but for some reason, that night his lady love could not sleep.

Leonore got up out of bed and went downstairs, being careful not to disturb Bobby Condon.

Leonore noticed that the outside light was off, and she turned it back on. "This was not the way that Reeves did things, and I turned the lights on," she would later say. Leonore fixed herself a drink and sat in the living room. It was shortly after midnight, and it was dark in the canyon, except for the occasional car that came speeding down the stretch of road in front of the house, its headlights raking the living room walls. That's when the doorbell rang.

This is what Leonore would tell the police and the newspapers. But this was only one version of events—her version. When Leonore opened the door, there were two figures standing there: Carol Van Ronkel and William "Bill" Bliss, a Benedict Canyon resident, though not a close friend of George's and someone Leonore hardly knew. The two had come for a party—Leonore had turned the front porch light on, which usually meant that the cocktail shaker was still in business.

Leonore let them in and started fixing drinks when George came downstairs in his bathrobe, cranky and sleepy and probably anxious about the impending boxing exhibition. Maybe he was tired of Leonore's nonstop, drop-in friends, though Leonore later claimed not to know Bliss at all. So George complained about their being there, and Bliss apologized, and then George apologized, and they all had a drink. Bobby Condon came downstairs and joined the party. Around 1:20 A.M., George went back upstairs to his room, leaving Leonore, Bliss, Bobby and Carol downstairs.

According to the police report, Leonore said at that point, "He's going up there to shoot himself!" They must have felt she was joking because nobody made a move to stop him—not Bobby, not Carol, not Bill Bliss. Maybe they were too drunk to care, or to move. Bliss and Leonore would also tell the police that they heard a drawer slide open, and

Leonore again said, "He is getting the gun out now, and he is going to shoot himself." Again, nobody moved. The silence was eerie. That is, until they heard a shot, and Leonore turned to Bliss—whom she barely knew—and asked him to go upstairs and see what happened.

That's when Bliss discovered the body, lying unclothed on the bed and covered in blood, with the .30-caliber Luger resting on the floor between his feet. Bliss called the Los Angeles Police Department, and two LAPD policemen, Officers Johnson and Korby, arrived around 2:00 A.M. Bliss let them in and showed them to the upstairs bedroom.

The two policemen made a hasty investigation of George's room, where they located the lethal bullet, which had passed through George's temple and lodged in the bedroom ceiling. They moved George's body and found the shell casing lying underneath him. That meant the casing was ejected from the chamber and landed on the bed before George's body fell, an unusual trajectory at best but not impossible, though George's biographer would later argue that it was feasible only if George had held the gun upside down against his skull.

Officer Korby picked up the gun while Johnson took statements from everyone present. Bliss repeated what Leonore had said about George going upstairs to shoot himself. Apparently that story rang true, for the two officers did not call in a crime squad to dust for fingerprints or take photographs of the body and scene of death. They dutifully wrote down Bliss's and Leonore's statements that George had been depressed about money and about his career. Actors and suicide? Creative types are unstable. Money problems? Why not? It happens all the time.

They arranged for the mortuary of Gates, Kingsley, and Gates to come by and pick up the body—in those days the coroner's office didn't have the funding to retrieve corpses even in suspicious cases, so mortuaries sent over hearses to pick up the bodies. Meanwhile, someone from the coroner's office showed up at George's house, oversaw the removal of the body, and advised everyone to leave the premises.

Bill Bliss returned to his house on Easton Drive, not far from Benedict Canyon. Carol Van Ronkel took Leonore home with her, about a mile and a half away. It's not known where Bobby Condon ended up. When the house was emptied, the coroner's representative affixed a seal to the front door.

Once George's corpse arrived at the mortuary, a sample of blood was routinely taken and forwarded to the coroner's office. Deputy Medical Examiner Alexander Griswold was sent over to Gates, Kingsley, and

Gates to make a cursory examination of the body. Griswold satisfied himself that there were no visible stab wounds or other signs of violence besides the fatal gunshot wound to the head. No internal examination was performed, as it had already been determined a "nonsuspicious death" by the investigating officers. After the brief physical examination, the body was washed and the entrance and exit wounds in George's temple were sewn shut with twine. The mortician then went about arteriorally embalming the corpse (that is, removing the blood but leaving the internal organs intact). Griswold did take photographs of the entrance and exit wounds and filed them away. By 3:30 A.M. Tuesday morning, June 16, the Los Angeles County Coroner had its case report #4546 on George Reeves: "poss. suicide."

"Then as now," Reeves's biographer Jim Beaver has commented, "it's absolutely normal for there not to be a full internal examination of the body unless there is some reason to suspect that it wasn't suicide." However, from the moment the police were called in, there were at least two occasions in which Reeves's body was treated inappropriately. In California in 1959, in a case of wrongful death, it was highly unusual to embalm the body without permission of the next of kin. And, before an official verdict of suicide was issued by the coroner's office, it was inappropriate to wash the body and sew up the head wound. The treatment of George's body was particularly unusual in that the death of a well-known personage is always treated with special attention as to preserving evidence, because too many people are in a position to ask questions in the case of a famous corpse.

Why didn't Officers Johnson and Korby check to see if there were any powder burns on George Reeves's right hand, the hand that presumably fired the gun? Because the body was washed, that bit of forensic evidence was lost forever. And why didn't Johnson and Korby find it suspicious that—in a house full of people—George's body was found nude? Most suicides do not undress before killing themselves. The alcohol content in George's blood was determined to be .27—three times the legal limit—and all those interrogated in the living room were clearly inebriated as well. Yet the police found no reason to question their tale of depression and suicide. After that night, Bill Bliss, Carol Van Ronkel, and Bobby Condon would fade from the scene. The police would never call them in to question their stories.

Other mysteries remain: Why did Carol Van Ronkel return to the house shortly after midnight with Bill Bliss? And who, exactly, was Bill

Bliss? None of George's close friends knew anything about him, nor did his closest neighbors have any idea what he did for a living. Why had he stopped by on a dark night and rung the doorbell? Years later, in a rare interview given over the phone to a fledgling journalist from Phoenix, Arizona, named Lee Saylor, Leonore would say "I had no idea who Bill Bliss was and what he was doing there."

She would also say about that night, "People lied. When the police got there, I looked at them. I remember one thing: a body going by me under a white sheet. That's all I knew . . . I was alone in the world in Benedict Canyon."

George Reeves as Clark Kent. A reader of Shakespeare and Shaw, Reeves was closer in temperament to the "mild-mannered reporter" than to the Man of Steel.
(Courtesy of Jim Nolt)

For Reeves, playing Superman was "the bottom of the barrel," though he brought immense likability to the role.
(Courtesy of Jim Nolt)

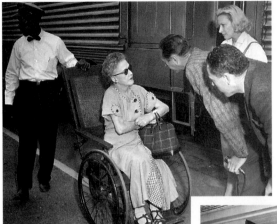

Helen Bessolo, Reeves's mother, inexplicably arrives in a wheelchair in Pasadena to force an investigation into her son's death.
(The Hearst Collection, Department of Special Collections, University of Southern Caifornia)

Sheriff's deputies photograph the broken coroner's seal on George Reeves's Benedict Canyon house.
(The Hearst Collection, USC)

The great Jerry Giesler, Hollywood's famed defense attorney, escorts Helen Bessolo from her son's death house.
(The Hearst Collection, USC)

Radio and screenwriter Alfred "Rip" Van Ronkel and his young wife, Carol, friends of Leonore Lemmon. Carol was present the night of Reeves's death.
(The Hearst Collection, USC)

Toni Mannix, Eddie Mannix's formidable second wife and George Reeves's longtime lover. The crucifix and wedding ring were prominently diplayed in the press by MGM publicist Howard Strickling during the scandal following Reeves's death. *(The Hearst Collection, USC)*

Long-suffering Bernice, the first Mrs. Mannix. Soon after filing for an expensive divorce from Eddie Mannix, Bernice met with a mysterious fatal accident in the Nevada desert. *(Bettmann Archive)*

MGM vice president Eddie Mannix, seated next to Norma Shearer at a Hollywood banquet. A tough guy from the New Jersey Palisades, Mannix used blackmail to hush up a scandal at MGM. *(Bettmann Archive)*

Mobster Mickey Cohen, looking bored, as he waits to explain his plush income to the U.S. Senate's investigation into organized crime. Eddie Mannix helped put Cohen back on his feet when the gangster was released from prison. *(Bettmann Archive)*

Leonore Lemmon photographed as the jilted bride after the bust-up of her marriage to a Vanderbilt, Jacob "Jakie" Webb. Lemmon's whirlwind romance with Reeves ended his ten-year love affair with Toni Mannix.
(Bettmann Archive)

Leonore Lemmon performing in New York City nightclub. She sang "I Was a Deb Caught in a Web," a novelty number capitalizing on her much-publicized break-up with Jakie Webb.
(Bettmann Archive)

Leonore Lemmon with Jakie Webb the day after their elopement. The honeymoon was cut short when Webb was arrested for passing bad checks.
(Bettmann Archive)

"She makes me feel like a boy again," Reeves said of his infatuation with Leonore Lemmon, shown here in a Miami nightclub six months before Reeves's death. *(Bettmann Archive)*

Leonore Lemmon caught leaving the house after Reeves's fatal gunshot wound to the head. Newspapers had a field day with Lemmon's "prediction" that George was going to shoot himself. *(Bettmann Archive)*

George Reeves with Joan Crawford and Sonja Henie at the Hollywood premiere of *The Egyptian*. By 1954, Reeves's hopes of becoming a movie star were derailed by the phenomenal success of *The Adventures of Superman*, which fatally typecast him as the Man of Steel.
(Bettmann Archive)

Phyllis Coates as the TV series's first Lois Lane. (Noel Neill, who originated the role in the Columbia Pictures movie serials, replaced Coates in the show's second year.) Coates was the first person Toni Mannix called in the hours following Reeves's death.
(Courtesy of Jim Nolt)

"**S**uperman" pictured with Jack Larson, aka Jimmy Olson. George and Toni called Larson "Junior" on the set. It was Larson who accompanied Toni Mannix to Reeves's house after the fatal shooting.
(Courtesy of Jim Nolt)

"Toni paid for everything we did those first shows. She owned George's house, his car, everything," Phyllis Coates said about Toni Mannix, shown here in this snapshot with George Reeves and two unidentified friends.
(Courtesy of Jan Alan Henderson)

Superman Agonistes: George was a physical culture enthusiast who enjoyed working out in his backyard. But he was forty-three in the last year of the series and was reduced to wearing a corset under his woolen costume.
(Courtesy of Jan Alan Henderson)

George with his beloved one-eyed schnauzer, Sam. Furious over being jilted, Toni Mannix kidnapped Sam from a Hollywood street, and the dog was never heard from again.
(Courtesy of Jan Alan Henderson)

A sad, prematurely gray George Reeves in this photo taken a month before his death. Was he mourning the end of his ten-year affair with Toni Mannix, or the derailment of his acting career?
(Courtesy of Jim Hambrick/Superman Museum)

"George was very ebullient when I ran into him on the street the week before his death," a friend recalled. "He told me he was getting behind the camera instead of in front of it . . . he would have made a great director."
(Courtesy of Jan Alan Henderson)

The Adventures of Superman has never been off the air since it stopped production in 1957. A triumphant Superman flies over Metropolis in a matt shot of Hollywood, circa 1951.
(Courtesy of Jim Nolt)

10

. . . .

BEAUTY SECRETS OF THE DEAD

Phyllis Coates, whom friends affectionately called "Gypsy," was used to getting phone calls from Toni Mannix in the middle of the night, ever since George had ended their affair. But there was something different about this early morning phone call. First of all, it was *very* early, even for Toni: She called around 4:30 A.M. the morning of June 16. "She woke me up," Phyllis remembered. "At first I didn't understand what she was talking about. She seemed hysterical. She was hyperventilating and ranting. She said, 'The boy is dead. George is dead. He's been murdered.' She wanted me to go over to the house with her. I absolutely would not go."

Years later, Gypsy would wonder how it was that Toni Mannix knew about George's death before the rest of the world, and why—when the police were calling it a suicide—she was convinced that it was murder.

• • •

After the coroner's men permitted the body to be removed and then placed a seal across the door to prevent anyone from entering, they cordoned off the house with yellow police tape, wrapping it around some bushes that grew up in front of the house.

Right away there were aspects of the news accounts of George's death that just didn't ring true. First and foremost, many of George's friends couldn't believe that Reeves had committed suicide. Fred Crane, who had become a popular radio broadcaster in Los Angeles, first heard about what happened to his old friend when the news came over the teletype machine in the studio. George had been best man at

Crane's first wedding, back in September of 1940, and though they were no longer close, Fred had always had affectionate feelings toward his former Tarlteton twin. Crane found it impossible to reconcile Leonore Lemmon's suicide verdict with the man he had run into so recently at that stoplight on Sunset Boulevard.

Pat Ellsworth had heard news of George's death coming over the radio the morning of the sixteenth, though the radio report had announced only that "actor George Reeves shot himself early this morning . . ." and no mention of murder or suspicious circumstances rode the airways. She told her father, producer Whitney Ellsworth, who phoned Robert and Bette Shayne to give them the news. At first Whit Ellsworth thought it had to be a mistake, that George was incapable of taking his own life. If it was true, then it had to have been some kind of temporary insanity.

When she read the newspaper accounts, Bette Shayne found it impossible to believe Leonore Lemmon's explanation of what happened that night. "For starters, it doesn't sound like George to become so angry at a guest unless he saw something he didn't like. And we were horrified to read, 'He's going upstairs to shoot himself.' What does that mean? Then why didn't she stop him?" And so the terrible news moved in concentric circles through the cast and crew of *The Adventures of Superman,* among the people George had worked with and who had come to love him as "Honest George, the People's Friend."

Gene La Belle, who had been helping George get back into shape for the last few weeks, was shocked to hear the news. He may have heard about the death from Whit Ellsworth, since La Belle had been on the payroll of *The Adventures of Superman,* or he may have picked up the June 17 edition of *The Los Angeles Times* with its banner headline: "Reeves, Superman of TV, Kills Himself in His Home." "I didn't know what to think," La Belle later said. "It was like losing a parent. George was like a father to me." La Belle was so skeptical about the verdict of suicide that he went to the Los Angeles Police Department and tried to tell them that George's fatal wound could not have been self-inflicted. He mistakenly believed that the wound was made by a left-handed person, and he was ready to testify that George was unequivocally right-handed. But the police brushed him off. "They didn't even want to talk to me—I was just a kid then, and they weren't interested." Thirty-seven years after Reeves's death, La Belle still does not believe the actor took his own life.

For character actor Milton Frome, who once played a villain on the show who fired a gun at Superman, Reeves's death was particularly discomfiting. The day Reeves died, the network reran that episode. "That night some neighborhood kids came by our house," Frome told Gary Grossman, "and told my son Michael, 'Hey, your father killed Superman.' . . . Michael said, 'No. My daddy's an actor, and don't forget, after my daddy shot him, Superman got up.' "

But Superman was not going to get up. The news that Superman had killed himself sent the 35 million young viewers of the show into a state of disbelief. One of the more disturbing images to emerge the day after Reeves's death was a news photograph of seven-year-old Charley Kephart, pictured in his Superman costume, his head leaning against his hand, his eyes downcast, staring forlornly at the floor, as he limply holds a copy of the *Mirror News* with the banner headline, "TV's Superman, Out of Work, Kills Self."

If the story of George Reeves's death was baffling to his young fans, it was no less a mystery to Reeves's friends, many of whom hadn't seen George since the close of the 1957 season. They thought back to the last time they saw him, they searched for signs in the George they knew and remembered: a look, a phrase, a thrown-away line, a remark that might have revealed something about his state of mind. But if he didn't commit suicide, then he had to have been murdered. George's friends— Art Weissman, Bette Shayne, Gene La Belle—were convinced of it. But everyone loved George—who could have wanted him dead? All they knew was that George had become estranged to them when Leonore Lemmon had entered his life. When they read the accounts in the newspapers, they knew two things: that George was dead and that Leonore Lemmon was somehow implicated. In the week following George's death, Leonore would begin to change her story, denying that she had ever predicted her fiancé's demise. And then she would disappear.

• • •

Leonore was hiding out in her friend Gwen Dailey's house in Burbank. But she must have had a feeling that something was left undone at 1579 Benedict Canyon, because she persuaded Gwen to accompany her to the house the following day. Leonore broke the coroner's seal and slipped into the house, telling her friend that George had "a little pussycat" that she feared had been sealed up in the house. While she was looking for the cat, however, Leonore managed to locate the $4,000 worth of traveler's checks George had purchased for their trip to Spain. She slipped them into her purse. According to Leonore, George's cat was wandering all over the house, and Leonore poured some milk into a platter, telling Gwen "that little pussycat is hungry." Gwen went upstairs, pulled the bloody sheets off the bed, and threw them into the bathtub. With Gwen upstairs, Leonore walked into the little den to the right of the living room. Gwen heard her scream.

Art Weissman was sitting on the couch in the den, sipping a martini, and scowling at Leonore, who by now had raided the kitchen and was holding luncheon meat in one hand and a bottle of scotch in the other. He had apparently slipped in the back door, without having to break the police seal. Weissman told her to put everything back where she found it. He told her that he was going to finish the job George had started: He was installing the rest of the new locks in the back doors leading to the patio. He was going to change every lock in the place so Leonore could never get back into the house. Weissman accused the two women of tampering with evidence and demanded that they leave the premises.

"We're just tidying up the house," Leonore barked back, not one to be intimidated by a middle-aged man in a goatee.

"You're disturbing a crime scene."

"Well, what the hell are you doing here, then?" she demanded to know.

"I'm George's executor. I have every right to be here, to protect the house. From vultures like you."

Art Weissman's biggest virtue was his loyalty to George. He had let himself into the house, fixed himself a drink, and had settled quietly in the darkly paneled den, which was George's favorite room in the house. He was trying to get his mind around what had happened that night to George, his only client, his friend. Some of George's other friends never quite understood why he kept Art Weissman around as his personal manager. "He certainly never got George any publicity. I would never have thought of going to Weissman and saying, 'Can you plant an item in the *Hollywood Reporter*?' " one of George's longtime friends confessed. "But what can you do? George was kind, and Art was a very devoted schmuck." But it was that devotion that would finally distinguish Weissman among George's circle of friends. He wasn't going to let Leonore have the last word on what—or who—killed Su-

Sam Kashner & Nancy Schoenberger

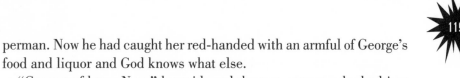

perman. Now he had caught her red-handed with an armful of George's food and liquor and God knows what else.

"Get out of here. Now," he said, and the two women, who had just raided a dead man's refrigerator, left the house. Whatever else Leonore had been looking for besides $4,000 in traveler's checks, she did not find it.

Gwen drove Leonore the mile and a half to Rip and Carol Van Ronkels' house and dropped her off. Leonore had already made her plans to get out of town, but she was going to leave with one final sally against the disbelievers and naysayers. She didn't like the way things had ended up, with Bill Bliss telling everyone that stupid story about how she had predicted George's death. Why had he shown up there anyway? Why did he take control of everything? There were too many things wrong with the way the whole sordid affair was reported to the police; she was going to try to get it right. She had always known how to handle the press, so once she settled herself at the Van Ronkels, she made two phone calls: one to her lawyer and one to Earl Wilson, the popular gossip columnist and longtime follower of the adventures of Leonore Lemmon.

The first call she made was to Edward Bennett Williams, just to find out what her position was and to "protect her interests." Williams was a powerful figure, one of the *shtarkers* who spoke Eddie Mannix's language. Described by *Newsweek* as "the country's hottest criminal lawyer," Williams was general counsel for the Teamsters Union who specialized in big shots charged with tax evasion, labor leaders charged with bribery, and gangsters being investigated by congressional committees. Williams was a big guy given to wearing splendid suits and expensive haircuts that set off a "noble brow" straight out of "Victorian literature," as described by *Newsweek*. He was responsible for beating the government's bribery case against Jimmy Hoffa.

Williams had only one thing to tell Leonore: Keep your mouth shut. But that was the last thing Leonore was capable of doing.

So Carol Van Ronkel made Leonore a potful of coffee and the two of them sat in the kitchen while Leonore put in a call to Earl Wilson at the *New York Post*.

"What I went through this afternoon," she sobbed, as she tried to tell her side of things. She told Wilson how she had returned to the house, not mentioning the broken coroner's seal, and "a man named Art Weissman was there and he was going to have every lock changed so I couldn't get in the place." Leonore wept crocodile tears. She then told the gossip columnist that she and her pal Gwen Dailey "pulled every bloody sheet off that bed."

Wilson, a seasoned journalist, knew that Leonore had at least created the appearance of tampering with evidence and had probably broken the law and should not have reentered that house. Until an official verdict was made, George's house was potentially a crime scene. Why did Leonore seem so confident that there wasn't going to be a criminal investigation? And why did she go into that house and pull all the sheets from the bed? Was she afraid that she had left something behind? What was she really looking for? But Wilson knew a good story when he heard one.

Wilson asked Leonore about those peculiar things she was reported to have said, according to the police report that became the basis of countless news stories already out on the street. He wanted to know how Leonore knew George was going to shoot himself and why she uttered those words that Bette Shayne and others found so particularly disturbing.

Leonore denied making the prediction, insisting that she was not clairvoyant. "I'd have stopped him. I'd have stopped him or he'd have gone for broke—he'd have gunned me, too."

She then reiterated her theme of how despondent George was before his death. "It was very simple," she explained. "He was so well known as Superman he couldn't get a job as anything else. So he was going to wrestle professionally. After twenty-eight years, you can't blow dignity. . . . He wanted to bring me the moon and diamonds and moonbeams and he just couldn't do it because he just couldn't get the job. Anyway, yesterday he brought me a carful of champagne and flowers and hotdogs. And he said, 'Mouse, walk on my hands. Princess, have I brought you goodies?' "

Leonore then repeated the story she and Bill Bliss had told to the police: that George had gone to bed around midnight, that shortly thereafter Bliss had shown up on George's doorstep with Carol Van Ronkel. Leonore let them in, but their voices woke George, who came downstairs and angrily told them to leave.

"We didn't have any beef. He just went upstairs and shot himself. It was that simple." Leonore then asked Wilson if he knew Clifford Odets's anti-Hollywood play, *The Big Knife*. "The theme of it was how Hollywood cuts them down. The system was what killed him!"

Sam Kashner & Nancy Schoenberger

When Wilson brought up the subject of Toni Mannix and her harassment of Reeves—without mentioning her by name but referring to her as "the wife of a Hollywood executive"—Leonore responded with a menacing "I'll take care of her in my own way." But she pounced on the subject.

She told Wilson that the unnamed woman had been calling Reeves as often as twenty times a day, at all hours. She was quick to say that those harassing phone calls contributed to George's despondency. She then added, "I can't tell you her name. I don't even want to talk about it." Of course, everyone who knew George knew who they were talking about. If people started to question the suicide angle, why not throw some suspicion Toni's way? After all, Toni really had harassed George.

In a final taste of irony, Leonore told Wilson that an offer "for some kind of witchcraft picture which he was to produce, direct, and star in" had been left on George's answering machine the morning after his death. Leonore must have heard it when she broke into the house. And Art Weissman must have heard it as well. With a voice pickled in sarcasm, Leonore added, "It came through finally this morning, wasn't that nice?"

"It's a shame," Leonore told Wilson, "but [Edward Bennett] Williams said to me, 'Lem, hold still, say nothing.' " Leonore wept more crocodile tears. "I'd better take his advice, because it looks from reading the papers like I've been kind of noisy." She added that Williams wasn't worried, and neither was she. He had looked after Jimmy Hoffa's interests when Robert Kennedy was poking his nose into Teamster business. This was a piece of cake in comparison.

So Wilson wrote that Leonore "bitterly denied by phone reports that she had forecast that he was to kill himself," adding "the New York-born and reared beauty . . . was to have married the handsome but unemployed, forty-seven-year-old [sic] actor on Friday. . . ."

"Leonore Lemmon could play the press like a violin," observed Peter Levinson, the music publicist who worked on behalf of jazz greats such as Artie Shaw and Miles Davis, and who befriended Leonore later on in New York. "She could be charming, entertaining, and she told a good story, even if it wasn't exactly a true one. You wouldn't really notice you'd been had because the whole damn experience was so entertaining," wrote the newspaperman Charles Robbins, who used to chronicle a much-younger Leonore's exploits along the Great White Way in the 1940s.

But why did Leonore feel she had to change her story? After all, her prediction that George was going to kill himself simply supported the verdict of suicide. And she would do everything she could to embellish the picture of a depressed George, about to take his life, even though she had told Gwen Dailey shortly before George's death how happy he was. So she pressed Rip Van Ronkel into service to shore up her view of a suicidal actor. After all, Rip was really *her* friend, not George's though he lived nearby; she had known him once in New York. She felt more confident crying on the shoulders of the press from his kitchen, with Rip nearby to help her give substance to her story. As writer Jan Henderson has suggested, "She's sitting in Rip's kitchen, and she's about to go on the horn with Earl Wilson—Rip can be helpful there, promoting this image of George, or at least exaggerating this image of George, as a nice guy who finished last." It was probably Van Ronkel who suggested the comparison with Odets's anti-Hollywood diatribe, *The Big Knife*. For all her worldliness, Leonore didn't read too much beyond the newspapers, especially if her name was going to be in them. Her description of George to Earl Wilson as a man "who just couldn't exist in this kind of world" would be the closest thing to a eulogy she could muster.

Whether Rip Van Ronkel ever figured out what his wife was doing at Reeves's house is not known. Carol Van Ronkel was never again questioned by the police, who were satisfied with the testimony of Bill Bliss—who gave his occupation as a heating-equipment manufacturer—about the so-called argument he had had with George. That argument would prove to be a smoke screen that would take thirty-seven years to disappear.

• • •

It wasn't a coincidence that Leonore's lawyer was the well-known defender of mobster big shots like Jimmy Hoffa and Mickey Cohen. Leonore Lemmon had often boasted of her connections to organized crime. In the interview she would give to Lee Saylor in 1989, she rhapsodized about the notorious gangster Frank Costello, whom she described as "the nicest of men, a businessman, you know." She liked to impress George with her tales of Costello and how he used to leave a hundred-dollar bill under the plate of all the ladies he lunched with. "I loved him," she said as she decried the fact that by the end of the 1950s, all the "good old gangsters" were dead or being deported. "I'm talking

about the good old gangsters. The guys who used to run the docks. . . .
They're a bunch of Puerto Rican hoodlums today who go around smack-
ing old ladies. They're not nice fellas. Not like Eddie McGrath, who ran
the docks. Nifty guy. They didn't walk around going boom, boom,
boom."

It was difficult for Leonore to take Williams's advice to stop talking
to the press, to keep her mouth shut. She loved publicity and found it
a strain to pass up her new romance with the journalism boys. Her interview with Earl Wilson raised more questions than it settled, and it
aroused the suspicions of Helen Bessolo. George Reeves's mother made
plans to take the train from Galesburg, Illinois, directly to Pasadena,
to be near her son.

• • •

Like the survivors of all suicides, Helen couldn't believe her son had
taken his own life. She read the newspaper accounts as she made plans
to return to Los Angeles, and found it particularly disturbing that she
didn't recognize any of the names—William Bliss, Carol Van Ronkel,
Robert Condon. They couldn't be George's friends—she knew who her
son's friends were. She claimed to have never even heard of Leonore
Lemmon, but that would later be disputed. Before boarding the *Super
Chief* to California, she told a Galesburg friend, "George needs me."

Helen knew she would have to make a decision about her son's
body. Why hadn't the police ordered a thorough autopsy? Why was there
no inquest into her son's "suicide"? Why did the police seem so satisfied with Leonore Lemmon's story, especially after she so publicly re-
canted part of it? Whatever secrets George's body contained, they
would remain secret until a second autopsy—a real autopsy—could be
performed. And unless Helen Bessolo managed to change the minds of
the Los Angeles Police Department, that just wasn't going to happen.

11

THE WOMAN IN THE WHEELCHAIR

Helen Bessolo, now sixty-five, was devastated by news of her son's death, and she refused to believe that he had killed himself. She had to bear the brunt of that news all alone in Galesburg, a Bessolo cousin remembers, because over the years she had alienated her neighbors with her eccentric behavior. She scared the local children and made a nuisance of herself reporting petty trespasses to the local police, so there wasn't the kind of outpouring of sympathy that one might expect in the wake of a sudden death.

Though Helen, in her obsessive love for her son, had never been willing to face the truth about George and the disappointments of his career, this was one truth she would unflinchingly stare down. Relatives claim that George spoke to his mother the weekend before his death and that he had asked her for one of her rings to give to Leonore as an engagement ring. So George did intend to marry Leonore, and Helen Bessolo's claim that she knew nothing of George's fiancée was not true.

Helen had already been troubled when she learned about George's crack-up in the Jaguar and the stitches he'd needed to close up the gash in his head. She had felt sure that George was in danger, and she had begun calling him frequently in the weeks before his death, expressing her concern. George reassured her that he wasn't in any personal danger, even though his own doubts were taking shape, sprouting in his consciousness like fungus after a heavy rain. "I have the situation under control, Mother," he told her, which was not exactly confidence-inspiring, nor was it true.

The first person Helen Bessolo called after receiving the news of George's death was Ellanora Needles Rose, George's ex-wife, with whom Helen had remained friends.

Edward Rose, Ellanora's current husband, had never really liked it when his wife talked about George Reeves, and he probably resented Ellanora's long conversations with Helen. Ellanora had been married to George for nearly nine years. It had been a long time ago, but the prosperous entertainment lawyer felt uncomfortable about the relationship Ellanora had had with George. Ed Rose wouldn't even allow their young daughter to watch *The Adventures of Superman,* and Ellanora, no doubt to keep peace in the family, went along with her husband's wishes.

Ellanora listened to Helen's conviction that George had not taken his own life. The fact that he was surrounded by people Helen had never even heard of seemed suspicious, people with strange names like Lemmon and Van Ronkel and Bliss. She told Ellanora that she was planning to go out to Los Angeles and needed someone who knew Hollywood and whose very name would be an "Open Sesame" to the gates of Bel-Air and Beverly Hills, as well as to the Hollywood demimonde. Someone, in Helen's words, "not afraid to get their feet wet." Ellanora asked her husband to suggest someone who could do some investigating on Helen's behalf.

Edward Rose, a former district attorney in New York City before moving to Los Angeles, recommended Jerry Giesler, one of the most powerful and flamboyant lawyers in Hollywood. Now that George was dead, Ed Rose could afford to help out Mrs. Bessolo. At the age of seventy-seven, most of Giesler's famous cases were behind him, but he still enjoyed the status of a formidable protector of reputations, and Ed Rose put Mrs. Bessolo in touch with him.

No casting agent would ever have cast Harold Lee "Jerry" Giesler as a criminal lawyer, with his weak eyes, high-pitched voice, and sirloined midriff. But in his heyday Giesler had handled Robert Mitchum's pot bust, Charlie Chaplin's paternity suit, and Errol Flynn's statutory rape charge. That case made Giesler's reputation and it made a folk hero out of Flynn—the swashbuckler was accused of seducing two underage women, one of them aboard his yacht, the *Sirocco.* Giesler, with his big belly and fastidious manners, resembled a decadent dauphin, or a cross between Alfred Hitchcock and Adlai Stevenson, as *Time* magazine once observed. But he was a carnivore in the courtroom—a relentless examiner whose take-no-prisoners style had kept Flynn out of prison. Giesler's successes won him another big client: Ben "Bugsy" Siegel retained Giesler to rescue him from the only crime for which

Sam Kashner & Nancy Schoenberger

Siegel actually was prosecuted, the 1940 shooting of an informer, Harry "Big Greenie" Greenbaum. Giesler was also responsible for getting an acquittal in the murder case of Norman Selby, the fighter known as "Kid McCoy" (object of that bit of American lingo, "the real McCoy"). Although Kid McCoy had confessed to murdering his mistress, Giesler argued that the Kid was depressed at the time, and his station-house confession was merely the expression of a death wish. Giesler had two specialties: murder cases and divorce suits, always taking the distaff side in the latter. He brokered Marilyn Monroe's divorce from Joe DiMaggio, Barbara Hutton's from Cary Grant, Lady Sylvia Ashley's from Clark Gable. He had one other spurious claim to fame: He originated the attack-the-victim defense of men charged with rape, finding ways to impugn the reputations of women who had brought charges of rape against his clients.

By the late 1950s, Giesler was legendary as a brilliant, relentless attorney who could bend people to his will. And he agreed to take Helen's case.

• • •

The *Los Angeles Times* was the first paper in the country to break the news that Helen Bessolo had retained Giesler to investigate Reeves's death. Within five days of the shooting, the press had begun to characterize the death as "bizarre" and "a growing mystery." The first controversy was how—and if—Leonore was able to predict her lover's death. Why did she make that statement, and why did she later deny it? The second was whether George was actually depressed enough to have taken his own life. There were many who could testify that he was not, including Helen Bessolo.

Helen told the fastidious attorney that she had spoken to George the weekend before the fatal shooting and that George had promised her he was going to make a stop in Galesburg to see her and to bring her a "surprise package" on his way to Spain. That surprise was no doubt going to be Leonore Lemmon: The two would be married in Spain and return to the States to a round of celebrations in New York and Los Angeles. It was these heady plans that at first led Helen to suspect that some violence had been done to her son. "I just can't believe that of his own volition George would do a thing like committing suicide!" she said.

Fred Crane, Gene La Belle, Phyllis Coates, Bette and Robert Shayne, and Dr. Paul Hanson had all seen George shortly before his death. They had felt that George had turned a corner and was optimistic about his career and happy with his new love. Among all of George's close friends and costars from *The Adventures of Superman,* only one believed the Man of Steel had been depressed enough to kill himself: Jack Larson.

Larson was traveling in Europe with his close friend, the writer and director Jim Bridges, when he heard about the shooting of George Reeves.

It had been an exciting time for the young actor, away from America where he was saddled with the identity of "Superman's pal." Being Jimmy Olsen wasn't the problem in Europe that it had been in the States. His friend Montgomery Clift was filming *Suddenly Last Summer* in London with Katharine Hepburn, and after visiting there, Larson and Bridges ended up in Rome.

"I was in Munich working at the Bavarian Film Kunst, and my next real destination was going to be Rome," Larson remembered. "And I had told people to write to me in care of American Express, Piazza di Spagna. The Superman Company had already exercised their option on me, and I knew we were going to shoot twenty-six more shows. I got to Rome, went to the American Express to pick up my mail. I was sitting on the Spanish Steps, right next to Keats's room, and I opened this tremendous amount of mail waiting for me. It was full of headlines and newspaper accounts of George's death. I was stunned. I just sat there on the steps."

Thirty-seven years later, Larson still believes that his friend committed suicide. "I felt that if he was as depressed as I was when I was in the United States trying to work, then he could have done it," Larson said. "George loved acting—but he didn't want to be Superman anymore. God, he was going to end up a wrestler and couldn't even get booking dates with that at the end of his life! It was a mighty come-down. And knowing that he'd split up with Toni, it just all made total sense to me. . . ."

"George had destroyed his relationship with Toni," Larson explained. "Alive, she never would have had him back. Dead, there was nothing more in the world she wanted than George alive, and back, and for them to spend the rest of their lives together. I felt bad about it."

George Reeves's death had thrown the ultimate monkey wrench into New York–based National Comics's most lucrative plans. Jack Leibowitz, who ran the company, tried to talk Larson into starring in thirteen episodes of a new show about "Jimmy Olsen, Superman's Pal." Larson said that "they figured out how they could run a muscle man in a Superman suit through a scene when they needed other shots." But Larson refused.

"I said to Liebowitz, 'No, the show is over. Even if I said I could, I couldn't. The sight of somebody else in George's costume would be too, too sad.' "

• • •

Larson may have felt that George was capable of suicide, but Helen was convinced otherwise. She now had to convince the LAPD to reopen the case. If her son was not a suicide, then what possible motive existed for murder? She latched onto Weissman's claim that a sum of $4,000 to $5,000—mostly in traveler's checks—was missing from the house.

Helen told Giesler—"the Hollywood lawyer," as he was often called in the media—about the funds George had set aside for his trip that neither the police nor Weissman had found in the house. Though her own personal fortune had grown to nearly $1 million by 1960, Helen was "a bit crazy on the subject of money." A cousin described her as having been "as obsessed about George's traveler's checks as she was about who killed him." Of course, until the checks were located, theft would loom large in her mind as a possible motive for murder, and she would try to get the Los Angeles Police Department interested in that angle.

Weissman told Mrs. Bessolo over the telephone about his encounter with Leonore Lemmon and Gwen Dailey in George's house, and how the two women had broken the coroner's seal and had left with their arms full of George's food and liquor. Weissman was sure that Leonore had taken the traveler's checks. So Giesler assured Helen that the first thing he'd do would be to look into the disappearance of the checks, and he added that if it could be proved that Leonore had indeed broken the coroner's seal, she could be held criminally liable. So right away Giesler offered up a suspect for his client.

Art Weissman had gone to Chief William H. Parker of the Los Angeles Police Department to protest Leonore's attempts to go through George's house "as if it belonged to her." Weissman's suspicions were aroused, and one of the things he privately accused her of was introducing guns into George's household. And George had taken to gunplay right away. Jim Beaver has said that "George used to get drunk at friends' barbecues and shoot people's hats off. I've got a couple of variations on that story. He had a lot of guns—he was a bit of a collector." Weissman concluded that some sort of fun-and-games with a gun had gone on that night, perhaps the playing of Russian roulette. He theorized that Leonore might have placed an extra bullet in the gun's chamber during one such game. "Leonore had more to do with George's death than with his life," he believed. The police agreed to question Leonore Lemmon on the whereabouts of the missing traveler's checks, but they were not going to reopen the case.

• • •

The mystery deepened by June 23, two days before Helen actually arrived in Los Angeles, when George's will, written eight years earlier, was filed for probate in a Santa Monica courthouse. Mrs. Toni Mannix was named as Reeves's chief beneficiary.

George had left Toni the Benedict Canyon house as well as the Oldsmobile convertible, and his entire net worth reported at $25,000. And nothing was left to Leonore. People were puzzled that Leonore and Helen were completely cut out of the will. And the fact that Toni Mannix was a married woman added to the drama. The cat was beginning to come out of the bag, as one of Toni's friends put it, and nobody liked what they saw.

To Phyllis Coates and Jack Larson, to George's inner circle and colleagues who knew Toni Mannix as someone who had "always been there," George's will came as no surprise. "It was all hers anyway—it all belonged to Toni and George. They built it up together," Jack Larson believed. He also believed that George and Toni still loved each other, despite the shenanigans of the past five or six months. But to everyone else—and especially the press—George's will only added to the mystery and introduced a titillating suggestion of scandal as well. Giesler felt that the tide was turning in his favor: The disputed suicide theory, Leonore's retraction of her statement to the police, the missing traveler's checks, and now the surprising contents of the will would be the groundwork for demanding a new investigation. He would orchestrate Helen Bessolo's arrival in Pasadena to attract even further attention to the case.

Leonore was especially infuriated when the contents of the will were revealed. She had allowed herself to be muzzled by Edward Bennett Williams, but the splash made by George having left everything to

Toni was too much of a temptation, and Leonore couldn't keep still. She insisted to Art Weissman, whom she confronted in a delicatessen in North Hollywood, that George had written another will naming her, Leonore, as the beneficiary. "He would never leave anything to that crazy woman" who had ruined their lives.

The will also put Weissman in an awkward position. It made George look guilty of something—at the very least of having had an affair with a married woman. "And in 1959—even in death—that's what you call bad publicity," Weissman knew.

There was one curious outcome, however: It put Helen and Leonore on the same side, as both women sought to overturn George's will. Both were appalled at the prospect of Toni Mannix walking off with all of George's personal belongings. "Her husband is worth millions," Helen said about Toni, "and I don't like the idea of [George] leaving money to a married woman." She insisted that everything George had, he had acquired on his own, including the house. "George built his own home in Benedict Canyon and paid $12,000 on it." She had never forgiven Toni for making her feel like the dog in the manger on that afternoon boat ride two years ago, at what had turned out to be one of her last visits with her son. But if she had wanted to make an ally out of her son's fiancée, it was too late. Leonore had flown the coop.

• • •

When Helen Bessolo got off the train in Pasadena, she was in a wheelchair. A woman who made the trip with Mrs. Bessolo found that very peculiar. "We got to Pasadena, and suddenly she needed a wheelchair. Never told me why." She may have simply been overcome by the events she would now have to deal with, but it's more likely that Helen was already beginning to try to shape public opinion, on the advice of Jerry Giesler, with whom she had spoken before leaving Galesburg. Donald Spoto has reported in his book *Marilyn Monroe, the Biography* that Giesler stage-managed Marilyn Monroe's announcement to the press of her impending divorce from DiMaggio. Giesler "wanted her to act for the reporters and cameramen. He worked like a good film director, explaining every mood and expression he wanted." Giesler would find that he had ready material in Helen Bessolo, who had spent her life reinventing herself for the world's approval.

So the arrival of George Reeves's frail, elderly mother—though she was only sixty-five—in a wheelchair made for a dramatic scene. Helen had years of rehearsal for this final, magnificent role that life had dealt her. She was in truth grieving, but she knew how to project that grief and make it larger than life. Her eccentricity and playacting would now take on the dimensions of heroism. Wearing dark glasses and an ankle-length cotton dress with gingham trim, being pushed along in a high-backed rattan wheelchair by a porter, Helen told a dozen reporters waiting on the train platform how her heart was broken. She ridiculed the theory that George was depressed because he couldn't get work. "It was so unlike my son to do such a thing. I had talked to him Sunday. He said, 'Mom, when are you coming back?'" she told a reporter for the *Los Angeles Times.* She mentioned that George had asked her for one of her rings, but he didn't say what he needed it for. She said that George "never had depressive moods" and "was in a splendid frame of mind" when they last talked, two days before his death.

She and Giesler would prove to be a formidable pair. Helen had her picture taken dozens of times right there on the platform, the mighty *Santa Fe Chief* idling behind her. The first thing Giesler did after Helen arrived in town was to arrange an interview with the *Los Angeles Examiner,* in order to "put this case on the map." And when Helen Bessolo insisted that Giesler take her to her son's house so she could see the "crime scene" with her own eyes, Giesler arranged for a photographer to accompany them.

They arrived at the house on a sparkling California day, driven there by Giesler's liveried chauffeur in a big-finned white Cadillac. There's no sign of the wheelchair, but Helen does look frail, and there's a photograph of her being helped up the front steps to George's door, flanked by Giesler and an unidentified man, probably an operative from the Nick Harris Detective Agency whom Giesler had hired to launch his investigation. In another photograph, the unidentified man points to the broken coroner's seal on the front door. There is an odd little smile on his face. There are no photographs of Helen Bessolo inside the house.

George's tiny, upstairs bedroom was terrifying. The mattress was blood-soaked, and the bloodied sheets that Gwen Dailey had stripped off the bed were balled up in the bathtub adjoining the master bedroom. The mattress, with its smears of blood and brain tissue, had been pulled from the bed and lay in the center of the room. How long did Helen gaze at the evidence of her son's violent death before she crossed the room

Sam Kashner & Nancy Schoenberger

to pick out a suit from George's closet, for him to be buried in, for the funeral that was now planned for the first of July?

Helen went into the house a lion but came out a lamb. If she was posing for the cameras on her way into the house, there was nothing posed about her exit. She had stood tall on her way in, albeit with some help; on her way out she stooped so severely that she appeared to be doubled over, as if crushed by the weight of what she had seen. Giesler helped her into the Cadillac, which was waiting for her on the sun-dappled street.

• • •

"All of the hoopla in the Reeves case," wrote a UPI reporter covering Hollywood in the summer of 1959, "had to do with Helen Bessolo, George's mother. She kept the seat warm for George. As far as the L.A. County courts and the police and the coroner's office were concerned— after all was said and done—this was an open-and-shut suicide, requiring no inquest, requiring no investigation beyond what had been done." But Helen Bessolo's dramatic arrival, Art Weissman's insistence that the police look into the missing traveler's checks, and Jerry Giesler's high profile were making it increasingly hard for the police to insist that George's death was indeed by his own hand. Though Chief Parker refused to change his verdict, he nonetheless agreed to reopen the investigation and order a second and more complete autopsy on the body, just to quiet George's mother.

Theodore J. Curphey, the county's chief medical examiner, would conduct the autopsy. Curphey was a progressive but arrogant pathologist known for stepping on the toes of county officials. He would receive his greatest notoriety in 1962 when he supervised the investigation into Marilyn Monroe's death, an investigation criticized for being slapdash and incomplete. Curphey was quick to publicly state that the police still considered Reeves's death "an apparent suicide." Why, one wonders, was Curphey willing to compromise his objectivity by insisting, beforehand, on a foregone conclusion of suicide? Why was the LAPD so insistent that there was nothing more to this case than a depressed, out-of-work actor shooting himself after a night of drinking?

Nonetheless, Curphey's autopsy took place on June 24, 1959, eight days after George's death. In the technical, Latinate language of forensic pathologists, George's wounds were described: "HEAD: 1. Perforating wounds with multiple . . . fractures of the skull. 2. Subdural hemorrhage and extensive laceration of brain. GENERAL: 1. Focal ecchymoses and abrasions of head, trunk and extremities. RESPIRATORY SYSTEM: Aspiration, blood."

One of the controversial bits of evidence in the case proving suicide was the high alcohol content of the blood, which Curphey duly notes: .27 percent. With a .27 blood alcohol concentration, most people could barely sit up in a chair, let alone hold a gun to their head and pull the trigger. Yet George had an amazing constitution and, as many have testified, usually showed little visible effects from consuming great amounts of liquor. The examination of Reeves's internal organs, including his liver, showed absolutely no organ damage due to alcohol or any other medical or toxic condition. George may have been that one in a million who could still function with such a high alcohol level in his blood.

The second controversial item on the autopsy report was the mention of multiple bruises—"focal ecchymoses"—and abrasions on the head and body. Page two of the autopsy states, "There are three blue-gray ecchymoses [bruises], measuring about 1 inch in diameter respectively and arranged over the right pectoral region." Further bruises are described on the "left olecranon region" and one three-quarter-inch bruise "on the left forehead." George's body was found on the bed, so it's not likely that he would have bruised his shoulder and forehead by falling at the time of death. So when did the bruising occur, and why? Was George involved in a struggle just before his death? Was the bruise to his forehead made by being struck by a heavy object? Curphey does not note whether the bruise on George's left temple was close to or caused by the left exit wound. Nor, curiously, did the presence of bruising on the body raise any further questions with the LAPD.

The third disturbing element is Curphey's failure to open up the head wound, which had been sewn shut with twine by the embalmer, in order to look for gunpowder residue in the wound track. Curphey performed a "monk's cap" removal of the top of the skull, and Reeves was slit open like a giant fish and his internal organs were weighed and examined, yet the coroner failed to open up and investigate the gunshot wound itself. Was this an intentional oversight? Or was Curphey so biased by Chief Parker's assertion that Reeves was a suicide that he did not want to discover anything to contradict that official verdict?

The absence or presence of gunpowder in the wound track would

Sam Kashner & Nancy Schoenberger

have been the only way to determine if the gun was held against George's temple or if he had been shot from across the room. Curphey failed to establish whether George's was a contact wound. Since it's impossible to shoot yourself from across a room, Curphey's failure to look for gunpowder residue seems a remarkable omission.

Fourth, Curphey does not state anywhere in his autopsy report whether he looked for gunpowder residue on George's right hand, the hand that allegedly fired the gun. In an open-and-shut case of suicide, the coroner might not bother to make that examination. But by June 24, after the questions that were being raised by Helen Bessolo and Jerry Giesler, Reeves's death was now suspicious. Since the body had been washed and embalmed prior to the autopsy, all the forensic evidence had been compromised, but, again, it's a curious omission on Curphey's part.

So two items of evidence that might have disproved suicide were not even investigated by the chief medical examiner of Los Angeles County: gunpowder in the wound track and gunpowder on the hand. And no one thought to ask about the bruises. Was Curphey *told* beforehand to confirm a verdict of suicide? Why did he make a public statement before performing the autopsy that the police already considered Reeves's death "an apparent suicide"? What was he afraid to find?

Many people have examined George Reeves's autopsy report since his death, including the chief medical examiner of Baltimore, Dr. John Smialek. Dr. Smialek, a youthful man with a Joe Friday manner, found Reeves's blood alcohol concentration "certainly high, but not inconsistent with suicidal behavior." One of the elements he found curious about the case, however, was the fact that the shell casing was actually found underneath George's body. Smialek wondered why Curphey never performed a ballistics test to find out how the shell casing landed there.

When asked about the lack of "tattooing" or gunpowder stippling on George's temple, Dr. Smialek explained that in a contact wound, all the gunpowder would be blown into the depths of the wound track, rather than being deposited on the skin. But there was no mention of gunpowder residue in the depths of the wound track because Curphey didn't bother to open up the closed wound and investigate. Dr. Smialek thought that was odd.

Though the autopsy was anything but thorough, Curphey announced that his findings were entirely consistent with the verdict of suicide.

Dodging a platoon of newspaper reporters outside his office, Curphey phoned the district attorney and issued his findings: "It is my opinion that the wound was self-inflicted."

Chief Parker was ready to let the matter drop, having gone to some length to satisfy Mrs. Bessolo. But Helen was still not satisfied. So Parker sent officers back into the house to look around one more time, again, just to make Helen happy so that she would pack up her tents and go away.

On June 25, the day following the autopsy, Sergeant V. A. Peterson went up into the bloody bedroom. He was looking around, and suddenly he thought about his cousin who laid carpet for a living. His cousin had once told him that whenever they rolled up an old carpet before installing the new one, they always found all sorts of weird things on the floor underneath. Old blood spots. Money. Once he found a ripped garter belt jammed into a hole in the floor. Peterson rolled up the area rug in the small bedroom, and there they were: two additional bullet holes in the floorboards of George's room.

12

A STORY, A HOUSE, AND A BROKEN HEART

Sergeant Peterson followed the trajectory of the bullet holes and looked around for the spent bullets. After searching the living room downstairs, he found one of them lodged in the paneling over the living-room fireplace and the second embedded in a beam in the downstairs ceiling. Both bullets had been fired from the Luger, the same gun that had struck down Reeves.

Police Chief Parker, however, was unmoved. He "attached no significance to the newly found bullet holes," insisting that he was satisfied with the conclusion that Reeves had shot himself. He did, however, tell the *Los Angeles Times* that Leonore Lemmon would be "re-questioned about the events preceeding the shooting—if and when she returns here from New York." Leonore had fled to Manhattan, where she was hiding out in her mother's apartment on East 63rd Street.

Leonore had no intention of returning to Los Angeles. Her mother told gossip columnists Walter Winchell and Earl Wilson that her daughter was "under heavy sedation" administered by a family physician. They dutifully noted Leonore's grief in their columns.

When Chief Parker reached her by phone to ask her about the additional bullet holes, Leonore had her story ready. She confessed that she had fired the gun only a few days before George's death. "We were just playing around and I wanted to know what a .30-caliber Luger would sound like," she said. Amazingly, Chief Parker was satisfied with her answer and refused to reopen the case, although she claimed that she had made only one of the two additional bullet holes. Chief Parker would tell the *Los Angeles Times* that "Miss Lemmon admitted to Det. V. A. Peterson that the bullet found in the fireplace paneling was fired by her 'accidentally' while she was 'fooling around' with the death weapon several days before the fatal shooting. The other bullet remains unexplained. . . ." Who, then, made the second bullet hole, and—since there were no holes in the rug in George's bedroom—who covered them up?

Art Weissman was not satisfied with the LAPD's conclusion—how could the police let Leonore slip away so easily? He agitated the LAPD with his inventory of the house, reminding them that $4,000 in traveler's checks were missing, and he accused Leonore of stealing them. Leonore, however, had an answer to that one as well.

Upon her return to New York, Leonore asked another attorney named Leon Kaplan to look into the existence of a second will, which she insisted George had made out before his death. Realizing that Weissman was gunning for her and that absconding with funds did not improve her position, Leonore asked Kaplan to "vehemently deny" Weissman's accusation that she had broken the coroner's seal. Before officially hiring Kaplan, she turned over the missing traveler's checks to him. Kaplan was furious. He felt "implicated, if not compromised," caught in one of Leonore Lemmon's webs. But she was just trying to show the world what a good little girl she could be and protect herself from Weissman's accusations. Curiously, she seemed more afraid of what Weissman would say or do than she was of Chief Parker and the LAPD, who seemed completely satisfied with her explanation of the additional bullet holes in George's bedroom, nor were they particularly interested in the missing $4,000. As far as they were concerned, the case was still closed.

She had won that little skirmish, but George's will continued to stick in her craw. She couldn't stand it that Toni Mannix would in effect have the last word on George and inherit all of his worldly goods. It was Leonore who needed the money, not Toni. She called up Detective Johnson and told him that "I was listening to George—with two other persons present—when he talked about making out a new will, with me as chief beneficiary. That will must be lost! It must be in the house somewhere." Perhaps that was what she was looking for that day when she stumbled upon Art Weissman having a baleful, farewell drink in George's den.

However, Reeves's attorney, Milton Tyre, insisted that there was no second will. "He just never got around to it," Tyre said. "It was one of those things that kept getting postponed."

• • •

Sergeant Peterson—the officer who took down Johnson and Korby's initial report of the killing—was not happy about Leonore Lemmon's explanation of the extra bullet holes in the floor of George's bedroom. Even if her story were true, she had still only accounted for one of the bullet holes; who was responsible for the second slug, one of the two that ended up in the downstairs living room? Sergeant Peterson suggested to Chief Parker that an inquest be held into Reeves's "suicide" to put to rest all of the competing stories and rumors. But Chief Parker wouldn't hear of it. He was satisfied with Theodore Curphey's conclusion, and he wanted a tidy end to the whole affair.

In Peterson's opinion, Chief Parker had gone out of his way to accommodate Leonore Lemmon, to avoid "adding things up." He felt that Parker had actually been bothered more than he let on by Curphey's discovery of multiple time-of-death bruises on the body. Those bruises should have opened his eyes, Peterson thought, not gotten his defenses up. Peterson was in a bind. There wasn't anything he could do without Chief Parker's support. But Reeves's optimism before his death, the additional bullet holes and Leonore's questionable claim that she had made one of them, the time-of-death bruises, the doubt in many people's minds that Reeves was even going to marry Leonore Lemmon—the fact that Gwen Dailey was to accompany them on their "honeymoon"—all roused Peterson's suspicions. So Peterson took his doubts to Jerry Giesler, whom he knew was representing Mrs. Bessolo. There had to be a reason why Chief Parker didn't call for an inquest, and he wanted Giesler to find out why.

Sergeant Peterson didn't care much for Chief Parker, the long-faced, gloomy übercop who was now the head of a five-thousand-man force thought to be the most effective crime-fighting machine in the country. But Parker paid a price for his effectiveness. Throughout the 1950s the city's Negroes and Mexicans put themselves to sleep at night hating him. He had a fearsome temper: "If subordinates failed to fulfill his directives they would feel the lash," observed the *Los Angeles Times*. One member of Parker's inner circle recalled the chief as possessing a rage "powerful enough to peel the paint off the walls." Parker was always talking about the "crooked rats" who were taking over the city, turning it into the "City of Diablos" instead of the City of Angels. Parker himself had been a captain in the U.S. Army during the war and had helped to draft the Allied prison system for the Normandy invasion. A fervid anti-Communist, it would be Parker, a few years later, who put the kibosh on Soviet leader Nikita Khrushchev's keenest ambition during his California trip: to visit Disneyland.

• • •

"This is not a conspiracy!" Chief Parker had announced after Dr. Curphey completed his examination of George Reeves's corpse. But Helen Bessolo and Jerry Giesler were satisfied with neither the results of the autopsy nor with Leonore Lemmon's claim that she had made one of those additional bullet holes. If Chief Parker was trying to appease Mrs. Bessolo and put the case behind him, he wasn't succeeding. And now there were others in the police department, including Sergeant Peterson, who were uneasy with the verdict of suicide. Everyone wanted to discount Helen Bessolo as at worst a nut, an obsessed woman, or at best as a typical survivor of a suicide, in complete denial that her son could have committed such an act. But there were other troubling aspects of the case that just would not go away.

First, Chief Parker and Dr. Curphey *were* disturbed by the bruises found on Reeves's body. A police officer who was present when Chief Parker took Dr. Curphey's phone call remembered that "Parker was unhappy to hear about those three bruises on Reeves's chest and head. He asked Curphey if those bruises could have been the result of George's drinking. I don't know what the doctor said." Parker questioned Dr. Paul Hanson about that little wrestling match the two had engaged in the Sunday before George's death. Hanson had sworn those bruises were not visible that night. Moreover, Dr. Hanson, head of emergency surgery at St. Luke's Hospital, thought those bruises could have been "made by a weapon, especially the head bruise." And, though Reeves was a heavy drinker, he was not the kind of drinker to stumble around and injure himself. Most people couldn't even tell when he'd had too much to drink. Still, Chief Parker refused to reopen the investigation.

Second, people don't usually commit suicide in the nude. George's body was completely unclothed when Officers Johnson and Korby found him in his upstairs bedroom in the early hours of June 16. That bothered Parker, though others have observed that Reeves had been interested in what was called "the physical culture movement" popular in the 1950s, a fad also known as nudism, that gave rise to nudist colonies, where middle-class accountants, secretaries, housewives, insurance salesmen, and the like flocked to summer camps where the only requirement was the removal of one's clothes. The photographer Diane Arbus has captured the banality of the physical culture movement in her grotesquely comic black-and-white photographs of suburban Americans relaxing in the nude at home, made even more ridiculous by the wearing of shoes and sunglasses.

"George didn't have any particular qualms about being naked," Gene La Belle remembers. The possibility that George had gone downstairs in his bathrobe, returned to his bedroom, removed his robe, and then shot himself "doesn't seem inconsistent with what we know about George," according to Jim Beaver. "George enjoyed walking around his house and doing yardwork with nothing on. He seemed pretty comfortable with his body."

Even so, the idea of a nude George Reeves in a houseful of clothed strangers drinking and talking downstairs was troubling to some of Chief Parker's investigators. But the chief still refused to reopen the case.

The final mystery was the lack of a suicide note explaining George's hasty exit from the world. But officers of the Los Angeles Coroner's Department specializing in suicide insisted that the existence of a farewell note is, according to Beaver, "the exception, not the rule. Only once in a while do we find a note. Usually not."

The people in George's house the night he died—Leonore Lemmon, Bobby Condon, Carol Van Ronkel, Bill Bliss—were not much help to police in clearing up the mystery. What the newspapers failed to report in their accounts of Reeves's death—and which was not even mentioned in the official police report, written by Sergeant Peterson based on Johnson and Korby's findings—was how drunk all the bystanders were. Why was that little detail left out of the police report? Didn't it call into question their ability to describe accurately what happened? But there would be no further investigation.

There are more puzzling aspects to Chief Parker's refusal to reopen the case. Why didn't he order an examination of the Luger to determine if more than one bullet was fired that night? Why wasn't he alarmed by the lack of fingerprints on the weapon? Why did he so readily accept Leonore Lemmon's over-the-phone confession that she had fired the gun prior to the night of George's death? And why was there no attempt to establish the provenance of the second bullet hole?

A few days after Lemmon's statement that she had accidentally fired the Luger, a news item appeared stating that "a female informant" notified Deputy City Attorney Noel R. Slipsager's office that she had witnessed Leonore Lemmon's firing of the gun.

Chief Parker pounced on this strange bit of testimony, taking credit for locating the unidentified witness and thus solving one of the riddles in this case that wouldn't go away. The unnamed "female informant" claimed to have been a guest in George's home about six weeks before his death. She said that she saw George take out a gun and begin brandishing it. She said that Leonore "gleefully took the weapon from Reeves and asked, 'Would you like to hear how this sounds?' She then fired into the living-room ceiling. The female informant said she knew both George Reeves and Leonore Lemmon well, and she agreed with earlier reports that George had been despondent over career problems, and was in financial difficulty." She also testified that George had been "drinking heavily" when she was a guest in the Benedict Canyon house.

The most curious aspect to this testimony is that the "female informant was granted immunity from prosecution in return for her cooperation." Who was this mysterious woman? And why would she ask for immunity in a case already closed, ruled a nonsuspicious death by suicide? And why did Leonore feel that she needed a witness to her claim that she had previously fired the gun?

And if Leonore fired a bullet into the living-room ceiling, where it lodged either in a ceiling beam or in a panel over the fireplace, how does that account for the *two* bullet holes found in the floor of George's room? They could only have been made by firing downward from the upstairs bedroom. Could the so-called witness—clearly one of Leonore Lemmon's friends—had gotten her story wrong in attempting to validate Leonore's claim? Having learned that the slug ended up in the fireplace, wouldn't she have assumed the gun was actually fired in the living room, and not in the upstairs bedroom? Her testimony clouds what really happened, based on the trajectory of the bullet, but it raises questions as to why Leonore felt she needed a witness to exonerate her from any suspicion.

And Chief Parker refused to investigate further.

Slipsager, however, had a theory. He had gone out on a limb for George Reeves once before, when Reeves had complained of constant harassment by Toni Mannix. Slipsager had written a politely worded

Sam Kashner & Nancy Schoenberger

cease-and-desist letter. Now he wondered if Toni or Eddie Mannix might have had something to do with George's death. There had been a couple of news articles unflattering to Toni Mannix—almost exclusively in New York–based newspapers—before MGM publicist Howard Strickling had a chance to clamp down on the coverage. The most damning was the *New York World Telegram and Sun* article, "Superman Slap at Woman Beneficiary Puzzles Cops," in which the question is asked, "Why did [George Reeves] complain to the city attorney's office that the woman to whom he left the bulk of his estate was harassing him with phone calls?" Larry Nathanson in the *New York Journal American* went even farther in asking "Did a 'Delilah' Drive Superman to Death?" But the press quickly dropped that angle, in part due to Strickling's influence and in part because no one in Chief Parker's office bothered to pursue the story. So it was dropped, replaced by Leonore Lemmon's much-publicized battle with Toni Mannix over George's estate.

• • •

It was Leonore Lemmon who tipped off the New York newspapers that Toni Mannix had been harassing George before his death, and that George had filed a complaint with the Los Angeles deputy city attorney's office. She was still mad as hell that Toni was going to inherit the house and all of George's worldly goods—"You've got your story now. Toni got a house . . . and I got a broken heart," she told the press—and she felt that the best way to contest George's will was to discredit Toni. She continued to insist that George had written a second will leaving everything to her, and she suggested that "anyone who's interested" ought to look into Slipsager's office to find out about those relentless phone calls. Those phone calls, she insisted, were part of what drove George to his death.

Leonore was out to cut the legs off of Toni's right to be George's beneficiary. "If not legally," Toni's friend Constance Shirley recounts, "then morally, or at least to create the illusion that George really must have wanted Leonore to have it all."

What followed was a war of images played out in the press, with Howard Strickling putting the best spin on Toni's role as George's beneficiary and the gossip columnists delighted to tell Leonore's side of the story. As serious coverage into the mysteries surrounding Reeves's death evaporated, the two women in his life fought their catfight through dueling photographs and insinuating remarks. "One thing Howard and Mr. Mannix *were* able to do," suggests a former assistant to Howard Strickling, "was to shore up Toni's image in the same newspapers that were printing stories of her harassing phone calls." These were movie men. They knew that a picture was worth a dozen columns of type. "One photograph could bring down all the negative newsprint against Toni." Therefore, a cropped photograph of Toni Mannix at a society luncheon began to appear in the Los Angeles newspapers. Toni is wearing one of the hats she liked to wear to those daytime charity events. In this photo, the rim of the hat looks like nothing so much as a halo. Her large, jeweled crucifix is prominently displayed, as is her wedding band. Toni is dressed up like a sister of mercy by way of the House of Chanel. Leonore Lemmon glowers at Toni Mannix from across the front page. Toni is smiling, Leonore is not. Leonore's picture was taken at a night-club, while Toni looks like she could be in church. In this battle of the newspaper images, Toni is clearly winning.

● ● ●

Helen Bessolo contested George's will with the L.A. County Courthouse, most likely on the advice of Jerry Giesler, who wanted to keep stirring the pot, to keep things hot for the LAPD and district attorney's office. Giesler and his young investigators from the Nick Harris Detective Agency took to congregating at Helen Bessolo's Pasadena house, which she had moved back into, meeting in her parlor over coffee and dough-nuts. Giesler, balancing his cup and saucer as he carried books and legal briefs from the kitchen into the parlor, told the men gathered there that he thought the "unidentified female informant" might be Leonore Lemmon herself. He sensed the hand of Edward Bennett Williams hanging somewhere above the puppets' theater that had become the Su-perman death case. Of course this "informant" knew of George's de-spondency, which dovetailed with the statements Leonore et al. gave to the police! Of course she knew of his heavy drinking!

But it's more likely that the "female informant" was Leonore's best friend and co-conspirator in cleaning up the death house: Gwen Dai-ley. The immunity she sought may have been immunity from the crime of breaking the coroner's seal and tampering with evidence. It was, after all, Gwen who had stripped the bed and thrown the monstrous ball of linen into the bathtub. She must have known that Leonore absconded with $4,000 in traveler's checks, which made her an accessory to the crime of theft. Was there another reason why she sought immunity from prosecution? As Leonore's best friend and confidante, did she know something about George's death that she was holding back from the police? Were there others in the house that night who, for whatever reason, had been left out of the police report?

She must not have conferred with Leonore before speaking to the police, because she placed the firing of the gun at six weeks prior to George's death; Leonore had claimed that she fired the gun "a few days" before his death. And she placed Leonore in the living room, firing directly into the fireplace panel, not in the upstairs bedroom. But even those discrepancies did not ruffle the feathers of the police department.

• • •

Jerry Giesler had become fond of Helen Bessolo. He knew she was a vain and difficult woman, but he admired her toughness and her flamboyance. That appealed to Giesler, who had once won a case by lying on the floor of the courthouse and pretending to be the corpse; he had successfully defended exotic dancer Lili St. Cyr against a charge of indecent exposure by prancing around the courtroom in the diaphanous costume she had worn on the night in question. The two were alike in other ways: Giesler saw himself as an indestructible winner who always came out on top. Helen was—well, she was Superman's mother! She had given birth to a legend, someone with superpowers.

Things looked bad for Leonore, whose story of playfully firing the Luger seemed lame at best. But Giesler wasn't interested in Leonore. His research was leading him in another direction. The detective agency was quietly working on the possibility that a fifth person was in the house the night that George died. Someone who slipped into the house, shot George, and let himself out as quietly as he had come.

• • •

It was time to say good-bye. Reeves's funeral had come at last. Helen had gone to her son's house, walked through the vale of bloodied sheets and smeared mattress, retrieved a dark suit from George's closet, and prepared herself for the ordeal to come. She had moved back into her former home in Pasadena, the home she had shared with George many years earlier, the home she had bought with her divorce settlement from the only man George had known and loved as a father.

Helen made up a list of pallbearers for her son's funeral that would baffle those who truly knew George. On that list were included Alan Ladd and Gig Young, actors who had but a passing acquaintance with the deceased. Alan Ladd and Reeves had barely even spoken, having only met casually when both men were under contract to Paramount. "George had a no-line walk-on when Alan Ladd was a major star," Jim Beaver has observed, and therein lies Helen Bessolo's method of madness. She wanted the world to remember her son as a big star, carried from the chapel to his waiting grave by other big stars. She knew the list of pallbearers would be published in any news coverage of the funeral. It was her last attempt to rewrite history, to give her son the movie star status that she was convinced was his true fate. She had appointed some of George's genuine friends as pallbearers, but with Gig Young and Alan Ladd included, it read like "a list of a star-struck girl who read the fan magazines," as Bette Shayne described it. Gig Young showed up at the funeral, but Alan Ladd did not.

Gene La Belle, Art Weissman, Nati Vacio, Phyllis "Gypsy" Coates, the Shaynes, Whitney Ellsworth (whom George had once called "Dad"), *Superman* director George Blair—they were all present at the Gates, Kingsley, and Gates chapel in west Los Angeles for George's funeral. Jack Larson was absent because he was still in Europe. But the most startling absences were Toni's and Leonore's. Neither one of them appeared.

Leonore had of course fled to New York, and perhaps her famous lawyer had warned her not to return to Los Angeles to attend George's funeral. After all, her "grief" had already been dutifully noted by the New York newspapers. Gwen Dailey—Leonore's stand-in, best friend, and shadow—did attend, however. Perhaps it was she who told Leonore to stay away, that the needle gauging Leonore's unpopularity in Los Angeles had gone off the meter. She was no longer the poor fiancée left at the altar, jilted by death, the weepy party girl whose heart had gone flat as soda water. Leonore knew that Art Weissman, the Shaynes, and Nati Vacio would all be there, and they all hated her. They all thought that she had had something to do with George's death, or at the very least was cold-hearted enough to have joked about it: "Oh, that's just George going upstairs to shoot himself." So Leonore stayed away.

So did Hedda Hopper and Louella Parsons, Hollywood's two aging divas of dish who went to more show business funerals than a professional mourner. They kept their distance, too, though they had once

Sam Kashner & Nancy Schoenberger

been charmed by the handsome young man who had flirted with Vivien Leigh on Tara's front porch, who had stolen Claudette Colbert's heart from his bed in a warship's sickbay. As an out-of-work TV actor, George Reeves's name had been taken off the star map as far as those two gossip mavens were concerned. Reeves's funeral didn't even rate a blind item—it wasn't worth the time it took them to open up their pocketbooks to look for a pen.

And Toni? In the wake of the news article naming her as George's beneficiary, she probably felt she couldn't risk the public exposure. But she was truly, genuinely grieving. Her love affair was over now. Alive, she would never have taken him back, Larson said. Now that he was gone, she wanted him back more than anything. Even if she had wanted to attend the funeral, Eddie would not allow it. And to make sure she didn't humiliate herself and her husband, Eddie called in Toni's physician and they gave her a barbiturate cocktail that would keep her heavily sedated in the weeks following George's death. No one was going to hear anything more from Toni, not for a long while.

The Reverend R. Parker Jones of St. Albans Episcopal Church officiated at the funeral. Gene La Belle, who was a pallbearer along with Art Weissman, was overcome by grief. "They put a wax mask on his face," La Belle remembered. "That gave me nightmares. I don't believe in open caskets. . . ." The wax mask might well have been one of the facial molds that makeup artist Harry Thomas had made of Reeves's face when he was doing the actor's makeup for *Superman.* Life masks always look eerily like death masks.

Bette Shayne remembered that there was a lot of crying at George's funeral. Phyllis Coates saw Mrs. Bessolo become hysterical; George's mother had to be escorted from the chapel. Curiously, there were almost no *Superman* fans gathered outside of Gates, Kingsley, and Gates that day—just a handful of strangers, mostly teenage girls. It was puzzling. Where were those legions of *Superman* fans who had been the mixed blessing of George's diminishing career? "Few Teens Attend Reeves Last Rites" was a typical headline. George's body lay for two days in the mortuary chapel before the body was temporarily placed in a Woodlawn mausoleum, and still the fans did not come.

Perhaps most of George's fans were simply too young even to understand what had happened to him, never mind attend a funeral with their parents. It's just as possible that the events of the previous week, with their whiff of scandal, had scared off the *Superman* mourners. "The element of suicide had something to do with it," one reporter who did cover the funeral explained. "People didn't know what the appropriate response should be." At the end of the 1950s, suicide and depression were stigmatizing. "There was something tainted about the Reeves death at that point." Only one little eight-year-old boy waited outside, standing on the curb a block away from the chapel, too stunned to cry.

• • •

After the funeral, Helen refused to have George's body interred. She felt that the minute she buried her son, the suspicions would stop and the case would be forgotten. Someone would have gotten away with murder. Giesler had told her, in his high-pitched voice, that the autopsy had raised more questions than it answered. "What about the bruises?" he had asked. As long as the rock could be rolled away, there was a chance she could find out what really happened and clear the stigma of suicide from her son's name. Giesler assured her there were answers "floating out there somewhere."

"Of course," says Jim Beaver, "we can't underestimate Helen's perversity, her strangeness. A part of her simply didn't want to give George up, period. If there was a way to do it, she probably would have lived with the body in her house."

13

YOU JUST DON'T WANT TO KNOW

She said she wanted to go back. Toni Mannix was being kept under heavy sedation in the weeks following George's death, but after Jack Larson arrived in Los Angeles, she roused herself to return to the Benedict Canyon house that she had helped George buy, where the two of them had spent so many happy years together. After Dr. Curphey's autopsy, the seal had been removed from the front door of the house, the house that was now Toni's, and Toni's alone.

But Toni didn't want to reenter the house by herself. There were too many ghosts. First she called Phyllis Coates and begged the actress to accompany her. She refused. Toni then called Jack Larson, fresh from Europe, and entreated him to return with her to the house.

In a way, Jack was like the son Toni and George would have had if they had met and married twenty years earlier. Barely out of his teens, the young actor was fond of Mrs. Mannix, impressed by her high style and her beauty. And Toni had done Jack Larson a big favor once. When Larson had taken ill on the set of *The Adventures of Superman* one day, the show's producer found a quack doctor who pumped him full of painkillers to keep him working. Toni found out about it.

"You can't treat the kid that way! You're not just going to keep him working like this," she complained. And so she brought in her physician—one of the best in the city—who kept the boyish actor at home until he had made a complete recovery.

"I appreciated it," Larson recalled. In fact, he never forgot Toni's motherly concern for him—Toni, who had never had children of her own. How could he refuse her now?

Larson knew that house well. He had joined George and Toni for candlelit dinners there, dining on Shrimp Newberg that Toni served with a silver ladle. Now Larson was about to reenter that house, where his friend had died a violent death, allegedly by his own hand.

For his part, Larson tried to keep a safe distance from the controversy swarming around Reeves's death. He certainly felt that George had had every right to be profoundly depressed about his acting career. Helen Bessolo contacted Larson when she heard of his arrival in the city. She had wanted to meet with him, to find out if he had any new pieces of the puzzle. "But I never phoned her," Larson remembered. "I was depressed about it all. I didn't know anything, and so I didn't want to talk to her. Out of politeness, I should have . . . but I didn't."

But refusing Toni was another matter. Larson remembered that George "had nearly always spoken of Helen and his ex-wife in a begrudging way. . . . George seemed to have very mixed feelings about his mother. He didn't speak well of her. . . . Toni he truly loved."

So Toni Mannix and Jack Larson drove up Benedict Canyon one bright day and entered the house. Larson recalled how there was "a lot of beautiful pine and maple, and Toni kept looking at things which 'this other woman' had done—such as painting all the wood furniture white enamel. She called her 'that whore. That whore did this . . . look what that whore did!' "

They went through the house, Toni incensed at Leonore's violations of her expensive décor. In each room Toni would pick up a particularly nice object and give it to Jack—a marble lamp, the silver ladle that had been a gift to George from Toni. Then she wanted to go upstairs.

"By that time," Larson explained, "I wanted out of the house very urgently. But I went upstairs with her, and she was looking at everything, figuring out what needed to be done."

They entered George's bedroom. Larson remembers that the only window in that room was in the adjoining bathroom, which must have made the small, thirteen-by-thirteen-foot room even more claustrophobic. The bedroom furniture had also been painted with white enamel. Larson began to hyperventilate—he did not want to be there. He went into the bathroom to get a breath of clean air and immediately laid eyes on the ball of streaked and stained sheets in the bathtub.

"They hadn't cleaned up the place. The bloody sheets were there. . . . With that, I started feeling very faint. I thought I was going to pass out. I got overwhelmed. While I was looking at all that dried blood, I began to hear a pounding."

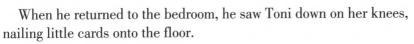
When he returned to the bedroom, he saw Toni down on her knees, nailing little cards onto the floor.

"What are you doing, Toni?"

Toni was tacking Catholic prayer cards over the bullet holes in George's room. "She was a very devout Catholic," Larson explained. "And she had gotten little cards that were exorcisms, little blessings against evil. . . . She had to point the bullet holes out to me, they weren't all that big, but I did see these two bullet holes. I saw them with my own eyes."

Finally, Jack insisted on leaving.

"No." Toni stopped him. "We have to figure out what we have to do with the house."

It dawned on Larson that Toni wanted the two of them to come back and do all of the patchwork and painting that needed doing. She wanted him to help her fix up the house. "Everything was very pulled together and polished in Toni's life," Larson recalled. "No ragged edges, certainly no bullet holes." He told Toni that whatever she wanted him to do, they would have to do it now. "I'm not going to come back to this house. And you and I are not going to fix up this house together, because I'm not coming here ever again."

When they left the house, they got into Toni's car. Toni just sat there for a few minutes. Larson was anxious to leave, overcome by the experience, but Toni couldn't bear to depart. She leaned back from the steering wheel in the sunlight and said in her Jean Harlow voice, "I never would have believed that my love affair would have ended in tragedy."

Larson was touched by that. He didn't say a word as they pulled out into the sparse traffic on Benedict Canyon and sped away, the wind in their hair and the sunlight reflected off the shiny hood of the car.

• • •

By the end of the summer of 1959, the police investigation into George Reeves's death had come to an end. Helen Bessolo still withheld George's body from burial, in the hope that someone, somewhere, might come up with the answer to the most fundamental of questions: Who killed my son? Many were horrified that Helen continued to refuse to bury George, including family members. It was strange enough that Helen believed that she could remove the stain of suicide by proving that George had been murdered by a disreputable woman involved in a love triangle. But she felt that the truth would be buried with her son, so she kept him aboveground.

• • •

In the weeks following George's death, Toni became convinced that George had been tricked into killing himself by playing Russian roulette. Jack Larson noticed the changes taking place in Toni, especially when she began telling him things that Larson knew were patently untrue, such as, "That boy was like a son to Mr. Mannix and me."

"I had heard them talk about their sex life—I'd heard them congratulate themselves on how good they were in bed the night before. But she got it into her head that George was just like a son to Mr. Mannix and her. But, of course, they were all in a state of grace then, including Eddie Mannix. They were very devoted and would go around to children's hospitals on Sundays after church."

Once the official police investigation had come to an end, Toni shared her theory about George's death with Jack Larson. "Maybe I'm the only one who knows her theory," Jack explained one evening after a long thunderstorm had damaged the roof of his house and soaked dozens of letters and photographs. "Actually, I recently found it written down on a damp piece of paper. It was in my bedroom for a long time. I wrote down some things Toni had said to me. She thought that they had all played Russian roulette that night. She thought that George was not going to marry Leonore Lemmon, so Leonore put [extra bullets] in the chamber so that it would kill him. That's what Toni believed."

Art Weissman would come to the same conclusion. But their explanation leaves one little detail unaccounted for: On her first day back in the house after George's death—her first visit back since Leonore Lemmon ousted her six months earlier—how is it that Toni Mannix knew exactly where to look to find the two bullet holes in the floor of George's bedroom?

"She had to point the bullet holes out to me, they weren't all that big," Larson has said. It had taken a return visit by Sergeant V. A. Peterson to find those bullet holes, and he had to lift up the rug in order to find them. Two things emerge from this: Since there were no holes in the rug in George's room, then somebody had covered up those holes after the bullets had been fired. And Toni—who arrived armed with Catholic devotional cards—knew exactly where to find them. Had Toni somehow slipped into the house that night—could she have been a witness to a killing?

Others wondered if Toni had simply visited the death house before she corraled Jack Larson into accompanying her. Constance Shirley thought so, but Phyllis Coates has always wondered how Toni knew so much about George's death just hours after the fatal shooting. The existence of the two extra bullet holes were, after all, reported in the *Los Angeles Times* on June 26. Toni could easily have slipped into the house, using her own key, after Peterson had rolled back the rug. She could have spotted those incriminating gouges in the floorboards of George's room and returned later with Larson to perform her ritual of salvation. Of all their mutual friends, young Larson would have asked the fewest questions.

On July 10, 1959, George Reeves's will was filed in Superior Court. Toni officially inherited the house at 1579 Benedict Canyon. Helen Bessolo tried to stop the transfer of property by filing a lawsuit that was eventually thrown out of court. When Helen Bessolo called Jerry Giesler's office to discuss her case against Toni, her discussion with his secretary gave her a funny feeling. She immediately sensed that the celebrity lawyer was avoiding her, although Helen had paid Giesler close to $50,000 to keep the investigation going.

By now, Helen had decided to remain in California where her son had spent most of his life, so she arranged to sell her house in Galesburg and ship her belongings west.

A curious thing happened by the end of the first week following Reeves's death. The story of the late-night shooting, the controversy over the will, the flurry of speculations as Toni and Leonore fought over George's estate, the dramatic entrance of Helen Bessolo and Jerry Giesler into the case, the results of the second autopsy: It all just slipped off the front pages.

The Hollywood writer and journalist Joe Hyams had become interested in the controversy surrounding Reeves's death, and he thought it was significant that the newspapers suddenly backed off, leaving all those questions hanging. Hyams familiarized himself with the official version of the case: how Reeves had politely excused himself from his guests, had gone upstairs, and had then fired a slug into his brain. It was the discovery of the two additional bullet holes that first caught Hyams's attention. "It just takes one to kill you," Hyams would later explain. "You don't usually fire two more after you're dead. Unless you're firing through the floor or up at the roof to get the attention of the people down below [before] killing yourself."

Hyams made an attempt to reach Leonore Lemmon in New York, but she refused to speak with him, at last heeding Edward Bennett Williams's advice to keep her mouth shut. But the name Mannix was a red flag to Hyams. He was used to men like Eddie using their power to put the truth out of reach. The studios had always exercised control over what went into the newspapers. Hyams knew that Mannix worked through Howard Strickling, the likable head of publicity for MGM who had very persuasive ways of handling the press.

The news announcement of George's will had been a public relations debacle for the Mannixes, seriously compromising Toni's reputation. What had been a Hollywood secret was now the subject of speculation for the whole country. So Eddie did what he had done hundreds of times before: He called up Strickling, the man they called "the fixer," and put him to work on damage control.

"Strickling usually came up with a cover story," Hyams explained. "He'd say, 'Lay off it if you can, I'll give you another story.' He was a very bright, very sharp guy." But it was too late to suppress news of the contents of George's will, so Strickling came up with a plan. George's will would be recast: No longer the residue of their long love affair, it would become a means of carrying on the charity work the two had engaged in throughout George's career as Superman. Eddie's name would appear prominently in the press release, and Toni would specify which charities would receive the proceeds from George's estate.

Toni had been strangely quiet through all of the news accounts of Reeves's death. The only peep heard out of her, thanks to Strickling, was her very ladylike statement: "Mr. Mannix and I have been friends of George Reeves for a number of years. I was particularly interested in and supported the work he was doing for children through the Myasthenia Gravis Foundation and the leukemia research work at The City of Hope, as well as the many appearances he made on behalf of charities and aid to stricken children. I intend to continue this work." That discreet little statement, written by Strickling, was accompanied by that beautiful photograph of Toni, a cross around her lovely throat, respectable, dignified, untouched by it all.

MGM was able to exercise power over the press because so many reporters, including Joe Hyams, were to some extent beholden to the studios. If they barred a journalist, he or she couldn't get on the lots to cover a story or interview a star. "All of us were competing for news. . . . We tried to maintain good relations with the studios," Hyams remembers. "No one breathed on me about the Reeves story, because

Sam Kashner & Nancy Schoenberger

I didn't cover it. But I was aware of pressure. I wasn't expressing an active interest in the case at the time, but the word was out, we were being shut down, or at the very least they were making it more difficult to get the story. Someone had picked up the telephone and was pulling in a favor."

"Now Strickling, Mannix—they never made those phone calls themselves," according to Hyams. "Someone who knew both men made the calls. Someone who worked for them. Strong-arm tactics wouldn't have worked. It was smooth. It was nicely done. 'Hey, you do this—we won't forget it.' "

Not only did MGM have influence over certain stories the newspapers did or did not cover, the long arm of the studio reached into the Los Angeles Police Department as well. Hyams found that out when he tried to get access to the photographs of Reeves's second autopsy, the one Curphey performed that revealed multiple bruises on the body. All the photos—inexplicably—had disappeared.

"You've got to see it working several ways," insists Hyams. "One way is that the LAPD has always had a close relationship with all the major studios. And when an officer from the LAPD retired in the late 1940s and throughout the '50s, he could be assured of a job as a studio security guard or with the studio itself. And therefore things that might have appeared on a police blotter, to say nothing of crime-scene or autopsy photographs, were cut off at the source. A friend from the coroner's office told me when I asked to see them that Reeves's autopsy photos were missing."

In the years since George Reeves's death, those photographs have never turned up. Who ordered their disappearance? If they were destroyed, who destroyed them, and why?

Hyams believes that Eddie Mannix was responsible for the disappearance of the autopsy photographs. "That was Eddie's department: the police and their relationship with MGM. A police officer might think, 'Well, I may be retiring in three years, I'll have a job, so I'll keep this one to myself a little bit, deep-six the crime-scene evidence, get rid of the photographs, make sure Mrs. Mannix is in no way disturbed.' "

But who was Eddie protecting? No one had brought up his name as a possible suspect in this case—Eddie Mannix's tolerance for his wife's affair was well known, and even if he had acted against George out of jealousy, why now? Why do so long after the affair had ended? Maybe Eddie just didn't want anyone coming around asking his wife any questions. She was losing it, and that scared Eddie. He certainly didn't want the nosy newspaper boys airing his bloody laundry in public; you can bet that "Delilah" story cost some poor schmuck in the MGM publicity department his job. Eddie saw to it that Toni was protected. George Reeves had no one protecting him. But Eddie didn't want his wife disturbed. Let her lose her marbles in privacy, if that's what she was going to do. It's humiliating enough to have everyone know you're a cuckold, but to have her carry on that way over some dead actor who wore tights for a living . . . it was too much. So the MGM machinery still worked, even now, when the studio had given up so much ground to television and with all the little nobodies making a fortune in the new media.

So for Joe Hyams—a pal of Humphrey Bogart, a fixture at Chasen's—the death of Superman was no big deal. Reeves was just another has-been actor who fell through the cracks and wound up entertaining kids on television, a guy who had had to spend his days trussed up in a harness pretending to fly. But the bloodhound in Hyams noticed how quickly Reeves and the death of Superman and all its unsolved riddles and contradictory statements dropped from the front pages, even as various stories of what occurred that night spun off into different directions and new bullet holes seemed to appear like stigmatas in the beamed ceiling and fireplace panel of George's Benedict Canyon home.

• • •

Meanwhile, Leonore Lemmon remained secluded in her mother's apartment on the East Side of New York. Edward Bennett Williams, who was seeing a lot of the ex-café-society girl, convinced her to drop her case contesting George's will and her futile search for a second will. He also destroyed a bizarre letter she wrote, demanding to take possession of George's corpse.

Leonore insisted to her lawyer that her wishes to have George's body cremated be honored by the family. She claimed that George had expressed the desire to be cremated and what Mrs. Bessolo was doing in keeping the body around "was a disgrace." Williams's secretary remembered that she sent a copy of her letter to the office, and that "Mr. Williams just threw it in the wastebasket. She had no legal rights in that matter." But Leonore persisted. She called Williams and demanded that he get her access to George's body—"It's my stiff!" she kept saying. "We were going to be married—you figure it out!"

Sam Kashner & Nancy Schoenberger

Was Leonore afraid of another autopsy? Was there something Cur-phey had failed to find that Leonore knew was there, waiting, just wait-ing for the right kind of investigation?

Within a few weeks of the killing, Leonore had given up the pretense of mourning—had "hung up her veil," as a friend put it—and she began going out on the town. She looked for an apartment to rent, ide-ally one where, on a clear day, "You can see Bergdorf's or Saks Fifth Avenue." Leonore had always liked to drink, but after George's death she began to drink more and more, with a kind of abandon that hadn't been present before. She liked to hold court at an Irish pub called Neary's, run by a fellow named Jimmy Neary, an old-style restaurateur in an old-style watering hole. She would sit at the bar and drink Jimmy Neary's whiskey and complain about how the people in California treated her "in a very bad fashion. I don't know the reason," she'd say, "but they were very bad to me."

Edward Bennett Williams knew that Leonore was incapable of telling the same story twice—in her own words, she was "a terrible blabber-mouth"—and he was concerned about her. He was, in fact, in love with her. In 1959, before the heavy drinking took its toll, Leonore Lemmon still had allure. The dapper lawyer who specialized in defending mob-sters had fallen for his client. Leonore could still exude tremendous lustiness and wit. Williams tracked her down one afternoon in a little dress shop on Fifth Avenue and, while she was trying on a suit, asked her to marry him.

"You're some kind of wacko!" was her sweet reply. "You're already married!"

"Don't worry about that," he implored her in his smoothest voice.

"I don't care how brilliant you are in court," she said. "You're not dealing with a full deck!" And with that, Leonore left the shop, the rich-est lawyer in America looking longingly after her. She liked Williams, she respected Williams, she needed Williams, but she found him "an exceedingly dull man." And that was that.

In the weeks following George's death, no one in the Los Angeles Police Department made a move to bring Leonore back to Los Angeles to answer questions. Nor did anyone bat an eyelash when she made her plans to leave the country, to return to England where she had made such a hit on the social scene following her divorce from Jakie Webb. But if she had wanted to get away from what happened in the Benedict Canyon house that night, she was not successful. The prominent English and American families—the Churchills, the Harrimans, the Vanderbilts, the ones who had once been so charmed by her—didn't treat her quite the same way. She wasn't invited to their country homes. "She was off-limits," recalled a girlfriend who made the trip with her. "They all wanted to know who really did it—it was a great mystery story—but none of them wanted to hear it from the horse's mouth. She had become too much of a scandal for them."

By the time Leonore returned to New York, Williams was even more worried about her, especially when she let it slip that she had started carrying a gun.

• • •

In the weeks following Reeves's death, Jerry Giesler had made a lot of public accusations, telling reporters that "the Reeves death case is full of phony angles." By mid-July, he dropped the case.

Helen realized something was wrong when her lawyer stopped returning her phone calls. The weekly jawboning sessions at her house in Pasadena had tapered off. By September, they had all stopped coming. Helen sat there among the coffee cups and sandwiches because no one had told her the meetings were over. There was just nothing more to discuss, until Giesler called her one day to say that he was withdrawing from the case. "It's in everyone's best interest to end the investigation at this point," he told Helen. Giesler agreed to send over one of his investigators to "clean up some loose ends," adding that he wouldn't charge her for that visit.

Helen was incensed. She couldn't believe that Giesler had just suddenly decided that the coroner was right all along and that George's death was by his own hand. Giesler was dropping the case because he was afraid.

Giesler didn't scare easily, but one of the detectives with whom he had worked on the case remembered that the unflappable lawyer had "gotten some letters that were a little frightening." And Wendy Barrett Levine, a former secretary in the defense attorney's office, explained, "I think Mr. Giesler had reached the point of believing that it was probable that George Reeves had been murdered." Whatever Giesler found out, however, he wasn't telling. "There are some dangerous people involved in this case," he warned Mrs. Bessolo. "It's better to drop it."

Giesler had made his practice by defending the rich and powerful and the wives of rich and powerful men. His antagonists had often been young women, without means and "without access to justice," in Giesler's cynical terms. The Reeves case was different, however. His client, Mrs. Bessolo, was rich enough, but she wasn't powerful. And the interests against her, Giesler discovered, were the ones with the power. The tables were turned on Jerry Giesler: He had always been on the side of Hollywood royalty and the studios, but now it looked like the "Reeves death case" was heading him in the opposite direction, and he didn't like it. "Drop the case, Mrs. Bessolo," he said. "You just don't want to know."

• • •

Giesler refused to tell Helen exactly what he had found out, but the case files soon to be locked away by the Nick Harris Agency pointed to one thing: that an element of organized crime was involved in George's death. The question was, who among George's intimates had the capability of using professional criminals? Leonore had always bragged of her love for "old-style gangsters" like Frank Costello.

It was more likely, Giesler discovered, that Eddie Mannix was the nexus at which Reeves and the hoodlum population of Los Angeles crossed paths. Milo Spiriglio, then a young detective on his first job for the Nick Harris Agency, thought that Eddie Mannix had in fact been originally brought to Hollywood by New Jersey Palisades Park owner Nicholas Schenck, to watch over his financial interests at MGM. Eddie had indeed worked for Nick Schenck when he was a young tough guy back in New Jersey. While his brother Joseph Schenck was founding Twentieth Century Productions, Nick Schenck developed the theater chain that became known as Loew's Consolidated Enterprises; he then became president of Loew's and financial controller of MGM. Nick Schenck hired Eddie to keep an eye on Louis B. Mayer; he wanted someone there who would be entirely loyal to him. But Mayer ended up hiring Eddie to do his dirty work. So Eddie Mannix was put in charge of the world's biggest candy store, in Culver City. It was always old-home week when any of the boys from New Jersey came out West to visit their old pal Eddie, to see how well he was doing.

But a new crop of even more dangerous boys had sprung up in southern California since the late 1940s. In fact, things had become so serious that the day George Reeves died, the California Assembly in

Sacramento released a report on a two-year investigation concluding that "organized crime exists to an alarmingly dangerous degree in California." The newspapers were full of the connection between the Hollywood studios and organized crime the week of Reeves's death. And though it never became public knowledge, Eddie Mannix was good friends with a runty ex-boxer and gambling czar named Mickey Cohen, who worked for Benjamin "Bugsy" Siegel and took over his smaller gambling interests after Siegel was rubbed out. The more powerful crime leadership of Frank Carbo and the Dragna family took control of the rest of Siegel's West Coast operation.

Cohen, described in the newspapers as "a pouty-lipped little ex-gambling czar," was barely five-foot-two, a hot-headed thug with a taste for beautifully tailored suits. He was being linked in the Sacramento State Assembly report on organized crime to everything from assault to bookmaking to a sprinkling of gangland murders. The plump, baby-faced gangster gained notoriety over his statements made on national television: "I've killed no one that in the first place didn't deserve killing," he said. "In all of these . . . I had no alternative. It was either my life or their life."

Cohen used to brag about the fact that he handled as much as $600,000 a day in illegal bets. Mannix had known Cohen back in Jersey when the two of them were fledgling boxers, roaming the Palisades with Cohen's manager, Harry Rudolph. The two men had remained boxing fans. Eddie used to visit his old friend at the Carousel, a Los Angeles ice-cream parlor Cohen ran as a social club for wise guys before he took a little side trip to McNeil Island Penitentiary in Puget Sound, in the mid 1950s, on income-tax evasion.

When Mickey got out of prison in 1955, he was broke. He couldn't raise funds anywhere, and he didn't want to get himself beholden to the East Coast mobsters he knew. Eddie was a big help, securing a large loan for his old pal so that Mickey could set up a nice little haberdashery business. Eddie would come away from Cohen's establishment with a new suit and an earful of stories about guys they had known back East. How Jimmy Utley got blackjacked in front of a lunch crowd at Lucy's back in '46 for trying to run some offshore gambling operation without Mickey's blessing. "Utley wound up in prison," Mickey told Eddie, "busted for conspiracy."

"Conspiracy? Conspiracy to commit what, Mick?"

"Illegal surgery," replied Cohen.

Sam Kashner & Nancy Schoenberger

Eddie asked about Mickey's former boxing manager, Harry Rudolph, also known as Matchmaker Babe McCoy. Besides Cohen, McCoy once managed the boxer Art Aragon. "Aragon would punch a guy through a wall and call it a work of Art," Cohen said. That one always cracked up Eddie Mannix. When a guy named Henry Maltin, a fountain man at Schwab's Drugstore over on Sunset, tried to fix a fight between Aragon and another "House of David" palooka named Dick Goldstein, McCoy complained to Eddie Mannix. Mannix told Cohen, who walked into Schwab's one day and attacked poor Henry, pouring an egg cream down his pants and lunging for him across the counter. "Start running or I'll be back with my boys and we'll take care of you," he growled at the hapless soda jerk. Eddie was at ringside, sporting a grin as big as a round card, the night Art Aragon cleaned Dick Goldstein's clock.

Their friendly conversations usually took place in front of a three-way mirror in Cohen's haberdashery while a tailor stuck a few pins into the hem of Eddie's pants leg. Somehow Giesler had found out that George Reeves had been a topic of discussion at one of those intimate little meetings. Why would Eddie bring George's name into anything, especially when talking to one of the boys? Maybe he was sick and tired of his wife carrying on about her "luv affahr," maybe he was sick and tired of her weeping and her raging, sick of having to hear "Faster than a speeding bullet . . ." coming from the television set in Toni's bedroom.

But how did Giesler find out about Cohen and Mannix's conversation? Giesler had once successfully defended Ben Siegel in a murder rap, and when Mickey Cohen took over a number of Siegel's gambling operations, he inherited some of Siegel's lieutenants—men whom Giesler relied on for information. Men like Harry Schwartz, a colorful figure from New Jersey who kept Jerry Giesler's business card in his wallet and who was a confidante of Mickey Cohen.

In 1959, the "assembly rackets committee" could barely bring itself to recognize the existence of the Mafia. They called it "the ruling house of crime, an international syndicate held together by bloodlines." Nowadays, there are no secrets in the ruling house. Nick Pileggi, the author of *Wise Guy* and an authority on organized crime, has said, "The Boy Scouts have more secrets than the mob these days." But in the 1950s, nobody talked and the secrets were kept.

14

WHAT HELEN KNEW

"Her gun began making little cameo appearances," remembered one of Leonore Lemmon's New York friends. "I knew she carried it all the time. I remember once waiting for her to get dressed for the evening and her saying that she was going to put it in her compact. I thought nothing of it until I saw the gun. That's what she was putting into her bag. A friend of mine, a physician, said that she shot out a street lamp once, at a party. He'd never seen anything like it from a woman dressed to the nines."

Her friends started noticing a change in Leonore's behavior after her return from Europe. She seemed nervous—paranoid, even. If she thought someone had followed her into a restaurant, there'd be the little snap of her purse opening up, with the gun nestled among her lipsticked tissues and five-dollar bills. Once a taxi driver had the misfortune to get lost with Leonore as his passenger. She got it into her head that she was being kidnapped, and she started screaming bloody murder. The cabbie dropped her off near Grant's Tomb on Riverside Drive, and Leonore just stood there, yelling her head off. Whatever had happened to Leonore that night in Benedict Canyon—whatever she had witnessed or participated in—it was clear that she was now the one afraid for her life.

Everywhere she went, the story of her doomed bridegroom preceded her. *The Adventures of Superman* had slipped quietly into syndication shortly after Reeves's death, so now the show was inescapable as well. If anything, the television show and George Reeves were even more popular now that he was dead. As always in show business, death had been the ultimate career move. But poor Leonore—the one thing that had now made her truly famous she wasn't even allowed to talk about. And she no longer wanted to talk about it. Something had changed. What had looked like guilt to many of George's friends, to Jerry Giesler, and even to Edward Bennett Williams, was, in actuality, not guilt but fear.

• • •

The lies had come full circle. Helen Bessolo had spent much of her life dissembling to "protect" George, to improve their situation, their standing in life. Now that he was dead, all she wanted was the truth. She didn't even care so much anymore who did it—who was responsible for her son's death. A rigorous Catholic all her life, Helen couldn't face the idea that her son had committed the mortal sin of self-murder. It wasn't that long ago that a suicide could not even be buried in sanctified ground. Maybe that was one reason why she couldn't bear to bury her son. What if somebody complained? What if the church came forward and forbad George's burial in holy ground? She had had an Episcopal priest perform the funeral rites, just in case there were complaints. And she waited a very long time before disposing of the body. She didn't want to get into the whole ugly business with a Catholic priest as to whether her son had committed a mortal sin against his soul. Anything would be better than that. But all they were able to give her—Chief Parker, Dr. Curphey, now Jerry Giesler—were lies.

• • •

Giesler, meanwhile, had spent the last year working up his memoirs with a writer named Pete Martin: a compilation of twenty-four of his most most famous and dramatic cases including defending Errol Flynn, Charles Chaplin, Ruth Etting, Kid McCoy, Ben Siegel, Robert Mitchum, Edward G. Robinson's son, and Busby Berkeley. In his memoirs, published by Simon and Schuster in 1960 under the title *The Jerry Giesler Story,* the criminal lawyer aired some of his pet peeves, including his dislike of the term "criminal lawyer": "If a lawyer is a criminal, he should be clapped into jail like any other offender. What I really am is a defense lawyer," he wrote. He also modestly refers to his reputation as "the magnificent mouthpiece," quoting the oft-used phrase, "If it's murder, they call Jerry Giesler first. Then they call the doctor. Then they call the police." (Giesler demurs: "the doctor, the police, *then* me.")

Curiously, there is no mention of George Reeves, Helen Bessolo, Chief Parker, or Theodore Curphey anywhere in his book, written in the throes of one of his most famous cases. Giesler loved publicity and always saw the benefit of good public relations. Why did he leave out all mention of the Reeves case? Had he been so scared off the scene by his discovery of Eddie Mannix and possibly Mickey Cohen at the core of the case that he no longer wanted any public identification with George and Helen? Giesler called up his old friend Edward Rose, husband to Reeves's first and only wife, Ellanora. Giesler warned his friend to stay out of it. Ellanora and Nati Vacio had, understandably, become interested in the truth about George's death, but Giesler suggested to Rose that he tell his wife to stop asking questions. "There are dangerous men involved here," he cautioned. Meanwhile, operatives from the Nick Harris Detective Agency, who were quickly dropped by Giesler (though Helen continued to pay for their services), noticed that Giesler—like Leonore Lemmon—had started carrying a gun.

So Helen took it upon herself to have George's body removed from the Westwood Memorial Cemetery mausoleum and sent to Cincinnati General Hospital. From there she planned to lay her son to rest in the family crypt in Cincinnati's Spring Grove Cemetery, but first she wanted one more chance to prove to herself that George had not committed a mortal sin. However, Helen had more battles to fight just to get a second opinion.

The Association of Cincinnati Morticians protested what they saw as the mishandling of George's body. They didn't want George's corpse brought to Cincinnati, and they didn't want to get involved in such a high-profile, controversial case. However, Helen persuaded the two pathologists, Dr. Alan Moritz and Dr. Frank Cleveland of Kettering Laboratories, to conduct a third autopsy on George's badly decomposing body. Maybe this time George's corpse would name his own killer.

Soon photographs of the Cincinnati autopsy were being shown around the hospital, illegally copied and passed around like dirty pictures in a schoolyard. They still crop up from year to year in strange places, such as Superman memorabilia shows, changing hands among avid Superman fans. Certain collectors who have stumbled across the gruesome photographs refer to them as "the summer camp photos," a cheery euphemism that adds irony to the cold facts of Reeves's death.

In the autopsy photographs, Reeves's skin is mottled like aged bark. Even though the body had been embalmed, the tissue had begun to crumble like old icing on a stale cake. The top of his skull had been surgically removed in a "monk's cap," revealing how little damage actually was done to the brain, packed tight as a walnut in the hard case of the skull. There's Reeves's unmistakable Roman nose, the neat, almost grim mouth. The skin and musculature of one calf has deteriorated badly, like a leg of mutton that's been picked at by a finicky diner. When public figures die, they simply disappear. They exchange one unreal realm for another. But the "summer camp photos" are absolute proof of George Reeves's mortality.

Dr. Moritz sent the horrific photographs to Helen Bessolo's home.

After the examination, Dr. Moritz walked down the corridor and into a small, cluttered office. The young medical examiner then did an extraordinary thing, according to Sergeant Peterson of the LAPD. He picked up the phone and dialed a number written down on the back of a skinny slip of paper that had come out of one of those fortune cookies that every Chinese restaurant in America serves up after a meal. A few nights earlier, an LAPD detective had arrived in Cincinnati and had introduced himself as someone from Chief Parker's precinct who was involved in the case.

The man had approached Dr. Moritz and arranged to meet him at a Chinese restaurant not far from the hospital. Over chop suey and moo goo gai pan, the detective asked that if the doctor's findings revealed anything that had been overlooked by Dr. Curphey's examination, would he call Chief Parker and let him know? As a courtesy, of course, before releasing his findings. Before telling Mrs. Bessolo.

Dr. Moritz had never been involved in a case like Reeves's before. At first glance, it still looked like a police matter, even though the LAPD had washed their hands of it. Dr. Moritz's only client here was the corpse's mother, Mrs. Bessolo. But here was this detective writing down the police chief's private number on the back of Dr. Moritz's fortune. The good doctor glanced at the phone number, then turned the slip of paper over and read his fortune: "It is better to deal with problems before they arise." He smiled a weak sort of smile as the detective got up to pay the check. The two men parted company, and the detective returned on the next flight back to Los Angeles. He had probably flown in on the very airplane that had carried George Reeves's corpse to Cincinnati: the detective sitting in coach class smoking a cigarette while Reeves's body, packed in dry ice, rode the air currents in baggage.

And so Dr. Moritz picked up the phone in his hospital office—a tiny, almost airless room with piles of old medical records stacked against

Sam Kashner & Nancy Schoenberger

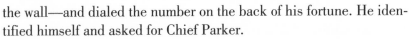

the wall—and dialed the number on the back of his fortune. He identified himself and asked for Chief Parker.

"Speaking," came the husky voice on the other end of the line. Every time the speaker breathed, a wheeze rattled from deep inside his chest.

Dr. Moritz told the voice on the telephone that there wasn't anything in his examination that could contradict Dr. Curphey's original findings. There was nothing there inconsistent with a verdict of suicide.

"That's good news," whistled the voice.

Dr. Moritz got off the phone feeling like he had just been given a good-citizenship badge.

When he heard about the phone call, Sergeant Peterson was disappointed that Dr. Moritz had found nothing inconsistent with Dr. Curphey's findings. Of course, the body was in such a state of decomposition, there just wasn't enough to go on.

Dr. Moritz told the *Los Angeles Herald Examiner* that he and his colleagues had found nothing to contradict the original findings of Dr. Curphey and the Los Angeles coroner's office. Once again, there was no mention of powder burns or stippling on Reeves's hands or temple. The autopsy was inconclusive. No one wanted to extrapolate on the absence of powder burns, especially since the corpse was no longer in pristine condition. Chief Parker had sent one of his police detectives to make sure that Moritz wasn't about to drop a bombshell. He was satisfied with the outcome.

• • •

Helen was, without doubt, disappointed in the results of the third and final autopsy. She could do no more, so she cancelled her plans to have him buried in Cincinnati and arranged to have George's body cremated, the ashes sent to her home in Pasadena, where for some time she kept them in an urn on her mantelpiece. It was still hard for her to give up her boy entirely. She had always kept a little shrine to George; now she papered her house with George's photographs, setting up what was effectively the world's first Superman Museum.

Meanwhile, Milo Spiriglio, the youngest operative with the Nick Harris Detective Agency in the Reeves investigation, got restless. He took out the files and began poring over them. He had done a lot of the preliminary research in the case, such as investigating the relationship between Eddie Mannix and Nicholas Schenck.

The young detective showed up at Helen Bessolo's door and offered to continue with the investigation. Helen had already enlisted her son's oldest friend, Nati Vacio, from their Pasadena Playhouse days, to help her continue the investigation on her own, now that Giesler was out of the picture. It was surprising to Helen to see how Nati Vacio had grown up and changed over the years. He was now a middle-aged man, still devoted to the memory of his friend and to Helen, whom he pledged to help. He was no longer the boyish youth who used to strum guitar and sing with George in more innocent days. Back then, a million years ago, the two young acting students were sure they were going to be stars. Helen sometimes wondered if her son's fame had made Nati feel passed over. Now George's career was finished, and Nati was the lucky one. He was alive.

So the three of them drove all over Los Angeles for the next few months, speaking with anyone who had had anything to do with George in the weeks before his death.

They spoke to the mechanic who had worked on George's Jaguar and who had first noticed that the brake fluid had been drained from the car. They spoke to the locksmith who had disappeared the day before George's death, leaving the original locks in place on the French doors leading out to the backyard. They spoke to the doctor at Cedars of Lebanon Hospital who had stitched up George's head wound and had given him Demerol for his pain after his car crack-up.

"Everybody was very polite, and sorry, and apologized for not being more helpful," recalled Spiriglio. He did remember, however, that when they queried Sergeant Peterson—who, alone among the LAPD, had felt that George's was a suspicious case—Peterson told them that the Luger was registered to Eddie Mannix and that the gun handle had been oiled so that no fingerprints could be lifted from the weapon. That fact alone, Peterson thought, was extremely unusual, and should have alarmed Chief Parker. But then, everything about this case should have alarmed the police chief.

The young detective would later conclude that Chief Parker willfully ignored the evidence and closed the case due to pressure from Eddie Mannix.

Just three years after George's death, Chief Parker would become embroiled in the debacle of the Marilyn Monroe case. Norman Mailer and others have suggested that Parker was promised a plum Justice Department appointment by the Kennedy administration if he sat on the

Sam Kashner & Nancy Schoenberger

Monroe dossier and made sure Curphey came up with a suicide verdict. Today it is only a matter of argument as to how far the official misconduct extended. But at the very least, Chief Parker was implicated in nearly every scenario involving the investigation of Monroe's death by drug overdose. "There was a lot of corruption in those days," explains Spiriglio, who now owns and operates the Nick Harris Detective Agency. "Parker was a heavy drinker. Depending on who you talk to, he was either well loved or well hated. There was a lot of corruption back then. . . ."

Spiriglio handed Mrs. Bessolo a list of about thirteen people whom the agency felt were implicated in George's death. But Helen felt that there wasn't enough to go on. "She didn't want to press charges against any of them," Nati Vacio has said. Vacio thought her reluctance was due to the fact that she didn't want to stir up any more trouble, she had just wanted to assure herself that her son had not committed suicide.

But it's more likely that she realized that chief among the list of names loomed the familiar name of Eddie Mannix. And Eddie Mannix—though weak as a kitten and confined to a wheelchair—was still very much alive. While it was clear to Helen and anyone else who knew the Mannixes that Eddie was too ill to show up anywhere, the Nick Harris Detective Agency had been pretty sure of one little fact that the police department showed no interest in pursuing: that there had been a sixth person present in the house that night.

• • •

By now Helen knew that the police would never question Eddie Mannix. That's what really galled her. Eddie and Toni sat up there in their gated mansion, like Olympic gods who had sacrificed one of their favorites, swatting him down like a fly, just because they could get away with it. Eddie had no doubt sent someone to Chief Parker, maybe meeting him behind the cabbage stall at the farmer's market, to tell him that Eddie might want to show his appreciation some time soon and that this case should stay a suicide. Parker was told before they ever discovered the bullet holes, before the case was ever reopened, that it had to remain that way.

Though physically and emotionally exhausted by the ordeal, Helen tried one more time to have the case reopened. By now, however, she was conveniently relegated to the status of "kook" by most members of the LAPD, and her continual complaints were dismissed. And, indeed, she was acting more and more like a kook. She took to attending séances, hoping to contact the spirit of her dead son. Maybe he could give her the lever with which to move the world. Now, she believed that it was Eddie Mannix behind the crime, but she wanted someone else to pull him down from his cloistered mansion. She was a little crazy, perhaps, but not crazy enough to go after her son's killer herself. She wanted someone else to finger him. But Giesler had dropped the case, the Nick Harris Detective Agency officially closed its files, and Chief Parker was not interested.

Gradually Helen Bessolo stopped wanting justice. "She seemed more content," recalled a Bessolo cousin. "Whatever she had found out seemed to satisfy her." She continued to devote her remaining days to building up her shrine to her son. She took to writing things down about George on the backs of photographs. She wrote down her theories and ideas about his death, like captions to a crime no one saw. She was convinced that Eddie had had her son killed, out of jealousy, to make sure that his wife would put the affair behind her and devote the rest of her days to taking care of him as he sank deeper into illness. But if that was his motive, it backfired in a colossal way, because Toni's grief began to unhinge her; she began to turn into a Beverly Hills Miss Haversham, mourning at the altar of a corpse.

Meanwhile, Helen's expensive Pasadena home began to fall into disrepair. She no longer kept up her lawn, her appearance, her status as the well-to-do mother of a television star. She took to buttonholing people who, out of pity, stopped in for briefer and briefer visits: "You know my son was murdered," she'd say, a Kleenex safety-pinned to her housedress and a baleful look in her eye, long after speculation about the Reeves case disappeared from the newspapers and the public mind.

• • •

What Helen Bessolo would never discover is that there were three important discrepancies between the official police version of her son's death and what must have happened that night. Some thirty years after George's death, Leonore Lemmon would give an interview to a young journalist, stopping just short of naming the killers but dropping three bombshells in her rambling discourse. The first bombshell was that William Bliss arrived *alone* on her doorstep, because Carol Van Ronkel was already in the Benedict Canyon house and,

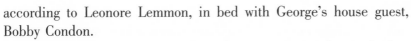

according to Leonore Lemmon, in bed with George's house guest, Bobby Condon.

The second is that George never came downstairs and never had an argument with Bliss, nor with any other persons gathered there that night. He remained alone in his bedroom and was shot just *after* Leonore went downstairs to open the door to Bliss.

The third is that Carol Van Ronkel wasn't present when the police arrived, but Leonore's good friend Gwen Dailey was.

• • •

Based on the evidence from Leonore Lemmon's tape—the so-called "confession" tape made by free-lance writer Lee Saylor over several sultry evenings in 1989, about six months before Lemmon's death—we can now draw conclusions as to what happened that night.

It all began the evening of June 15, 1959, when Leonore Lemmon's party had fizzled out, turning into a gathering of a handful of neighbors. Leonore just wasn't well liked in Beverly Hills. George had stopped seeing his old friends from *The Adventures of Superman.* John Hamilton was dead. Bette and Bob Shayne were too loyal to Toni, and Leonore didn't want anyone throwing her disapproving looks behind George's back. Jack Larson—everybody's favorite kid actor—was in Europe. Nati Vacio, Art Weissman, and Gene La Belle? They made no secret of their disapproval of Leonore. Henny and Jim Backus had shown up the previous night, did not like what they saw, and left. So if a party had been planned to celebrate the couple's impending nuptials, there weren't too many people around who felt like celebrating.

That evening the Van Ronkels—the patriarchal Rip and his young wife Carol—dropped by around 9:00 P.M. Bobby Condon had already flown in from New York, in order to research Archie Moore's autobiography, though it was probably at Leonore's invitation that he was staying with George. Leonore liked to have a lot of people around her—and big good-looking guys were her specialty.

Earlier that day Carol called her friends the Blisses—Bill Bliss and his wife, Jan, who lived farther up Benedict Canyon and were good pals of hers. "Come over to 1579," she told them. "We're having cocktails with some neighbors—you know George, don't you? Used to be Superman? He's marrying a great gal . . ." So Bill Bliss showed up a little after 9:00 P.M., expecting to have a few drinks with Carol, Rip,

Bobby, Leonore, and George, though George seemed to be in a grouchy mood and he spent most of the evening upstairs in his bedroom. At one point he came downstairs completely naked, got into a little argument with Leonore, then went back upstairs. Nobody was fazed; George liked to walk around in the nude. Jan Bliss showed up about twenty minutes later, and caught a glimpse of George through the opened front window just as she was about to knock on the door. It made her uncomfortable— George walking around with his shirt off (which was all she could see through the window), having an argument with Leonore in front of everyone. She decided to skip this particular party and she went home.

Leonore slipped upstairs and came down a little later, dressed to the nines. She was a big woman, and when she went all out, she could knock your socks off. George came downstairs, dressed this time, and the two of them had another cocktail and then left their guests and went out to Chasen's for dinner. Bill Bliss and the Van Ronkels soon left, leaving Bobby Condon alone in the house.

Leonore held court at Chasen's, asking for the house phone and calling up everybody she knew. George drank his scotch straight; Leonore downed a few more vodka martinis. By now George had entered that state of euphoria, as if the top of his head were floating somewhere near the noisy chandeliers, but, as usual, he didn't show it, except for a slight drooping of the eyelids. It was amazing how much he could put away.

While George and Leonore were still at Chasen's, Carol Van Ronkel returned to the Reeves house. Carol—beautiful, clear-eyed Carol with the strong jawline, dark eyebrows, and soft, light hair—waited for Rip to retire for the evening before she drove the mile and a half from her house to George's. It must have been around 10:30 P.M. According to Leonore Lemmon, Carol wore nothing but a negligee as a surprise for Bobby, because, in Leonore's words, "Carol and Bobby were having an affair." They retired to the tiny, upstairs guest bedroom and were apparently asleep in each other's arms when Leonore and George returned from Chasen's around 11:30 P.M.

George was tired and he wanted to sleep. He was scheduled to go two rounds with Archie Moore in two days, and he needed his beauty rest. So George climbed up the carpeted stairs and went to bed around midnight. Leonore lingered in the kitchen for a while, fixing herself another drink, lighting a cigarette, watching the smoke float like a cloud above the empty liquor bottles by the sink. Soon she would be married. She had fallen for that out-of-work actor the moment she'd clapped eyes

Sam Kashner & Nancy Schoenberger

on him. "A helluva nice guy," she liked to say. He never even bothered to wipe her lipstick off his cheek—she liked that about him. He was as big and relaxed as a sofa. She had felt safe with him, upstairs in that suburban bedroom, there in the arms of her Superman.

So Leonore went upstairs and got into bed with George, being careful not to wake him, but for some reason she couldn't sleep. She was uneasy about their upcoming wedding—after all, George was still accepting money from his mother. That made her nervous. And the house was eerily quiet—too quiet. So she got up and went downstairs, noticed that the front porch light was off, and she flipped it back on. She had a funny feeling. There's something strange about tonight, she thought, but she didn't know what it was.

It was nearly midnight. Nobody knew that a guy had shown up in a car and was parked just up the road, on Philbert Drive. He'd been watching the house. He saw people coming and going; he saw some dishy dame in a nightgown knock softly on the front door; he saw George and Leonore return to the house. He knew there were people at home, but by twelve-thirty all was quiet and the lights were off. He was going to go into the house.

Suddenly the man saw a car come roaring down the canyon and park across the street from 1579 Benedict Canyon. It was Bill Bliss—he just seemed to have come out of nowhere, and he walked right up to the house and knocked on the door. The porch light was on, the usual signal that drinks were being served.

"Is the party still going on?" he asked Leonore when she opened the door.

"Who are you?" she said. In her intoxicated state, she barely remembered the guy who described himself as a "heating installations man" but who now seemed very suspicious—even downright shady— standing at the front door.

"Come on, this is Bill Bliss. Remember, I was here earlier? Looks like you still have a party going on. Can I have a drink?"

Those were the magic words for Leonore. She invited Bliss in. As soon as Bliss entered the house, the quiet man biding his time just up the dark street quickly slipped around to the back of the house, taking advantage of the distraction that Bliss had suddenly provided, like manna out of heaven.

"Come in, you nut," Leonore barked. "But George isn't going to like it. . . ." She knew George would be furious with her for inviting someone into the house while he was asleep. She knew how nervous he was about the exhibition match with Archie Moore. Sleep meant more to him now than even staying in shape. But Bliss kept her chatting there by the front door, making small talk, quietly, so as not to wake up George.

Leonore did not know or like Bill Bliss; it's one of the few things she makes clear in her later interview. She had no idea why he was there, but his presence seemed suspicious, even to her, a "drinking girl" from New York who doesn't know how things are done in Beverly Hills. "He was a bad man," she later said, but still she let him into the house.

The back door that led to the patio was locked, but the old lock was still in place because earlier that day, the locksmith had been unable to work on it. The "sixth man," as the Nick Harris operatives referred to him, opened the door with a key that had been given to him and made his way easily upstairs and into George's bedroom at the top of the house. He knew just where to go; he slipped by Bill Bliss and Leonore chatting at the front door.

The Luger was lying right there on the dresser, shining dully in the faint moonlight that seeped in from the bathroom window. He did exactly as he was told, and he picked up the heavy gun.

George woke up, startled to see a stranger in his room. He lunged for the fellow who had suddenly slipped on the floor but rose up on one knee as if he were proposing marriage, in a scene from a romantic comedy at the Pasadena Playhouse. That's when the gun went off, sending a slug through the floorboards in George's room that lodged in the ceiling beam in the living room below.

"I heard a thud," Leonore would later remember. "I heard a thud, and then I heard a shot."

The two men struggled briefly. But George was groggy from sleep and drink and he was quickly overpowered. The gunman pressed Toni Mannix's gun up to George's temple and pulled the trigger. He'd been wearing gloves, but the gun was over-oiled, leaving splotches on his gloves but no fingerprints on the handle of the gun. There were no windows in George's bedroom, but there was one in the adjacent bathroom, so the gunman climbed through it and dropped softly to the ground below. Neighbors would later report that they'd heard a shot, followed by the sound of a car careening off into the night. In a heartbeat, the gunman was history.

Leonore—still trying to figure out why Bill Bliss was standing in her foyer—looked up at the ceiling. What had she heard? "A thud or a shot, or a thud followed by a shot"—she would never be sure.

She turned to Bliss with a look of surprise on her face, and, in a jokey voice, said, "Ah, that's just George, shootin' himself." Before Leonore could think of what to do next, Bliss bounded up the stairs. "I'll check on George," he said over his shoulder. He walked into George's bedroom. George was slumped on the mattress, blood splattered on a wad of sheets at the foot of the bed. A gun lay on the floor at his feet.

The thud Leonore had heard was the muffled sound of the first bullet slamming into the floor. But directly following that thud was his second, fatal shot, and all of a sudden the small house began to fill up with the smell of sulfur.

In the struggle, a single bullet entered George Reeves's right temple just above the ear, exiting the left temple one and three-quarters of an inch above the left ear and lodging in the ceiling. There were now two bullet holes in the floor: one made earlier by Leonore Lemmon and one newly made by the gunman.

Downstairs, a shudder went through Leonore. She just stared as Bliss came downstairs with a grim look on his face. Silence hung in the air like smoke, as if whatever he had to say to Leonore didn't need saying.

By now, Bobby Condon and Carol Van Ronkel had come downstairs, asking what was going on. When they'd heard the muffled shots, Carol probably thought it was just a car backfiring. She lived on that same street and was familiar with the sounds of the night that ricocheted off the canyons and came back like gunfire. But Bobby must have heard voices, so he went downstairs and Carol followed.

Bill Bliss—who was a good friend of Carol's though not especially friendly with Rip Van Ronkel—glanced over at Bobby and Carol and said that George had just shot himself and that he was about to call the police. If he was shocked to see Carol in her nightie with another man, he didn't let on. Death trumps all other scandals. Leonore Lemmon later claimed that Carol wanted to get out of there—she didn't want her husband to know where she was, in a dead man's house in a negligee, so she asked Bliss to wait until she left the premises. But Bliss told her not to worry, he'd take care of everything.

Leonore was in shock. She couldn't believe what had just happened. She had no idea what to do or who to call, so Bliss phoned an old friend at the Beverly Hills Police Department who rushed over, quietly—no ambulance was called, no sirens were heard that night on Benedict Canyon.

When the officer arrived, he and Bliss went upstairs to survey the scene. George looked like a man floating on the surface of a pool, turning his head away from the sun. But the pool was a pool of blood, and a little plaster fell from the ceiling onto the dead man's shoulder.

They seemed to have been upstairs for a very long time. When they finally came back down into the living room, the officer told the assembled group—Leonore, Carol, Bobby—that this really wasn't in the jurisdiction of the Beverly Hills Police Department, that they'd better call the LAPD. With that, he left the premises.

That's when Carol Van Ronkel became upset. "I want to get out of here," she said.

"Not dressed like that, honey," Leonore told her, snapping out of her daze. Even Bliss seemed a little nervous then, not knowing what to do next. This is where Leonore began to figure out a few things, and she knew it was going to look bad for her, with or without Bill Bliss as her alibi. There were people who could testify to the way she and George used to like to play around with that gun. She remembered the bullet hole she had already made in George's bedroom floor. "Didn't I tell you George was going to kill himself?" Leonore reminded Bliss. "Tell that to the police."

Leonore, still overwhelmed, figured she needed some help in dealing with this, so she called up her best friend in Los Angeles, Gwen Dailey—and she persuaded Gwen to drive over from Burbank and help her out. She told Gwen that George had just killed himself, but there were people there who didn't want to be around when the Los Angeles police arrived.

Gwen couldn't get over soon enough to suit Carol, however, so Leonore racked her brains some more. She remembered another old pal living nearby—Polly Adler. Polly had been through shit like this before, she thought, so Leonore called up the notorious ex-madam from New York and got her to come over, too. Bobby Condon knew Polly and didn't mind having that tough old broad around to smooth things over.

When Polly showed up, Leonore gave Carol a coat to wear over her negligee, and Polly whisked Carol out of the house and back home. According to Leonore Lemmon, Carol was too shaken up to make the brief trip by herself. Condon was rubbing his head and wondering what the

Sam Kashner & Nancy Schoenberger

hell was going on. He poured himself a drink. He asked Bliss, "Who the hell are you?"

When Gwen Dailey arrived from Burbank, she took over. Leonore wanted to cry, but she was still in a kind of suspended animation. Inwardly, however, she was pissed off. Who was this guy Bill Bliss, and why did he show up when he did? And if he hadn't shown up, maybe George would still be alive. She didn't know if she should smack him or kiss him—maybe whoever shot George would have gunned her down, too. "The man upstairs just didn't want me," Leonore would say with genuine relief, many years later, when she was finally willing to talk about the events of that night. "The man upstairs" wasn't a reference to God but to the gunman who shot George, and who, she believed, would have shot her as well had she been lying next to her fiancé in his tiny bedroom at the top of the stairs. Whatever her feelings about Bliss, Leonore believed that if he had not shown up when he did, she would have been just as dead as George. "I think to myself, had that doorbell not rung, had I not turned that light on, what makes me think he might not have shot me as well?"

• • •

Bliss's involvement in Reeves's death remains a mystery. Did he unknowingly create an opportunity for the gunman to slip into the house, or was he part of the plot, sent by George's killer to keep Leonore occupied while George slept? Bliss and his wife were friendly with the Beverly Hills Police Department, because Bliss had installed the heating system in police headquarters. Jan Bliss sold real estate to a lot of movie stars. Everyone seemed to like her; the Blisses had a lot of bridge parties and even some singalongs in their home off Benedict Canyon. They had three kids, including a set of twin boys. They were friends with Carol Van Ronkel, but then Leonore didn't really know Carol—it was Rip who was her friend. Leonore just knew that she didn't like Bill Bliss, even though he had a pleasant, open countenance. In fact, he looked like the picture of a man you get when you buy a frame from the drugstore: the last guy you'd expect to wind up in a house surrounded by yellow police tape. Leonore didn't like him, and she would go to her grave believing that he was implicated in George's death. But it's just as likely that Bliss was exactly what he seemed to be: a decent guy, a family man, who simply was in the wrong place at the wrong time and who unwittingly created the distraction for a killer to make his way upstairs.

"When did this happen?" Gwen asked Leonore.

"Just after midnight."

"You'd better call the police. They can tell if you've waited too long, and that looks bad."

Leonore took Gwen upstairs to George's bedroom and the two women looked slowly around the room. That's when Leonore saw it: the bullet hole on the floor, at the foot of George's bed. Not too far from the one she had made herself, a few days earlier, fooling around with George's gun. Now she knew. She knew George hadn't shot himself. He would not have missed like that. She knew someone had gotten into the house. And she knew why, and who had sent him.

She turned to Gwen and said, "Help me move this rug."

The two women looked at each other for a long moment, then Gwen helped Leonore cover the two bullet holes with the rug in George's room. Leonore spied the spent shell casing and slipped it into the pocket of her robe. Let the police think it was a suicide. It was going to be too dangerous for anyone to think otherwise.

Once Carol was out of the house, Bliss called the Los Angeles Police Department. Gwen wanted to make sure Leonore was all right, but she didn't want her name mixed up with a shooting.

"We've got to get our stories straight," Leonore said. "I don't want Carol to get in trouble, but I want to keep you out of it, Gwen. Bill, or whatever your name is, you say Carol came with you because you thought there was a party going on. Gwen, you tell the cops you're Carol Van Ronkel. You live at 2300 Benedict Canyon. You came over with this guy here for a party. Let's say George came down and got mad and went back upstairs and did the deed. Let's say that."

Maybe Bliss didn't want Carol's name dragged into this at all, but he kept his mouth shut. Gwen knew how to play along. Once they'd called the cops, Gwen didn't want to be seen leaving the scene of a suspicious death.

So Officers Johnson and Korby of the Los Angeles Police Department answered the call. They took a look at the body and poked around George's room. They took everybody's statements, but Bliss did most of the talking. Bliss told the officers that George had been depressed and that Leonore had predicted he'd do something like this. She'd actually *predicted* that he was going to shoot himself. Leonore even embellished the story by saying she had heard the opening of a drawer as the gun was retrieved. Leonore didn't remember what else happened that night. She would only remember seeing George carried out under a white sheet, and her feelings about Bill Bliss, and her sense that something was very wrong with this picture. From that moment on, Leonore would be haunted by a heretofore unfamiliar emotion: fear.

• • •

By the time Toni Mannix had realized that the gunman she had hired was on his way to Benedict Canyon, she panicked and saw her life in cinders. She ran into her husband's room, crossing "the red sea" that had always separated them, to plead with him to put the genie back in its bottle. But Eddie, this week, this day, this hour of all hours, was out of commission, like a busted traffic light at the intersection of Toni and George. She tried feeding him some Louis Sherry ice cream, thinking that she could bring him out of his stupor. But it was like spoonfeeding a mummy. There was no hope of stopping this terrible thing, this plan that her unhappy life had set in motion.

Toni stood in her black pajamas and forgot her own name. She looked out the window and thought the vast lawn was an ocean and she was drowning in it. She began to lose her breath. She called up her friend Phyllis Coates—Gypsy—though it was *"very* early that morning." She said, "George has been murdered! The boy's been killed. Someone shot my darling boy!" Gypsy thought that Toni must have been drunk. Suddenly Gypsy heard only Toni's rapid breathing. It seemed to fill the room. But in the early morning hours of June 16, no one could have known that George had just been murdered. By the time Detective Johnson was calling in his report to Sergeant Peterson, Gypsy was listening to Toni hyperventilating over the telephone.

"She . . . told me the gun had recently been oiled, so no fingerprints could be taken from it. She implied she had been at the house earlier that evening!" Gypsy later recalled. The dam had broken. It was too late for Toni to undo what she had done. God knows, Toni had the brains to cover it up, but in those early hours her conscience, her regret, her love for George betrayed her.

The gunman was told that George always kept his Luger—the one that she had given him—on the bureau next to his bed. She knew George kept his guns heavily oiled, but she knew the gunman would take precautions anyway. And if for some reason the gun was not on the bureau, he was to do nothing and slip out as quietly as he had slipped in. It was important to use George's gun.

She had wanted it to look like Leonore had shot her fiancé in a drunken rage, but no one had considered Leonore's reaction to the shooting: that it had to have been a suicide. And now that's what the world would believe! That was unbearable, almost more unbearable than the fact of George's death, which she had caused. Like Helen Bessolo, Toni couldn't bear the fact that her "boy" would now be forever stigmatized as a suicide. Somehow the world would have to know. Toni was caught in an unspeakable dilemma: She had to hide her crime, but she had to let them all know that he was murdered. That's why she had to return to the house with Catholic prayer cards and say her hopeless prayers over the dead.

• • •

If Phyllis Coates guessed the truth, it would be Lois Lane's greatest story, but she couldn't share it with anyone. Not unless she wanted to spend the rest of her life gazing into rearview mirrors and being afraid of the trees and their long shadows in the middle of the day. Toni Mannix was not a killer like her husband Eddie, but, in her rage and her grief, she had killed what she had most loved.

All these years, Leonore knew. She knew enough to be scared, to keep to her story that "happy, jolly, normal" George was depressed enough to kill himself. She knew that Toni was "very, very angry" with her and that Eddie was "a union man, a strong-arm guy." And that she was "alone in the world in Benedict Canyon." It didn't take her long to look up Edward Bennett Williams, the one who had the crush on her and wanted to marry her and would maybe give her good advice for free. Williams told her what she had figured out for herself: Keep your mouth shut. So she covered up the extra bullet holes, left the hills of Beverly, and never looked back. She never changed her story, either, of how "Superman killed Superman," but it's clear from her midnight confessions that she believed all along that Toni and Eddie were behind it and that she had reason to live in fear for the rest of her life.

15

FLIGHT OF THE BUMBLEBEE

By the close of 1959, Mrs. Bessolo officially ended her association with the Nick Harris Detective Agency. Giesler had persuaded her to give the appearance of going along with the suicide verdict. He had originally told her that he identified with her plight and felt as if it were he who had lost a son. Now he convinced Helen to drop the case by telling her that her life was in danger, as her son's had been, and that there wasn't much she could do to clear George's name. He had heard things through the contacts he'd made defending Siegel; he had heard about conversations between Eddie Mannix and Mickey Cohen at The Carousel, after Cohen had gotten out of prison. They referred to George as "the bumblebee"—that was their code name for him. The bumblebee who flew from Toni's honey pot to Leonore's, all trussed up in a Superman costume. When Mickey Cohen entered the picture, it was like turning up the Grim Reaper in a deck of tarot cards: George Reeves's future was all used up.

Giesler's secretary Wendy Barrett Levine remembers, "Jerry began to worry that he would get back a little more meanness than he bargained for. I thought [he] came around very quickly to believing it was suicide, after all those accusations about criminal offenses being committed. He made a 360 [*sic*] degree turnaround."

The ordinarily unflappable, almost effete attorney had found that some of the people he'd interviewed about George's death were terrified to talk to him. The fear that had changed Giesler's mind would cling to the case for a long time. Even the sober-minded Jim Beaver, who began researching George Reeves's life in the late 1970s, knew that fear. "I interviewed some people who were terrified to talk to me," he said. "As late as 1980, I went to a couple of interviews carrying a gun." Even Jan Bliss, who broke a thirty-six-year silence to speak about her late husband's involvement in the case, had to first ask: "Who is still alive?"

Jerry Giesler was the first person connected to the investigation to die. On New Year's day in 1962, three years after George's death, the seventy-seven-year-old defense attorney died of a heart attack in his law office, found sprawled across the carpet as if he were imitating a corpse, the way he had that one time during a murder trial when he lay on the courthouse floor to the delight of the jury and spectators. *Time* had called him an "ambivalence chaser" but gave him an otherwise respectable obituary.

Two years later, on June 19, 1964, Helen Bessolo would die in her home in Pasadena, a home that had become a mausoleum, full of tattered and scribbled-over photographs of her son. While the rest of the house decayed around her, she kept his funereal urn as shiny as a bowling trophy. Before her death, however, she finally removed her son's ashes from her mantelpiece and placed them in a Pasadena cemetery, between her own plot and her sister's. She would eventually be laid to rest next to the ashes of her son. On her son's urn she had had engraved "George SUPERMAN Reeves," lest anyone forget his claim to immortality. She went to her grave knowing three things: that her son was murdered, that the LAPD had failed to investigate the crime, and that the Mannixes were somehow behind her son's murder.

Helen Bessolo outlived Eddie Mannix by one year. Mannix died on August 30, 1963, nine years after his first heart attack. Like everything else about "the Bulldog," even his heart attacks had become legendary. Harry Schwartz, who used to work for Mickey Cohen at The Carousel and was probably the man who had tipped off Giesler, would boast to his customers about how many heart attacks Eddie had survived— "maybe fifty angina attacks, six or seven heart attacks . . . I dunno, maybe more." The year of George's death—1959—had been the beginning of Eddie's real decline. He would slump in his wheelchair and be out of it for days, then he would rally and get his minions to take him to the Santa Anita racetrack. Out would come the cigars, and Eddie would tell his friends that he was going to outlive his doctor—"Dr. Putz," he called him, a Yiddish word for "penis" that he'd picked up from Mickey Cohen. It was as if he were taking a farewell tour of his old life, the life he knew when he was still powerful and in charge.

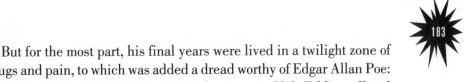

But for the most part, his final years were lived in a twilight zone of drugs and pain, to which was added a dread worthy of Edgar Allan Poe: the fear of being buried alive. In his last years of life Eddie suffered from narcolepsy. A story circulated that right after Eddie died, his doctor had to call in one of his colleagues for a second opinion.

Harry Schwartz recalled that "you never knew with Eddie. It could've been the dropsy. Eddie was like that character in the Poe story—the one everybody thinks is dead, but is only in a coma. Eddie had those kinds of problems." Eddie was reduced to telling his wife, "Make sure I'm dead, Toni. Make sure you bury a dead man."

Shortly after her husband's death, Toni paid a desperate visit to the MGM lot, to clean out her husband's office. The studio guards refused to let her on the premises. That made her furious, and she screamed and fought her way into her husband's office. Security tried to prevent her from clearing out Eddie's files, but she eventually had her way. "If you know what's good for you, you'll stay the hell away from me," she yelled at the hapless guards. "Don't fucking trifle with me! I know who you all are—you panty-waist motherfuckers! Get out of my way!" They let her pass.

She told Jack Larson about it later, how the hairdressers, the makeup girls, all the old-timers came out to watch the confrontation. "They were all there, and they watched Toni just barrel her way through," Larson described. "She just went in and did what she wanted to. She took no prisoners."

Howard Strickling, MGM's director of publicity, would eventually retire to a ranch in Chino, California, and contemplate accepting a big advance to write his memoirs. Toni Mannix was the last person Strickling expected to hear from in his retirement, when the biggest mess he had to clean up wasn't Joan Crawford's reputation but an old tool shed behind the house. But there it was, that unmistakable voice on the other end of the telephone. Sam Marx had called that voice "imperious," Jack Larson called it "faux English." Toni was demanding that Howard drop everything and come to see her immediately, that it was urgent, and she wouldn't take no for an answer.

Strickling picked up his old friend and former MGM colleague Sam Marx in a battered old car, a vintage Pontiac Estate Wagon. During their drive to the Mannix home, Strickling had characterized Toni as belonging to that species of snob who can't accept the fact that times have changed, that the old studio system was history, and that men like

Eddie Mannix, and the carnivores before him, no longer roamed the earth. "She was in a highly nervous state," Sam Marx remembered, "loud and shrill." Even before entering the house, Toni made her demands known to the man they called "the fixer" but who hadn't bought off so much as a traffic ticket in ten years. Toni went on about how some reporter for a supermarket tabloid had called her early in the morning to ask her questions for an article he was writing about George Reeves and his unusual relationship with the Mannixes.

"I hung up on the son of a bitch," she said. "We've got to stop it. You can do it, Howard. You must."

Experience had taught Strickling one thing about the tabloid press: You can't possibly do anything to smother a tabloid story, because if you do, they know they've struck paydirt. The more you squirm, the better they like it. The trick was to distract them with another story, the way you distract a petulant child. Or bargain with them: Give them one scandal in exchange for another. But Strickling was no longer in the scandal-control business. He tried to explain to Toni how her resistance and threats would simply become part of the story and that she'd be playing into the reporter's hands.

Back in the car, Strickling told Sam Marx how Reeves ". . . had an affair with Toni. There was a hot rumor around town that Mannix had the guy killed."

"Is that all you want to tell me about it?" Marx pressed his old colleague.

"Well, Eddie did it, of course." Sam Marx never learned that it was really Toni who had made that phone call.

Howard Strickling never wrote his memoirs. Sam Marx kept no notes when he wrote *Deadly Illusions,* his exposé of the Paul Bern murder and the modus operandi of MGM's executives. In fact, the old MGM employee prided himself on his memory. Both men are dead now, but that sentence—"Eddie did it, of course"—is haunting in its chilling weariness, its detachment.

Toni Mannix finally told Howard Strickling everything, after Eddie died, after the whole business quieted down and the town had something really big, like the Manson murders, to occupy its collective mind. She trusted Strickling—they all trusted him. Despite many offers to write his memoirs, Strickling still refused to do so. It didn't matter how much money the publishing houses threw at him, he just wasn't going to put anything on paper. But he did confide a number of company secrets to a protégé at MGM, including a final piece in the puzzle that was George Reeves's death. A young man named Leo Boroskin worked closely with Strickling in the publicity department during the studio's declining years.

From his home in Honolulu, Boroskin insisted that Eddie Mannix was never really in the business of killing people. He wasn't working for Murder, Incorporated, he was working for MGM. They made movies. That was his life. But he knew some pretty nasty people who knew even nastier people. Through Mickey Cohen, he knew a circle of fixers—some ex-prizefighters, some policemen who weren't getting by on the money they'd saved up for retirement. Mickey and Eddie called them "the blonds," for a few reasons.

One was that in polite company, an unsavory conversation could just as easily have been about some comely ingenues under contract. Two: to a lot of the Jews and black Irishmen from the New Jersey Palisades, everyone they met in California seemed blond, like aging beach boys. That's how Eddie's "fixers" came by their nickname. So Toni called up one of Eddie's blonds—a young man, a kid, really, that Mickey Cohen had gotten to know at McNeil Island—and the gates of heaven were opened.

By the evening of June 12, 1959, Toni Mannix had resolved to put George Reeves beyond all desiring, even her own. Eddie kept a few telephone numbers under the glass that covered the top of his desk at home. He once told Toni in case of emergency, she should take those names from under the glass, commit them to memory, and throw the pieces of paper away. One evening while Eddie was upstairs watching a ballgame, Toni lifted the heavy glass and pulled the papers out, like a world-class thief heisting the Hope Diamond. She probably had little idea what she was doing, who she was speaking with, what they were telling her. But after the plan was hatched, when she finally realized what she had done, it was too late.

Earlier in the week, Eddie had suffered a serious episode with his heart, which required Demerol among other drugs to help him relieve the pain and his anxiety about the seizure.

By the time Toni had hung up the phone, the world was a different place. For when Toni tried to speak to her husband about calling off the dogs, about reining in the blonds, about putting the killer back in his box, Eddie was nearly comatose. The only thing Toni could hope for now was that Leonore Lemmon would be implicated in George's death. At least she would have revenge against her hated rival. Leonore would be accused, if not of George's murder, then at least of being in some way involved. After all, it happened on Leonore's watch. She had driven George to "this craziness," to ending his long romance with Toni. She probably thought she was doing George a favor, giving him a chance to escape from that "terrible woman."

What Toni had wanted was to punish George. If it meant the ultimate punishment, so be it. If it meant that Leonore Lemmon would spend the rest of her miserable life fending off rumors that it was she who killed Superman, then so much the better. The rumors, the innuendos, would destroy Leonore's sanity and her life, like a jar full of fire ants emptied out in her skull. All the madness of the last few months would be worth it.

Toni was hysterical, full of grief and regret. At first she didn't care who knew—she didn't want to live without George, with that knowledge locked up in her heart. Strickling had to get in there and tell the newspapers how George left her his estate to carry on the charities they did together. Strickling really knew how to press all the right buttons.

In those first terrible hours, Boroskin explained, like any good Catholic she wanted to confess. But what she really wanted was for Leonore to pay for Toni's crime. She became like Helen at the end of her life: telling everyone that "the boy was murdered, you know." But by then people could see that Toni wasn't herself anymore; she had undergone a sea change, she was out of reach. She told Jack Larson and Gypsy that she knew that Leonore had murdered George. She agreed with Art Weissman's discredited theory that Leonore had slipped an extra bullet or two into the Luger so that George would get a big surprise when he played Russian roulette.

When Larson was interviewed by Tom Brokaw on *The Today Show* in the 1970s, he told Brokaw that he believed that George Reeves had committed suicide. When he returned to his hotel room after the show, Toni was on the phone, fuming at him, shrieking her sense of betrayal. Jack had to promise that he would never publicly say that again.

"Out of deference to Toni, I never say that he committed suicide. And maybe he didn't. Maybe he was murdered. I didn't want to make her unhappy," he remembered. "She had had enough unhappiness already."

So Howard Strickling's comment outside the Mannix estate, more than twenty years later, that "Eddie did it, of course" was closer to the heart of what happened than anyone realized. It wasn't so much that

Eddie "did it," thought Boroskin, as Eddie "hid it." With Strickling's help, he hid what Toni had caused to be done, with his name as an "open sesame" to the darker places: the places that George himself knew to be real, and, as he told Noel R. Slipsager at the deputy city attorney's office, potentially deadly. A place where you went looking for trouble and nearly always found it.

• • •

Leo Boroskin was a tall man in a small plane. As Strickling's protégé, Boroskin had been asked to fly to a dusty little town in Montana, to check in on a fellow who had done some favors for Eddie once. Strickling wanted to make sure the guy was doing all right, find out if he needed anything, so he sent Boroskin, then a young man in his mid-thirties. It was 1965. Eddie had been dead for two years. Boroskin got the impression that Strickling was just tying up some loose ends, and he didn't ask questions.

The twelve-seater was not to Boroskin's liking. The lanky PR man, originally from Yonkers, New York, could barely fit into one of those sardine-size seats; his legs stuck out into the aisle, and the grim hostess—not one of the beauties they reserve for the big jets but a hard-working gal just the same—had to ask him to move his legs on more than one occasion.

The view from the little prop plane was not a confidence-inspiring sight: a lot of short, brown, rounded mountains with a frosting of old snow, then a big flat prairie. Flattest land he'd ever seen, rimmed by those endless mountains. And nothing on the ground but a lot of little houses laid out in neat, even grids. He was supposed to rent a car at the airport, drive to an address Strickling had given him, check in on the guy, and then return that same afternoon. Nobody said anything to Boroskin, but he figured that the guy he was checking up on was one of the "blonds" Strickling had told Boroskin about.

"Howard did send me out of town once to check on somebody, and he never told me why, except that I understood it was for Toni," Boroskin recalled. "He just said, 'Go see so-and-so, ask if he needs anything, make sure he's happy.'"

• • •

Boroskin got directions from the airport, but it wasn't hard to find the address because the streets were laid out in such an orderly fashion.

He found the little house on a dusty street—not the best part of town but not the worst, either. A middle-aged, bland-looking guy opened the door and invited him in. He didn't seem surprised to find Boroskin on his doorstep. He looked completely ordinary, a little defeated, a little resigned to the way his life had turned out. Boroskin walked in and sat down on the man's yellow couch. It was a modest house, with bedsheets tacked up over the windows instead of curtains, so it was dark inside, though it was the middle of the day. The only thing those bedsheets let in were motes of dust.

Boroskin excused himself and went into the man's bathroom, right off the tiny living room. He noticed that there was an out-of-date calendar tacked to the wall, with a picture of a scenic mountain view.

"Is that a special date you're remembering?" Boroskin asked.

"Nah, I like the picture."

Boroskin thought that was odd, because if he'd just lifted up the makeshift curtains and looked out the window, he would've seen the real mountains outside.

He offered Boroskin a piece of pie and some coffee.

"My wife's away," the man said, but Boroskin had gotten the idea that maybe she'd left him.

"So how are you doing? Are you making out okay?" Boroskin asked.

"No complaints." The man smiled. The two of them sat there in the darkened living room, gulping down hot coffee, when the man's son came home. He was a nine- or ten-year-old kid—good looking, blond. Quiet and polite. When the conversation slowed down a bit, the boy turned on the television. The three of them just sat there, staring at the set. All of a sudden *The Adventures of Superman* came on the air.

Boroskin, who'd figured out a few things, started feeling a little nervous, and he glanced over at the man on the yellow couch. But he looked completely blank; he turned to Boroskin and said, "This is my boy's favorite show. He just loves it. Superman is his hero."

About halfway through the show, Boroskin just got up and left. He didn't think they even knew he had gone. He left the two of them sitting on a yellow couch watching Superman on television: a nice kid and his father watching Superman fly through the air as if nothing had ever happened. Boroskin drove back to the airport, carefully reversing the directions that had brought him there, and caught the next plane back to Los Angeles. This time he managed to get himself on a DC-10 and he slept the whole way home.

"It later occurred to me that this guy probably didn't even know George Reeves was Superman. He probably never got a good look at him. They wouldn't have told him anything. So it dawned on me that out there in God's country, in that sad little house on the prairie, this guy sitting there with his son probably didn't even know that he killed Superman. That would make the irony hall of fame, wouldn't it?" Boroskin asked, from his safe retirement home in balmy Hawaii.

"Poor Toni, she didn't have the balls to go through with it. That's what Howard said. That's why she called Howard out of retirement, appealing to his loyalty to the studio. Maybe she was afraid someone was going to dig up this guy in Montana, or he was going to go after her and ask for more money. But nothing like that ever happened. From time to time she wanted reassurance, but then, toward the end, you know, she wasn't playing with a full deck."

The Bulldog and the Lady. Those were their nicknames. Toni and Eddie are long dead. Helen Bessolo is dead. Jerry Giesler is dead, as is Sergeant Peterson, who believed Reeves was murdered, as is William H. Parker, chief of the Los Angeles Police Department and not known for his scrupulous honesty. Head medical examiner Theodore J. Curphey, M.D., is gone. John Hamilton and Robert Shayne—aka Perry White and Detective Henderson—have departed this earth, as did Whitney Ellsworth, who produced *The Adventures of Superman* and whom George Reeves had called "Dad." Leonore Lemmon—who outlasted her rival and outlived her era—is remembered only by the Superman fans who hate her. There's really only one person who still lives who was a key player in the whole mystery, and that person is Superman. You can see him on television every night in nearly every corner of the world, you can see him on film, you can read about him in DC Comics, you can go to The Super Museum in Metropolis, Illinois, and stand at the feet of his fifteen-foot, 4,440-pound statue in the middle of Superman Square. You can dream about him, you can call on him, you can wish him well. He's going to be around for a very long time.

EPILOGUE: THE HAUNTING

LEONORE LEMMON died on January 1, 1990, having never returned to Los Angeles. By 1971 she was living in an apartment on West 57th Street and had become involved with Jack Whittemore, a well-respected musician's agent who had represented some of the greatest jazz artists in the country—Miles Davis, Stan Getz, John Coltrane, Art Blakey. Whittemore was married but was separated from his wife. He eventually shared his apartment at 39th and Park with Leonore, though he would never divorce his wife and marry her. She was far gone into alcoholism by the time Phil Terman and Peter Levinson got to know her. "They started their day at 9:00 A.M. at Neary's. She never stopped drinking. She would wake up in the morning and drink all day," Levinson remembered. By the mid 1960s, her knockout looks had begun to slide—Terman remembered that "her face became like a soft grapefruit. All the years I knew her, she was suffering a rapid personal decline. It was like a rock falling off a ledge. When I first met her, she had these great looks. But they were fading as you'd watch. I would say almost within weeks, I watched her looks go." Soon the only thing that connected her to the image of the sultry debutante sitting on a love seat with Jakie Webb was her artfully made-up eyebrows.

In her 1989 interview with Lee Saylor, undertaken at the end of her life, Leonore railed against the thirty years of changes she'd witnessed in her beloved city. "If I go out at night to get a newspaper . . . 39th Street and Park is like living in the desert," she said boozily. "I'm in the middle of three hotels—now you take my word for it, because I don't come up with crazy stories. But you take the Doral, the Slattery, or whatever the hell it's called, and all I do is giggle, because every guy who

191

checks into one of these chic hotels wears white socks. What the hell is that about? You can tell a man's from out of town if he's wearing white socks! Now, does that sound strange? Well, it isn't. The Statler, the Doral. The doors are locked at midnight. I'm a born New Yorker. I've walked all over this town, but I don't anymore! Park Avenue is strange, there's nothing here. . . ."

She laughed derisively about the stream of out-of-towners: geeky guys who have filled up the hotels and ruined the neighborhood, but the truth of the matter is, she needed those men to keep her bar bill current. In later years, after Whittemore's death, there were rumors that Leonore was desperate for cash and that she was reduced to hanging around the Doral and other hotels along 39th and Park, waiting for one of those out-of-town "guys with white socks" to help her keep body and soul together—or apart. She had, at the last, become a small-time prostitute.

Leonore talked about Jack Whittemore, the man she lived with for ten years. "He just plain up and everyday died," she told Saylor, as if it happened yesterday. "Bang. That's all. Wasn't even sick." That was the man she was mourning for, not George. Reeves's death had given her notoriety; Jack Whittemore's death had devastated her. In her interview with Lee Saylor, Leonore occasionally forgot herself and referred to George as "Jack." She wound up the interview by saying "I've just lost a good friend and I have a case of downers. . . ."

In her last years, she seldom talked about what had happened to George Reeves, and people in her circle knew better than to bring it up. No one who knew her thought she had murdered George. The most she would say if the subject ever did come up was, "The people in California treated me in a very bad fashion. I don't know the reason, but they were very bad to me."

In May of 1989, thirty years after George Reeves's death, *Entertainment Tonight* and *A Current Affair* produced nearly identical segments on the unsolved mystery of Superman's death. Both programs interviewed Leonore Lemmon, then living in Whittemore's apartment at 39th Street and Park.

In both segments, obviously filmed the same day in the same setting, Leonore has gone to the trouble to tie her white hair back at the nape of her neck and apply lots of blush to her sagging cheeks. A heavy dewlap hangs below her chin; her nose is a W.C. Fields drunkard's nose, red as a strawberry. She looks stupefied by drink, or else she has recently suffered a mild stroke, causing her features to sag on the left side of her face. At the end of her life, Leonore looks like Charles Laughton in drag, every glamour girl's nightmare; years of booze and not caring who you go home with have made the flesh lumpy and deadened the eyes.

When she speaks, her words are slurred, but they are forceful. Something of the old "Lem" comes through—her style, her penchant for drama. She sounds like a punch-drunk ex-boxer with a one-way ticket to Palookaville.

"It was Superman who killed Superman," she announces, emphasizing each word and staring, blinking slowly, at the camera. "George is dead, and the subject is just as dead," she adds with hatred and disgust in her voice. She has told this story before; she knows the words by heart. It is her official story and she will never change it, though she found ways to implicate the Mannixes in her Saylor interview. "It was Eddie's gun," she told Saylor. "What do you think of that?"

There's an unforgettable photograph of Leonore making her night-club debut at the Beachcomber, circa 1943, singing "Jake's a Fake" and looking fresh and dewy and slim as a willow. No makeup but dark lipstick and a strong brow line. It's hard to believe she's the same person as the coarsened, fleshy woman on *A Current Affair*. The debutante has been nearly obliterated, swallowed up by the boozy woman who has lived and seen too much.

One wonders if that "case of downers" played a role in her death six months after speaking with Lee Saylor on a couple of sultry summer nights, the air conditioner going full blast. Always the ultimate party girl, Leonore Lemmon died on New Year's Day.

• • •

JERRY GIESLER published his memoirs the year before his death, an "as-told-to" book called *The Jerry Giesler Story*. At least one operative in the Nick Harris Detective Agency—Milo Spiriglio, whose first case was George Reeves and who has ended up running the agency—believes that Giesler was killed by mobsters. "The kind of men he liked to represent," Spiriglio has said, referring to Giesler's involvement with Ben Siegel. By the time of his death, Giesler was one of the richest men in the cemetery, having collected $100,000 in fees from his famous clients in the days before income tax.

• • •

SERGEANT V. A. PETERSON retired from the Los Angeles Police Department and moved to Texas. Never happy with the way Chief Parker had handled the investigation, Peterson kept copies of the department files and his own notes on the case. Sometime in the 1980s, he sent his Reeves file to Jim Hambrick, founder and owner of The Super Museum in Metropolis, Illinois, the only museum in the world devoted to Superman memorabilia and boasting a collection of over 40,000 items valued at $3 million. Hambrick, long interested in the mystery surrounding Reeves's death, proudly displays one of the woolen costumes Reeves wore in *The Adventures of Superman*—a rarity because George used to burn his costume at the end of each season, after carefully removing the emblem and giving it to a friend. In 1993 one of Reeves's original costumes sold at auction for nearly $80,000.

Sergeant Peterson went to his grave believing that Leonore Lemmon killed George Reeves.

• • •

CHIEF WILLIAM H. PARKER died of a heart attack in the middle of making a speech about the incorruptibility of the police department at an awards banquet in the Pacific Ballroom of the Statler Hilton. Over a thousand Marine Corps veterans had just given him a standing ovation when he collapsed. Parker was a controversial figure; many believe that under his tenure the Los Angeles Police Department was deeply associated with organized crime.

• • •

HELEN BESSOLO was laid to rest in a Pasadena cemetery, next to her sister and the funeral urn containing George Reeves's mortal remains. An auction was held after her death, and an urn containing ashes was taken from her mantelpiece and sold to a young man, who later tried reselling what he believed to be George Reeves's ashes to Jim Beaver, then doing research for his biography of the actor.

"When I heard about those ashes, I smiled," Beaver recalled. "I knew what they were. They belonged to Helen's dog—she had had him cremated and kept his ashes there, long after George's were lovingly placed in a cemetery in Pasadena."

JACK LARSON spent many years trying to make peace with the character of Jimmy Olsen, which typecast him so severely that it virtually destroyed his once-promising acting career.

By the time Larson was flown to New York to be interviewed by Tom Brokaw on *The Today Show*—more than a decade after Reeves's death—Larson had become a highly respected playwright and librettist, having collaborated with the American composer Virgil Thomson on the opera *Lord Byron.* He continued his long-term association with the director Jim Bridges, coproducing such films as *The Paper Chase, The China Syndrome, Urban Cowboy, Mike's Murder, Perfect,* and *Bright Lights, Big City.*

Larson continues to receive hundreds of fan letters for his portrayal of Jimmy Olsen, Superman's pal; he is continually amazed at how much *The Adventures of Superman* is still loved around the world and what an impact his character has had on so many people's lives. Whenever he's asked about George Reeves, Larson invariably says, "I admired George and I miss him." Larson once admitted that "I feel badly that he didn't live to have all the blessings from the show. People love you for it through the generations. I feel badly that George was cheated out of that. He only got the bad things; I got all the good things."

Strangers often approached Larson in the years after George's death, telling him that they, too, were somehow connected to the mystery. "I couldn't go anywhere," Larson remembered, "without somebody coming up and saying 'I was the ambulance driver'—or 'I sat at the morgue and this is what happened.' Or 'I was the carpenter who was hired to repair the bullet holes.' " Larson said that a man actually once went up to Helen Bessolo in an ice-cream parlor and introduced himself as "a friend of the man who shot your son."

Larson remained friendly with Toni Mannix in the decades after George's death. He, too, was witness to her decline. "She certainly exemplified 'Hell hath no fury like a woman scorned' when George left her for Leonore," he said. "After Eddie died, I'd go see Toni. We'd go out to La Scala in Beverly Hills, or I'd go up to the house, and she'd start to complain to me. She'd say, 'You only see the people you don't want to see. They're the only ones who want to see you.' "

Once Toni called Jack at six-thirty in the morning and asked if he would like to have George's alligator shoes. She had, of course, inherited all of George's worldly possessions, and she kept George's clothes in Eddie's closet after her husband's death.

"I don't want the alligator shoes, Toni," Larson told her.

"Well, then, would you like the gun? I can give you the gun, you know. You should have the gun."

"No, Toni. I don't want the gun, either."

Toni kept the Luger in her house. "Naturally," Larson observed, "she inherited the gun. It was not considered to be a murder weapon. It was in his house, so she inherited it. Then she'd find little things she tried to give me, like George's books. We didn't talk for a while because it was making me feel so bad. I just couldn't go on with it."

Sometimes Jack would get her late-night phone calls, usually around 1:00 A.M.—around the time of death established for her former paramour. "She'd be lying awake and hearing things, fearful that someone was in the big empty house with her," Jack remembered. Eventually even the phone calls stopped, and Toni lived on alone in her mansion like Norma Desmond, awash in her memories. "She was haunted," Larson remembered. "She was definitely haunted by it all."

• • •

TONI MANNIX tried renting the house on Benedict Canyon after George's death, but tenants would move in and then suddenly move right out again. She eventually put the house up for sale, but when real estate agent Gail Bertoya held an "open house" several weekends in a row, nobody even came to look.

"It was a very eerie, weird house," she told Jan Alan Henderson. In the years following George's death, it got the reputation for being haunted. Tenants would report hearing the sounds of a party going on in the middle of the night. Once the police were called in to investigate mysterious shots heard emanating from the house, but they were unable to determine who—if anyone—had been firing a gun. Joe Hyams became interested in the subject of haunted houses when he and actress Elke Sommer, to whom he was married at the time, were living in a Benedict Canyon house believed to be haunted. Hyams wanted to include the Reeves house in an article on haunted Hollywood residences, but when he asked Toni for permission to look around, she became incensed.

"Absolutely not! Over my dead body!" she shrieked, but Hyams managed to gain access through real estate agent Bertoya. He promptly received an attorney's letter from Toni Mannix, who unsuccessfully sued Hyams and the *Los Angeles Times* for running the piece. She accused the inveterate newspaperman of "ruining my life by writing such terrible things."

Hyams remembered that he had seen what looked like bloodstains on the floor, "But it was hard to tell by then whether they were bloodstains or stains from a hamburger."

Toni let the house fall into disrepair. Tenants continued to move in and to quickly move out again, grumbling about strange noises in the bedroom at the top of the stairs. The Reeves house—once the charming love nest Toni and George had made for themselves—was now an empty creep show, eventually becoming the first stop on the Hollywood "Grave Line" tour of notorious Hollywood houses. The second stop would be the Sharon Tate death house, not far away in Benedict Canyon.

But the house was finally sold and restored to its former beauty. Bought in the 1950s for $12,000, the house has recently been put back on the market for the asking price of $600,000.

Toni lived a long time after George's death. "She was a recluse, you know," confided Bette Shayne, who had once counted Toni among her friends. "She just watched him on television constantly." Before his death, Art Weissman paid a social call on Toni, in the mansion on El Retiro Way that Toni continued to live in after Eddie's death. "By this time her beauty had faded," remembered George's manager. "She lived as a recluse in her Beverly Hills home. At her insistence we spent most of the time watching reruns of George as Superman. Through it all, she sat transfixed, staring at the TV screen as if George was still alive. For the few remaining years of her life," Weissman recalled, "she still had George."

"She was always a bit like Medea," Jack Larson believed. "But now she was Medea without an audience. She was playing to an empty house . . . she never remarried, she never had any children."

She also denied having a sister, so when Larson got a phone call from a woman named Florice Talley claiming to be Toni's sister, he was very surprised.

Toni had spent her life keeping the existence of her sister a secret to all her friends. Constance Shirley believed it was out of a kind of jealousy: Toni—like Lana Turner, like Norma Jean Baker—had turned herself into her own glorious creation, and she didn't want any family members showing up and betraying her roots. Or upstaging her as a potential rival who looked like her, talked like her, and seemed to have inherited her flair for the dramatic.

Florice Talley called up Jack Larson one Christmas Eve and introduced herself as Toni's sister. "Toni wants to see you," she said. "She's in St. John's Hospital."

Larson was surprised. He hadn't seen Toni in a long while; the last time they spoke he had asked her to stop calling him in the middle of the night. He just couldn't take those phone calls anymore.

"I went down on Christmas Eve and visited her," Larson remembered. "It was very poignant because she was on oxygen, old and dying. She was lying in bed. And there we were: an aging juvenile and an old beauty queen. We'd known each other and had been through so much together. And there wasn't much to say. Whatever she had to say, whatever was still in her heart to say to me, it was too late to say it now."

INDEX